The Making of
Tory Education Policy
in Post-War Britain
1950–1986

379.42 KNI

This book is to be returned on or before
the last date stamped below.

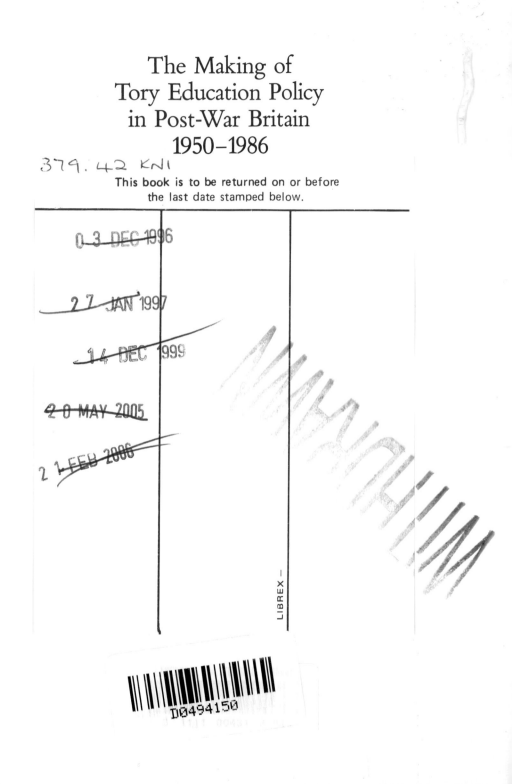

0 3 DEC 1996

2 7 JAN 1997

14 DEC 1999

2 0 MAY 2005

2 1 FEB 2006

LIBREX —

D0494150

Dedication
For my parents, Laurence and Evelyn, and my wife Cherry.

The Making of
Tory Education Policy
in Post-War Britain
1950–1986

Christopher Knight

 The Falmer Press
(A member of the Taylor & Francis Group)
London ● New York ● Philadelphia

UK   The Falmer Press, Falmer House, Barcombe, Lewes, East Sussex, BN8 5DL

USA   The Falmer Press, Taylor & Francis Inc., 1900 Frost Road, Suite 101, Bristol, PA 19007

©Christopher Knight 1990

All rights reserved. No part of this publication may be reproduced, stored in a retrieval system, or transmitted in any form or by any means, electronic, mechanical, photocopying, recording or otherwise, without permission in writing from the Publisher and copyright holders.

First published in 1990

British Library Cataloguing in Publication Data
Knight, Christopher
  The making of Tory education policy in post-war Britain 1950–1986.
  1. Great Britain. Education. Policies of Conservative Party
  1. Title
  379.41

  ISBN 1-85000-676-8
  ISBN 1-85000-677-6Pbk

Jacket design by Caroline Archer

Typeset in 11/13 Bembo by
Chapterhouse, The Cloisters, Formby L37 3PX

Printed and bound in Great Britain by
Redwood Burn Limited, Trowbridge, Wiltshire.

Contents

... The party has always been a coalition of left- and right-wing Tories, who have been forced to coexist with one another (much like the right- and left-wings of the Labour Party) ... On only a few occasions during the last century have the reactionaries actually dictated Conservative policies: contrary to the claims of the Right, the self-appointed guardians of the so-called 'true Toryism', successive Conservative leaders and governments have seldom been motivated by ideology, dogma or doctrine. Neither have they — in the main — been opposed to reform. Their hallmark has been a pragmatic adaptability to shifting circumstances, a willingness to pursue progressive and enlightened policies and a determination to steer a moderate course, a middle way between the extremes of Right and Left in politics. (Russel, 1978, p. 7)

List of abbreviations

ACE	Advisory Centre for Education
ACP	Advisory Committee on Policy
AEC	Association of Education Committees
AGLB	Anthony Greenland's Letter Books
AMA	Association of Metropolitan Authorities
APS	Assisted Places Scheme
APU	Assessment of Performance Unit
ASC	Adam Smith Club
ASG	All Souls Group
ASI	Adam Smith Institute
CCO	Conservative Central Office
CE	Conservative Educationalists
CEA	Conservative Education Association or Council for Educational Advance (as appropriate)
CEC	Conservative Education Committee (also referred to as the PEC)
CNACE	Conservative National Advisory Committee on Education
CPA	Conservative Party Archive (Bodleian Library, Oxford)
CPC	Conservative Political Centre
CPES	Council for the Preservation of Educational Standards (later the NCES)
CPG	Conservative Philosophy Group
CPS	Centre for Policy Studies

CPSESG	Centre for Policy Studies Education Study Group
CPVE	Certificate of Pre-vocational Education
CRD	Conservative Research Department
CSC	Comprehensive Schools Committee
CSE	Certficate of Secondary Education
CQS	Critical Quarterly Society
CTANAC	Conservative Teachers' Association National Advisory Committee (later known as the CNACE)
CTU	Conservative Teachers' Union
CUTA	Conservative and Unionist Teachers' Association
DES	Department of Education and Science
DoI	Department of Industry
FCS	Federation of Conservative Students
FEVER	Friends of the Education Voucher Experiment in Representative Regions
GCE	General Certificate of Education
GCSE	General Certificate of Secondary Education
GLC	Greater London Council
HMI	Her Majesty's Inspectorate
IEA	Institute of Economic Affairs
ILEA	Inner London Education Authority
LEAs	Local Education Authorities
MEP	Micro-Electronics Project
MSC	Manpower Services Commission
NAFF	National Association for Freedom (the Freedom Association)
NCES	National Council for Educational Standards
NCW	National Council for Women of Great Britain
NEA	National Education Association
NIESR	National Institute for Economic and Social Research

OECD	Organization for Economic Cooperation and Development
PEC	Parliamentary Education Committee
PEST	Pressure for Economic and Social Toryism
SAU	Social Affairs Unit
SG	Salisbury Group
SJS	St James Society
TES	Times Educational Supplement
TVEI	Technical and Vocational Education Initiative
WFD	Women and Families for Defence
YCs	Young Conservatives

Acknowledgments

In guiding my study of Tory education policy-making, I wish to thank my three academic mentors, Dr Michael Hickox, Dr Pamela Young and Professor Miriam David. Their criticism and counsel over a number of years has helped bring the present work to fruition.

Many individuals assisted in the collection of materials on which this book is based. I owe a special and obvious debt to the many people who kindly agreed to be interviewed. As the key actors in the issues and events described in the book, their assistance was invaluable. Those who expressly wished to remain anonymous will find their contributions suitably disguised.

Special thanks are due to the following: to John Selwyn Gummer, former Chairman of the Conservative Party, who granted me permission to consult Party papers for the period 1960–74 held in the official Party archive at the Bodleian Library, University of Oxford; to Drs Stephen Stacey and Sarah Street, Conservative Party Archivists, Bodleian Library; to the staff of the Department of Western Manuscripts and Modern Manuscript Reading Room, Bodleian Library; to Mr D. Cox, former Keeper, and Mr P. Morrish, Sub-Librarian (Special Collections), Brotherton Library, University of Leeds, and Dr Ann Gold (Lord Boyle's sister) for granting me permission to examine the papers of the late Lord Boyle of Handsworth; to Miss Jane Roscoe, Cataloguer of the Lord Boyle Papers; to Joan West, former Librarian, Conservative Research Department; to the staff of the Conservative Central Office and Conservative Political Centre; to the staff of the Department of Education and Science Library; and finally, to those individuals who graciously loaned me their papers and correspondences (each of whom are acknowledged in the chapter references and bibliography). Without their help, much of the story of the making of Tory education policy in the post-war period could not have been told.

For translating the original manuscript into book form, I wish to thank my editor at Falmer Press, Christine Cox, and to Malcolm Clarkson, Managing Director of

Falmer Press, I would like to record my special thanks for his warm encouragement and his belief that the work on which this book is based was deserving of a wider audience.

Chapter 1

Introduction

Though historians, political scientists and sociologists are now beginning to focus attention on aspects of contemporary educational policy and practice, this is the first documented account of the formation and formulation of Tory education policy in the post-war period. Drawing amongst others on the official papers of the Conservative Party Archive, the private correspondence of the 'Black Paper' authors and former Conservative ministers, the book attempts to provide an objective account of how individual groupings of Conservative educationalists came to shape Tory education policy between 1950 and 1986. In so doing it reveals for the first time both the genesis of modern Conservative educational thought on state secondary schooling and its evolution up to the conclusion of the 'Joseph years'. It is the belief of the present author that there has been much misunderstanding over the modern Conservative Party and education policy. Whilst some commentators (see the following section) have suggested that the Party (even if it had an identifiable education policy) has displayed nothing more than a nonchalant attitude to schooling, others still have been aggressively dismissive of the Conservatives' approach to state education. Much of this may be explained by an ignorance of the facts or, at least, by an unwillingness to study in any great depth the Conservative Party's performance on education policy. Either way never has the time been more ripe than now (in this Margaret Thatcher's eleventh year in office as Prime Minister) to help set the record straight. This study will show that in the period between 1950 and 1974 the Conservative Party failed to fashion an educational policy in line with Conservative philosophy, but that, in the period between 1975 and 1983, it formulated such a policy (of sound basic skills, choice of schools and academic excellence) largely at the behest of the *Conservative Educationalists* (CEs).[1] For the present author, the failure of the Tories to develop a clear conservative educational policy before Mrs Thatcher's Party leadership was of considerable interest and a spur to investigating the period 1950–1986.

The perspective of educational politics and policy studies

Educational politics and policy studies as a field of study has, to date, focused upon macro-sociological theory.[2] Such studies, whilst offering insights into the dynamics of educational change, do not fully address the question 'Who makes education policy?' To this area of theoretical weakness, can be added the empirical weakness of other accounts to fully probe the educational policy-making machines of the main political parties. There has been little or no discussion of how 'ideas' become 'policy' — the relationship between thought and practice.

Students of educational politics and policy studies have only very recently (since 1980) been attracted to analyzing the educational policies of the modern Conservative Party. However, in the main these commentaries have seemingly come from people largely unsympathetic to the Conservative case for education. For example, Davies (1986) and Green (1988) have both suggested the Conservatives' revolution in schools has lacked invention, systematic planning, direction and political imagination, and far from making opportunities real has, in fact, merely accentuated the rhetoric and reality of vocationalism as a widely acceptable counterpoint to an expansion of 'de facto' selective provision and given more power to often unrepresentative groups of parents. Likewise, Tapper and Salter (1986) and Fitz, Edwards and Whitty (1986) in their studies of one particular aspect of Conservative educational policy (the Assisted Places Scheme) have criticized the Tory government for reinforcing belief in the inability of public sector schools to match the quality of private provision or to develop creditable alternatives to the type of education which the scheme has so powerfully sponsored. This concern with political intentions and state intervention is also common to the critique offered by Sharp (1986) which suggests that no other capitalist country experienced quite the same 'rape' of its educational system as Britain between 1979 and 1985. The seven studies mentioned offer useful insights into the politics of education but their weakness is their assumption that the existence of economic constraints on educational provision demonstrates the primacy of capitalism in policy-making.

A number of other studies have also covered various aspects of Conservative educational policy. Wright (1977) has analyzed the Black Papers and their impact upon Conservative educational thinking; Tapper and Salter (1978) have assessed the response of right-wing educationalists to the education debate and their contribution to contemporary educational ideology; the Centre for Contemporary Cultural Studies Education Group (1981) has produced a radical critique of educational policy-making since 1944, documenting the emergence of an aggressively populist Conservatism and showing how, between 1970 and 1975, there was a gradual convergence between Conservative Party policy on education and the new educational-right; Jones (1983) has described the themes of the Conservative offensive and examined the success of the Black Papers in capturing the highground of debate, especially their impact upon the revival and redirection of Conservative education policy; Dale (1983) has offered a descriptive account of the various strands of Conservative educational thought contributing to Mrs Thatcher's educational policy — a theme developed in the collection of essays edited by Wolpe and Donald (1983). Edwards, Fulbrook and Whitty (1984) have examined continuity and change in recent Conservative discourses on education and the role of individuals and groups in and near the Party in the formation of Conservative educational policies; and Salter and Tapper (1985) have studied the recent political history of private schooling, drawing attention to the role of the new right intellectuals as an influence on this particular area of Conservative education policy.

The problem with all of these studies is that they do not fully address the genesis of Conservative ideas about education or, in any way, attempt to quantify the support given to these ideas within the modern Conservative Party. Wright's study was, according to its publisher, intended to provide little more than a broad survey of the facts for the general reader. The two books by Salter and Tapper are more concerned with the process of educational change (i.e. the way in which education translates the pressures placed upon it into new policies and practice) than with the actual process of educational policy-making. The authors do show the barriers ideas have to cross between their original conception by individuals and their final implementation by government but they do not offer convincing evidence in appreciating the relationship between ministers and their departments.

The CCCS Education Group study — to date the fullest account of the Conservative educational *counter-revolution* — may be criticized for restricting its analysis almost entirely to the effects of the Black Papers; little account is taken of other events and participants contributing to the Conservative education offensive. A notable omission is the Group's treatment of Mrs Thatcher's ministry which fails to pinpoint her personal contact with the Back Paper authors. The Jones work rehearses yet again the main themes of the Conservative offensive but offers no new insights and is based almost wholly on secondary sources. In contrast, Dale's essay makes an original attempt to locate the various Conservative positions concerning education and describes how each emerged to influence education policy during the first Thatcher government. The main weakness of Dale's account is its failure to show how the various strands of Conservative educational thought were absorbed by the different branches of the Conservative Party central organization (see chapters 4–9 of the present study). The collection of essays edited by Wolpe and Donald is devoid of any references, and though it has a comprehensive account of Thatcher's record on education until the 1983 General Election, it can make no claim to objectivity given its polemical intentions. The essay by Edwards, Fulbrook and Whitty (in Barton and Walker, 1984) has the same weakness as Dale's account (upon which it is heavily reliant). By concentrating on the historical outcomes, as opposed to the historical roots, of policies their analysis fails to show who the architects of Conservative education policy (affecting state and private education) actually were. In part this study seeks to identify the architects and the genesis of their thought (see chapters 2–9).

It is important to note that much of the existing politics of education literature (including the studies cited above) concentrates upon the recent emergence of *New Right* ideology. For example, the work of David (1980) and Levitas (1986) has focused attention on the Tories' treatment of education and the economy and how initial Tory concerns (1970-74) with the fabric of education and the links with broader social policy have been superseded (under Thatcher) by a preoccupation with the accountability of state schooling, whilst the work of Finn (1987) has highlighted how, since 1979, the Conservative government has acceded to a number of *New Right* proposals and redefined the relationship between education, training and work.

It is observed that those commentators who have most usefully helped to identify the antecedents of recent Conservative educational policy, have not been political scientists or political sociologists. The work has been the product of educational historians. For example, Simon (1985) has suggested that the Conservatives' failure between 1951 and 1954 to modernize the educational system and their policy of hostility to secondary reorganization on comprehensive lines between 1950 and 1960, inspired the Labour Party to campaign more vigorously in favour of comprehensive education; and that the focus of official Conservative policy on the massive expansion of the secondary modern school laid the foundation for Labour's 'breakout' of the sixties to transform the secondary system. Simon has further argued (1986) that the 1944 Education Act did not signpost a 'new order' in English education but the old order (i.e. the perpetuation of educational privileges through the protection of the independent/public schools, through the direct grant schools and through the protection of the grammar schools as a separate system within the maintained sector) in a new guise. Here, Simon's work is of interest because it allows us to appreciate how subsequent Tory administrations have sought a policy direction for education removed from their earlier aborted attempts.

Griggs (1979) has shown how the Conservative philosophy of education has been the direct product of Conservative philosophy in general. His account of how the Conservative belief in inequality is fundamental to the Conservative view of education (especially in terms of support for private schools or attempts to maintain and restore selection in secondary education) is a useful reminder of how pervasive an influence Conservative philosophy has been over modern Tory education policy. Finally, Jefferys (1984) has offered important new insights into the making of Conservative education policy in the inter-war years. His observation that before 1939 most Conservatives opposed the extension of state power in education and with it the creation of a more flexible social order, but that R. A. Butler was genuinely concerned to apply the Baldwinian concept of *one nation* to education policy (especially by creating equal opportunities at the secondary stage) is of particular relevance to the present study. It is suggested by the present author that these were the roots of the dilemma facing the CEs from 1950.

The literature to date reveals a need for a detailed historical account of the development of Conservative educational thought in the post-war period and the role played by the CEs in that development. In particular, such an account should show how the thinking of the CEs was drawn upon by the Conservative Party and its relation to the formation of modern Conservative educational policy. The present work seeks to address the omission, in particular by testing two principal hypotheses found in the existing literature: the belief that the Conservative educational *counter-revolution* began in 1969 with the publication of the first Black Paper (Cox and Dyson, 1969a) and that this movement operated outside, and without the support, of the Conservative Party; and the belief that there has been no one identifiable body of Conservative opinion shaping modern Conservative educational policy.

Outline of the study

The term 'CEs', following Lord Maude's usage (given in an interview with the author), is here applied in its educational not its political sense. This is necessary because, although many CEs have been members of, or have had close affiliations with, the Conservative Party some (notably Dr Rhodes Boyson, Professor Brian Cox, Baroness Caroline Cox, Anthony Dyson, Paul Johnson, Dr John Marks and Lord Vaizey) have had earlier associations of support for, and/or membership of, the Labour Party; whilst others still (for example, Lord Beloff) have been members of the Liberal Party. It is also appropriate that the term is used in its educational sense since a number of CEs (for example, Dr Rhodes Boyson, Patrick Cormack, Dr Elizabeth Cottrell, Lord Elton, Harry Greenway, Alan Howarth, Tom Howarth, Dame Kathleen Ollerenshaw and Maurice Venn) have themselves been practising teachers in the state and/or independent school sectors.

Chapters 2 and 3 examine the ideas which brought the early CEs together to state their 'sober and careful analytical presentation of the conservative case' (letter from Professor Bantock to Professor Cox, chapter 3). Chapter 4 shows how one grouping of CEs (the preservationists) formulated and promoted their philosophy of *excellence in education* and successfully lobbied the Conservative Party central organization, which gradually absorbed the philosophy into official Party thinking. Chapter 5 explores how the philosophy was adopted by the Party as the strategy to oppose (unsuccessfully) the Labour government's 1976 Education Bill. Here the Conservative Central Office (CCO), the Conservative Research Department (CRD), the Conservative Political Centre (CPC), the Conservative Education Committee (CEC) and the Conservative National Advisory Committee on Education (CNACE) worked together, exploiting what they perceived to be, the intellectual bankruptcy of Labour's education policy, with its apparent inability to deliver sound educational provision for the lower 40 per cent of the secondary school population.

Policy formation, it is suggested, proceeds by politicians learning to adapt their thinking and operations to emerging problems. In chapters 5 and 6 the role of the Conservative Research Department between 1974 and 1979 is shown to have been crucial, acting as it did as the intellectual repository for the ideas of the preservationists. Under the guidance and direction of Angus Maude (Chairman, 1975–79), Chris Patten (Director, 1974–79), Alan Howarth (Director, 1979–81), John Ranelagh (CRD education desk officer, 1975–77), and Biddy Passmore (CRD education desk officer 1977–79), the key tenets of the *excellence in education* lobby were popularized in and outside the Party by Norman St John-Stevas, Leon Brittan and Dr Rhodes Boyson. Also significant was the role of Stuart Sexton (Education Adviser to the Conservative Opposition, 1975–79) who was instrumental in formulating much of Tory education policy for the 1979 General Election, including the Assisted Places Scheme (APS). It is argued that one of the principal architects of the changed climate within the Party, allowing for the reception of the ideas of the *excellence in education* lobby, was Sir Keith Joseph who, in 1975, became Chairman of the Advisory Committee on Policy (ACP) and took special responsibility for the development of Party policies, initiating a review of Conservative Party philosophy. This change, it is argued, set the ideological framework within which the CEs promoted their particular approach to education after 1975.

Chapter 7 examines how the Party implemented its newly-developed conservative educational policy under Mark Carlisle and Lady Young. They were aided by individuals prominent on the CNACE and together they set about marginalizing the more extreme tendencies and claims of the educational radical-right. Chapter 8 assesses the push towards *excellence in education* during Sir Keith Joseph's early period as Secretary of State for Education and Science. Finally chapter 9 shows how, during the second Thatcher government, the Party sought to rethink the whole area of secondary education and how some of the ideas formulated by CEs of the educational radical right were beginning to be incorporated into the mainstream of Conservative educational thinking.

Notes

1   Lord Maude, to author, 19 February 1986. According to Maude the term 'Conservative Education-alists' denotes and describes 'that body of individuals (intellectuals, academics, politicians, education-ists, journalists and others) who stood for the preservation of, what they saw as, the best and most effective of traditional educational methods and structures, whilst granting the necessity to adapt these to the perceived changing needs of pupils and society'. In the main they have been those individuals who have fought to preserve the grammar school ethos (i.e., strong discipline, high educational standards and streaming by ability). They each believed post-war educational policies to have been increasingly dominated by the socialist principle of compulsory equality — one type of school for all and no selection either within or between schools. This body of individuals was united

by a conviction that creativity comes from discipline and individual excellence is best promoted by selection in education.

2   See, for example, James (1980), Ranson (1985) and Howell and Brown (1983).

Chapter 2

First groupings and the meeting of like-minds, 1950–64

Introduction

In this chapter the first CE groupings, and the ideas underpinning their establishment, are traced. It was around these ideas that various networks of CEs developed with the resolve to lobby the Conservative Party to give effect to their particular prescriptions for educational change. In the early post-war period party political interest in the purposes of education was, at best, marginal. The preoccupations of ministers, LEAs, Parliament, press and public were with buildings and teachers, needed to cope with the rise in the birth-rate which first hit the schools in 1951. Oversize classes (forty or more pupils) and inadequate buildings were the dominant issues for politicians, civil servants and parents alike. Thus, the pressing needs of the schools took priority over all else. A wider vision of schooling was not yet developed.

All this began to change with the arrival of David Eccles at the Ministry of Education in 1954.[1] He believed that Britain needed not only more scientists and engineers but also a better trained workforce. He acted against the advice of his civil servants and educationists and forced a new conception of *technical education* upon the schools. He desired to see state schools work within the framework of the 1944 Education Act and to introduce new goals for educational institutions. Reflecting upon his period as Minister of Education, Lord Eccles has written:

> In 1954 I hoped to raise the quality of education in the sixth-forms of the maintained schools to a level where on academic grounds parents would not have to prefer fee-paying schools. We failed. First, because policies brought comprehensive education in and, secondly, because the number of teachers were doubled and their quality went down. More meant worse as I always said it would. Thirdly, it became more and more obvious that the curriculum was out of date.[2]

As will be shown in the following section, the early CEs were to be characterized by their conviction that the variety of schools which the 1944 Education Act envisaged had to be defended against the enforced uniformity of comprehensive education.[3]

Historians are generally agreed that Eccles was the first Conservative minister to register a growing public concern with the content of education (what was to be taught, and how, and to whom) and a growing belief that such questions could no longer be left to the professionals (see Judge, 1984, p. 56). However, one historian — himself of the same generation of CEs as Eccles — has been less than complimentary to the former Conservative Minister of Education, suggesting that whilst he was markedly more dynamic than his predecessor, Florence Horsburgh, his promise to preserve the grammar schools was a pledge he failed to fulfil and that, during his ministry, secondary modern schools were starved and neglected (see Howarth, 1985, p. 193).[4] This criticism seems strange given Kogan's assertion that it was Eccles who legitimized and stimulated the social demand for education, (Kogan, 1971, p. 22) who put large sums of money into the secondary modern schools which for a long time featured significantly in the Ministry of Education building programmes (Kogan, 1978, p. 30) and who set about increasing public support for public education (Kogan, 1985, p. 12).

The genesis of the CEs

To understand the genealogy of the first groupings of CEs it is important to appreciate that their concerns were borne out of the direction taken by education programmes administered by the Conservative governments (1951–1964). They were not all as convinced as Eccles that levelling-up educational opportunities was a good thing, though they were supportive of his attempts to improve the quality of schools, technical education and the training of teachers. Rather, they perceived that Butler's formulation of his 1944 Education Act as a giant umbrella under which all sorts of experiments could flourish, hardly suggested a coherent Conservative policy for education. They wanted shifts in emphasis in secondary education but they did not want these determined by what was, in their view, a misguided egalitarianism and equalitarianism.

It has been suggested by Seldon (1981) that education in the early 1950s was not bereft of controversy. Not only had the organization of secondary education not been definitively tackled in the 1944 Act, but a serious debate was beginning in the Ministry and in education circles on the value of comprehensive schools. Seldon has also noted that this debate had transcended the Conservative Party and that it was Angus Maude who proposed a motion, passed unanimously at the 1953 Conservative Party Conference, deploring the attempt to replace the tripartite system with comprehensive schools (*ibid.*, p. 277).

The true genesis of the CEs may be found within that alliance of nine Conservative MPs, first elected in 1950, who wrote the book *One Nation — A Tory Approach to Social Problems*.[5] The nine authors were Cuthbert Alport, Robert Carr, Richard Fort, Edward Heath, Gilbert Longden, Iain Macleod, Angus Maude, Enoch Powell and John Rodgers. Of these, Longden, Maude and Powell may be identified as CEs. Each would be committed to defending, what they would later call, 'standards of excellence'. Each would seek to preserve the grammar schools. Such would be their influence in helping to determine a conservative educational policy that even journals more often associated with support for the Labour Party would come to note their ascendant voice (see Corbett, 1969, pp. 785–7).[6]

The original One Nation group (which was a dining-club) focused on national welfare and in that sense they were considered to be to the left of the Conservative Party. The foreword to their book *One Nation* was written by Rab Butler. He wrote:

> They (the authors) have boldly squared up to the defects in the adminis-tration of the present vast system of social services. What is more, they have made positive suggestions with the object of remedying certain crying needs.

As well as housing, health, insurance and assistance, and the care of the elderly, the book also considered a social policy for industry, methods of paying for the social services and education. The essay on education was written by Angus Maude. A brief study of certain key passages in this essay will indicate the embryonic thinking of the early CEs.

First, we can read a statement of their general philosophy:

> ... (state) schooling can, and must, be provided economically; it can never be provided cheaply . . . . An average standard of education which is main-tained by lowering the highest standards of quality is worse than inade-quate; it cannot even be long maintained.[7]

Maude quoted with approval from the White Paper on *Educational Reconstruction* (Cmnd. 6548 of 1943) which preceded the introduction of the Butler Act:

> ... The new educational opportunities must not be of a single pattern. It is just as important to achieve diversity as it is to ensure equality of educational opportunity . . .

This insistence on opportunity for all and the acknowledgement of the diversity of human nature and talents, are threads which have run through Tory policy since Disraeli sought to heal the schisms and injustices of a modern industrial society.

In his essay Maude reviewed how the 1944 reforms had worked out in practice and made a number of observations about teaching and learning, the organization of the school curriculum and educational standards, each of which would become central tenets of the thinking of CEs in the period between 1950 and 1986.

On teaching and learning, he wrote:

> The modern insistence on 'humanizing' teaching methods . . . must not be made an excuse for abandoning the traditional disciplines of

learning . . . . We deplore the present tendency to drag down the brighter children to the level of the dull ones . . . [8].

We shall see in chapters 3 and 4 how the CEs set about formulating their own critique of what they termed 'modernism' (later more commonly termed 'progressivism') in education and how they used this critique as a basis for developing a conservative educational policy for the Conservative Party.

On the curriculum Maude emphasized the important role of religious teaching:

Under the Butler Act, special recognition is given to the place of religious instruction and worship in the daily life of children. A system of education in which religion found no place, which concerned itself purely with material things without cultivating the spiritual element in man's nature, would create a vacuum in which Communism would soon spread.[9]

The preservation of the denominational schools and the defence of religious education in the curriculum would become major issues for the CEs — men and women who would urge upon the Conservative Party the need to keep the religious experience central to schooling.

On educational standards Maude noted:

We believe it is essential that there should continue to be schools outside the State system. The best of them provide both a yardstick for educational standards and salutary competition for University Open Scholarships . . . . So long as they survive, and maintain good educational standards, we can see no reason for politicians to interfere with them.[10]

The belief in a diversity of educational provision, in and outside the state system, would prove common to CEs throughout our period of study.

The endorsement by later CEs of much of what the One Nation group advocated suggests that the thoughts of some Tory backbenchers in 1950 were the catalyst for that philosophy of *excellence in education* which evolved inside the Conservative Party during the succeeding thirty-six years. Specifically, the *One Nation* theme in Conservative philosophy — particularly the belief that the state should provide, in the area of social policy, a minimum standard above which people should be free to rise as far as their industry, their thrift, their ability or their genius might take them — was to provide a number of CEs with a doctrine that would convince them that theirs was the better way.[11]

It is an old Tory principle that 'unless it is necessary to change, it is necessary not to change'. Conservatives are pragmatic, and they have wanted educational changes to come about organically. As we have seen, the early One Nation CEs put 'excellence' high on the agenda for a Tory policy on education and opposed the notion that the state should provide an average standard of schooling. They did not want a uniform national plan and saw no reason why good grammar schools, technical or modern schools, should be swept away for something else that may have been no better and might have been worse.

It should be remembered that, during the thirteen years of Conservative government (1951–1964), the number of comprehensive schools rose from five to 195; and that long before *Circular 10/65*, sixty-eight LEAs had begun to implement concrete proposals for reorganizing secondary education, and twenty-one more were contemplating such proposals. Only fifty-nine were not even considering them — probably because it was not necessary to do so in their territories. This background of comprehensive school development particularly irked those CEs who were determined not to see the destruction of existing schools which had proved their worth and who would not, on any account, agree to the abolition of all selection.

Though the CEs would comprise numerous factions and tendencies, they were to successfully cohere around a set of ideas and causes. They would be both elitist and populist: elitist in their celebration of the virtues of selection in education; populist in their endorsement of certain aspects of popular culture and morality.

While not advocating drastic changes some CEs were, in the late 1950s, claiming that it was essential for the Conservative Party to clarify its thinking if it were to influence the future development of the social services. Brendon Sewill, then an economist working as a research officer in the economic section of the CRD, sought to signpost what he saw as 'the right direction' (Sewill, 1959). In education, he advocated giving parents more freedom in choosing their child's school which, he believed, would tend to create more interest and responsibility (*ibid.*, p. 59). He also urged that state schools should continue in exactly their present form (*ibid*).[12]

It has been generally assumed that the modern Conservative Party has not favoured intelligentsias as a basis for policy formulation. As two leading analysts of the Conservative Party have written:

> . . . Conservatism is a habit of mind which naturally disposes members of
> the party to perceive what is necessary in changing circumstances. (Norton
> and Aughey, 1981, p. 16)

Thus, what has commonly been stressed has been the belief of Conservatives in the superiority of enlightened pragmatism and their distrust of intellectualism (*ibid*).

Between 1950 and 1960 the early CEs had not yet formed an intelligentsia. While the small community of CEs before 1960 had a common shared experience no one issue or event had yet caused them to come together formally as a group.

Any shared experience can create a network within and without a political party. The more persistently and deeply an experience is shared, the more effective the network is likely to be. 1961 may be seen as a turning point, a year when orthodox educational thinking was already coming under critical scrutiny and when the Ministry of Education was having to respond to an increasing disquiet concerning the *state of the people*. Those who had guided education policy after 1951 had presumed a fundamentally civilized, moderate and caring quality of schooling aimed at securing the 'ladder of opportunity' for all. As Finch (1984) has argued, the period was essentially one of consolidation, but also a time when the beginning of the important challenges to the operation of the 1944 Act were developed (p. 21).

In 1961 the Minister of Education was starting to express a personal concern that educationists might perhaps consider a change to more exacting standards in their work. In a letter to the principals of all training colleges he observed:

> Public opinion in general is disturbed by the signs of lower standards of conduct, and people are looking to the education service for help in this matter. Reflecting on what we could do, I have thought first of the training of teachers.[13]

With his letter Sir David Eccles sent a personal memorandum in which he posed some questions and asked for assistance. What he desired was an exchange of information on the practical methods by which student teachers might be encouraged to rethink the teaching task and consider the importance of moral values. Within this memorandum, itself symptomatic of the Conservative Party's growing unease about the tendency towards permissiveness in the young, are to be found many of the concerns and beliefs that were being shared by a widening circle of CEs.

Thus, Eccles questioned the trend towards the teacher as a neutral educator:

> I have often heard it said that not so long ago it was considered right that all subjects should be taught in as neutral a manner as possible. One can see how this neutrality came into fashion. The nineteenth century escape of knowledge down a thousand new paths left the old landmarks deserted, and made it a matter of genuine doubt whether one set of values or tradition had more authority than another.[14]

Eccles considered this neutrality towards absolute values to be misguided and that the will was growing to define more clearly the ends in life. He was particularly disturbed by what he saw as 'the juvenile delinquency, which so disfigures our affluent society', which, in his view, was partly the result of parents being too indulgent with their children and their failure to provide moral protection at a critical stage in the child's life.

Eccles' quest for a return to the 'old landmarks' and his desire to see that children should find firmer moral principles at a time when their elders appeared to be making the pursuit of material interests their chief occupation, led him to assert:

> The schools themselves — as Plato and Aristotle first told us — have a special responsibility in shaping and upholding the ends which society should pursue. (*ibid.*)

From this Eccles affirmed that 'the school should be a place where good citizens are formed and where discipline is maintained'. Whilst there was nothing new in this philosophy its public statement by the Minister of Education may be seen as signalling that moment from which the CEs' case against modernism in education was given official Party sanction.

The distinguishing mark of CEs now was their search for stable schools, with firm patterns of discipline and strong moral standards. The most persistent and deeply felt experiences concerned the struggle to move away from the style and priorities of the *comprehensive school*. This concern would be manifested in the various networks of CEs established during the 1960s and 1970s (see chapters 3–6).

The second alliance of CEs took place in London in 1961. It was then that two London teachers — Rhodes Boyson (a member of the Labour Party and Headmaster at the Robert Montefiore School) and Harry Greenway (a member of the Conservative Party and Head of English at the Sir William Collins School) — met at the Oxford University Settlement in Bethnal Green. According to Greenway this was the initial encounter between those two strands of thought (the educational-right and the educational centre-right) that were to mark many of the later networks of CEs.[15] The meeting of Boyson and Greenway (two educationalists united by their conviction of the primary role of the school as a moral force in society) gave birth to a mutual friendship that was to hold a special significance in the light of future developments.[16] The immediate product of their meeting was the establishment of the 61 Society, which first met at the St James Hotel, Buckingham Gate, later moving to the St Stephen's Constitutional Club, Westminster.[17] Co-founded by Boyson and Greenway, this dining club group also included Russell Lewis and Dr James Koerner, both avowed critics of the egalitarian impulse and, what they saw to be, the attempts both in Britain and America to establish the standards and the ethos of schools by the average instead of the best.[18]

The founding of the 61 Society may be seen as an example of how effective intellectual weight was brought to bear on a question (how could schools escape educational mediocrity?) at a time when a small but growing number of people were beginning to appreciate the failure of policy-makers to look abroad, to see what might be learned from other countries about comprehensive schools. This grouping of like-minded individuals reflected the sense of urgency about education felt by those CEs who perceived that comprehensivization was threatening to destroy existing good schools. For the members of the 61 Society, changing schools in the name of egalitarianism was simply the triumph of purblind political dogma over educational common-sense. As Greenway has put it:

> ... our thinking evolved as a grass-roots drive against the pace of change
> from the tripartite system to comprehensive education without any proper
> research.[19]

As we have seen the whole tormented question of the comprehensive school had troubled the Conservative Party for several years. The Party's policy had been firmly stated on the issue and appeared unequivocal:

> What matters in education is the development of the child's talents and personality, not the forwarding of a political theory. To prepare for the increasing opportunities of the modern world we need all three kinds of secondary school, grammar, modern and technical, and we must see that each provides a full and distinctive education. We shall not permit the grammar schools to be swallowed up in comprehensive schools. (Conservative Party manifesto, 1955)

For the Party, the most urgent problem in education since the war had been to provide for the huge rise in the school roll. Between 1955 and 1960 the Party had sought to provide at least another million new school places, mostly in secondary schools. In this period it had intended to complete the reorganization of all-age classes in the rural areas and make good progress with reorganization in the towns. Additionally, the Party had pledged that it would tackle the problem of slum schools (*ibid*). Thus, the Conservative way had been to encourage far-sighted educational policies to augment the nation's scientific and technical skills. The Party had particularly denounced, what it saw as, Labour's desire to use the social services as an instrument for levelling down (*ibid*).

Given its conviction that the social services were not to be a levelling instrument and its questioning of the concept of the social services as an equalizing force[20], the Conservative Party's pronouncements on the comprehensive school may be seen as stemming from a belief that uniformity would not help the weak by its repression of the opportunities and independence of the strong. Thus, the Party considered that, by endeavouring to eliminate differences of educational opportunity wholesale, comprehensivization might threaten the standards of the ablest.[21]

Between 1960 and 1962, the Conservative government was still not giving much support to the comprehensive school (see Fenwick, 1976, p. 162). However, it was tolerating *comprehensive school* experiments and was prepared to acknowledge that some comprehensive schools were doing well (*ibid.*, pp. 118–9). This may explain why other groupings of CEs (see the following section) were now formed by those who were alarmed not only by the egalitarian impulse to change the social pattern of schooling but by, what appeared to them to be, the possibility of an ill-considered, headlong rush towards a monolithic system of comprehensive schools. These CEs would argue that there was a strong case to be made in Britain for maintaining multiplicity in types of schools, for avoiding massive standardization, for leaving room for heterodoxy and choice and dissent, even within the state system. They would suggest that there was an even stronger case to be made for the survival of those schools, both independent and maintained, which had earned over many years a reputation for excellence.

Dons and schoolteachers

Greenway has suggested that a marked feature of the widening range of CE groupings in the early 1960s was the fusion of 'intellectuals' and 'experience'.[22] Two CEs who were then already united in the belief that education should have a genuinely civilizing purpose, encouraging children to want to learn more, were Charles Brian Cox and Anthony Dyson.[23] Both were advocates of the *traditional school*, where children were instructed in real subjects and disciplines by teachers claiming authority, and where they were trained gradually to criticize as well as to receive. They believed the rules and regulations of the *traditional school* introduced children to the business of civilized living and moral duties, and encouraged them to enrich themselves as members of a culture older and larger than themselves. They also believed the values of civilization acted both as reward and incentive — while selection, competition and examination were a healthy preparation for real life.[24]

Cox and Dyson had met as undergraduates at Pembroke College, Cambridge, in 1949.[25] As we shall see in chapters 3 and 4, both would play a major role in locating and organizing those individuals who were prepared to fashion a conservative educational policy that ran counter to modern orthodoxy. This activity, which would formally begin in 1968, was pre-dated by their work in *The Critical Quarterly*.[26] Here their objective was to advance the view that high standards of lucid English and a wide appreciation of great literature remained powerful elements of the nation's common culture.

It was in 1961 that Cox and Dyson began their *Critical Quarterly* conferences for teachers at Bangor. The *Critical Quarterly* was not just a literary journal. From the beginning Cox and Dyson put the journal at the centre of an educational campaign.[27] The teacher conferences allowed for open debate on the teaching of English and literary appreciation but a special feature of these meetings was their questioning of writers' attitudes to Marxism. In 1963 Cox and Dyson organized their first *Critical Quarterly* conference for sixth-form students at Manchester.[28] Its educational purpose was to increase the number of people who enjoyed and appreciated literature. It was also in 1963 that Cox and Dyson established the *Critical Quarterly Society*, and started a new journal, *Critical Survey* (discontinued in 1973), which placed emphasis on the educational needs of schools.[29]

These early years of collaboration between Cox and Dyson were formative to that educational philosophy that each would shortly represent in their Black Paper writings, and which Cox, in particular, would state in speeches to CPC conferences and to CNACE regional groups, following his admission to the Conservative Party in 1972: namely, that creativity comes from discipline, and selection is the best promoter and measure of individual excellence.[30] The tendency of traditional Conservatives (partly because of their attachment to the past) to be authoritarian, anti-egalitarian and elitist, and to adapt to modern times the Renaissance ideal of education as largely the imitation of patterns of conduct depicted in literary works, was to be displayed in a number of later CE groupings (see chapters 3 and 4) who would seek to impress their vision upon the Conservative Party.[31]

The evolution on early CE thinking

The first groupings of CEs were established, and operated, in isolation. The important interactions between like-minded individuals, so essential if opinions are to be developed and fed into the grapevine of politicians, committees and party lobbies through which policies are made, would begin to occur when the Conservative Party was in opposition (1964–70), a period in which a 'loose-nexus' of CEs, linked by personal friendships, emerged.[32] These CEs, largely operating outside of mainstream politics, would associate *ad hoc* and contribute to a variety of books, journals and pamphlets to bring forward their opposition to, what they increasingly came to see as, the injustices committed in the course of an educational revolution: the shift to comprehensive schools and the rejection of clear academic standards (with *child-centred* teaching to enable each pupil to go at its own rate and *mixed ability* classes to prevent the differentiation of the brighter). They would be an 'invisible college'[33] of people fundamentally committed to an educational *counter-revolution* which would seek (amongst other things) to reaffirm the principle that civilized, harmonious society, cannot be imposed by government but must rest on the power of individuals to decide the degree of acceptable coercion.[34]

The evolution of early CE thinking and its gradual assimilation by sections of the Conservative Party (see chapters 3 and 4) would be determined by that body of people actively concerned with teaching at all levels, together with interested media correspondents, parents and other supporters who wished to campaign for a change in educational attitudes. This campaign would be the precursor to that more developed form of a conservative educational policy which the CEs were to fashion during the Conservative Party's third post-war period of opposition (see chapters 5 and 6).

Notes

1 Minister of Education (1954–57 and 1959–62).
2 Letter from Lord Eccles to author, 17 June 1986.
3 For a full statement of the argument, see Eccles, Lord (1967) pp. 114–6.
4 It may be noted here that David Eccles was educated at Winchester, the same school at which Tom Howarth taught much later after the Second World War as Second Master. Eccles' pledge on the grammar schools was made on 30 December 1954 when he told a joint meeting of the Associations of Assistant Masters and Assistant Mistresses 'My colleagues and I will never agree to the assassination of the grammar schools. We want you to continue and flourish'.

5 *One Nation: A Tory Approach to Social Problems*, CPC, 1950. The book's main thesis was that the best immediate means of improving the social services was to establish priorities. That portion of the nation's wealth dedicated to the social services was being partly wasted because the policy for applying it was ill-formulated. Each of the social services was therefore examined in some detail in order to elicit a rational scheme of priorities. One Nation was compatible with statism but did assert a Conservative emphasis upon private enterprise and voluntary services as essential for prosperity, vitality and welfare.

6 Corbett coined the term 'the preservationists' to describe those Conservatives who opposed the 'vested educational interests', the 'educational bureaucracy', and Tory orthodoxy on the importance of state education.

7 *One Nation* (1950) *op. cit.*, p. 39.

8 *Ibid.*, pp. 46–7. Maude warned that 'The new host of "experts", each with a specialist axe to grind, must be held in check'.

9 *Ibid.*, p. 47.

10 *Ibid.*, p. 49.

11 For a reflective account of the history of the One Nation Group and its place in the One Nation tradition of the Conservative Party, see Sir Gilbert Longden (1985) 'The original "One Nation" ', *Crossbow*, August.

12 It is interesting to compare Sewill's view with that of Sir Keith Joseph (PPS to Cuthbert Alport, CRO, 1957–1959). See chapter 5, note 44.

13 Letter from Sir David Eccles to principals of all training colleges, 6 October 1961, *The Longden Papers*.

14 Memorandum by Sir David Eccles to principals of all training colleges, 6 October 1961, *The Longden Papers*.

15 Harry Greenway MP, to author, 23 January 1986.

16 It was Greenway who sponsored Boyson into the Conservative Party in 1967 (and later on to the Parliamentary candidates list), the same year he co-opted Boyson on to the NACE (to which Greenway himself was elected in 1965). Later both Boyson and Greenway were to figure prominently in the work of the NCES, Boyson serving as its Chairman (1974–79) and Greenway serving as a member of its Executive Committee (1980–85). Both were to become North London MPs, Boyson (Brent North, 1974–) and Greenway (Ealing North, 1979–), and both were to rise to influential positions in the Conservative Party educational establishment: Boyson becoming, respectively, Vice-Chairman Conservative Parliamentary Education Committee (1975–76), Honorary Secretary CNACE (1975–78), an opposition spokesman on education (1976–79), and Parliamentary Under-Secretary of State, DES (1979–83); and Greenway becoming, respectively, Chairman, Greater London Area NACE (1970), a member of the Parliamentary Select Committee on Education, Science and the Arts (1979–), Vice-Chairman, Conservative Parliamentary Education Committee (1983–), and Parliamentary Secretary CNACE (1981–).

17 A venue which was later to host several Conservative groupings and key-note speeches, including meetings of the Salisbury Group, CPS talks and Norman Tebbits' First Disraeli Lecture. Both Boyson and Greenway have been members of the St. Stephen's Constitutional Club.

18 Russell Lewis, to author, 22 August 1986. Russell Lewis would become Director of the CPC (1967–75), an editorial writer on *The Daily Mail* and a biographer of Margaret Thatcher. Dr James Koerner was an American academic at MIT who had written a doctoral thesis on the destruction of the English grammar school. The 61 Society was disbanded in 1978.

19 Harry Greenway MP, to author, 23 January 1986.

20 For a description of post-war Conservative thought about the social services, see Powell (1953).

21 Though the modern Conservative Party has long held to the principle of an 'Educated Democracy' and insisted that a liberal education should hold first place in the opportunities available to every citizen, it has not acknowledged the existence of any real consensus in British society in support of the equality of classes.

22 Harry Greenway MP, to author, 23 January 1986.

23 Cox and Dyson were both English dons (Cox at the University of Hull and Dyson at Bangor).

24 In place of this, Cox and Dyson believed, Progressive Educationists proposed to put contempt for rules and traditional learning, and a total and obsessive concern for the 'self'. The 'self' was to be neither systematically instructed nor tested, but to be allowed to develop 'aptitudes' in a void. The formula was one of carefully nurtured ignorance and self-indulgence; sanctioned waywardness; hatred of customs, loyalties, duties; disregard for the claims or indeed the realities of the social world. Morality would become 'personal' in a manner divorced from tradition, and 'art' the mere outpouring of the 'self'. For a full exposition of the threat to traditional education posed by the Progressives, see Dyson (1969).

25 Professor Cox, to author, 21 February 1986. Significantly, they would both choose their old college for the inaugural meeting of the Council for the Preservation of Educational Standards (CPES) in January, 1972. It was their classics tutor, W. A. Camps, who acceded to their request for assistance in organizing a suitable venue.

26 *The Critical Quarterly* journal was co-founded by Cox and Dyson in 1959, from which date each acted as co-editor.

27 See Cox (1984). The journal was first planned by Cox and Dyson at a British Council summer course in Cambridge in 1958. Their interest was literary criticism. Through the journal they were able to propagate their ideas for changes to the teaching of English.

28 Since 1963 these school conferences have been held twice-yearly in Manchester.

29 In 1966 Cox moved from his lectureship at the University of Hull to a Chair in English Literature at the University of Manchester, and Dyson moved from his post at Bangor to a part-time lectureship at the University of East Anglia so he could co-edit *Critical Quarterly* from an office in London.

30 Professor Cox to author, 21 February 1986. In their contribution to the formulation of this philosophy both Cox and Dyson would be reacting primarily in opposition both to the decline of traditional authority and the permeation of contemporary culture by equalitarianism.

31 For a critique of traditional conservatism and its representation in English and American education, see Kueller (1984) pp. 219-33 and Phillips (1978) pp. 109-22.

32 John Barnes to author, 22 March 1985.

33 John Burton to author, 5 July 1985.

34 A number of the propagandists of the educational 'counter-revolution' would be participants in the more global intellectual counter-revolution that also developed in the late 1960s and 1970s. For example, Rhodes Boyson and Russell Lewis would meet and collaborate with Ralph Harris, and all three would assemble in the Mont Pelerin Society — a venue in which educational policy has been discussed on many occasions — founded by Hayek to further the post-war revival of classical liberalism. For an outline of the intellectual counter-revolution and its impact upon government in Britain, see Seldon (1983).

Chapter 3

'What we need is a sober and careful analytical presentation of the Conservative case': The preservationists state their philosophy, 1964–70

Introduction

The Conservatives' election defeat in October 1964 gave sign of the ascendancy of socialist ideas (for example, the concepts of human equality and social justice). We saw in chapter 2 that these ideas were, in the view of early CEs, hostile to traditional conservative views and so it had been necessary to attack them. We shall now see how this attack was levelled against individual Conservatives who showed themselves sympathetic to such ideas.

Traditional conservative views, with their emphasis on preserving existing institutions and the authority of the state, had found a ready echo in the small circle (but not as yet network) of CEs who, since 1950, had advanced a belief in diversity, elitism and selection. These CEs believed in ruling classes and in a quite powerful state because they saw it in the role of the father, with all kinds of duties and responsibilities towards the children, who were the people. There was also a moral dimension to the attitudes of the early CEs, a very strong belief in moral values founded for the most part on Christian religious principles. To these CEs, socialism and socialist practices were immoral; each had become nothing more than secondhand charity or doing good at other people's expense.

One CE who felt this was Rhodes Boyson and he believed socialists, in 1964, were propagating what they saw as good for others (comprehensive education and progressive schooling) but not what was good for themselves.[1] Socialists were treating 'the people' as though they had 'expendable consciences'.[2] The conviction that socialism and socialist practices were institutionalized bribery, linked a growing number of CEs after 1964.[3]

The Wilson victory (narrow in 1964 but decisive in the follow-up election of 1966) marked the start of the second, and most important, formative period of CE thought. The early CE line (1950–1964) had had a *One Nation* provenance. It was political reality in 1964 which caused the CEs to adjust their thinking and provide fresh approaches to the education debate.

Describing the Conservative Party's failures of planning in the years before 1964, one CE has suggested (Butt, 1986a)[4] that the Tory government was not defeated simply because of internal dissensions nor because the public had become bored with it (though both were true) but because it had turned to economic and social policies which were a diluted form of its opponents' ideas. There had been a belief that Britain had lost her momentum because her institutions had become outmoded — a 'What's wrong with Britain?' mood had prevailed which was undoubtedly heightened by the growing disillusion with the performance of the Conservative government under Macmillan in the first years of the 1960s (Butt, 1969, p. 6).

According to one historian (Blake, 1986, p. 416) the period 1963–64 saw the Conservative Party not only bereft of policy and purpose but divided between those who believed in tradition and those who wanted to modernize Britain. As we shall see, this division in the Party would be especially marked in the area of education policy and would be represented in the opposing views of Angus Maude and Sir Edward Boyle.[5] Maude was one of the foremost publicists for a Conservative Party representing the voice of English history, English traditions and experience; Boyle was an enlightened Tory and, like R. A. Butler, adhered to the liberal Conservative tradition with its tendencey to seek radical alterations in existing social welfare systems. Their uneasy relation would be symptomatic of the divergence of view in the Party on how best to manage the quality and content of education.

Both Maude and Boyle regarded selection as an essential part of the education system. Although they could find agreement on several points — especially on opposing socialism — they disagreed over the comprehensive school issue. Boyle represented a changed attitude to the 11+ in the Party and defended the movement by local authorities towards more informal methods of selection, and to a less rigid conception of the role of the grammar school (Fenwick, 1976, p. 12). This approach was opposed by CEs like Maude who saw egalitarian attitudes and enmity to tradition as a cause of Britain's malaise.[6] However, Heath's appointment of Sir Edward Boyle as Shadow Minister in charge of policy formation in November 1965 and Deputy Chairman of the ACP was to severely restrict the permeation of the Maude-view into Party policy-making in opposition.

It has been suggested (Brittan, 1968, p. 73) that dissenters against any of the front-bench policies of the moment are too easily written off as extremist, far removed from the middle ground for which the Conservative and Labour parties are supposed to be fighting. However, in Maude's *Good Learning* (1964),[7] possibly the most important CE statement prior to the Black Papers, we find neither evidence of a dissenter facing pressure to support the conventionally enlightened policies of the moment nor of an extremist Tory intent to make unreasoned ideas fashionable. What we do find is a

CE believing that what education is all about is *teaching and learning* and proposing that any genuinely educational policies (as opposed to all those *policies for education* which are directed at trends not essentially connected with education) must be concerned with what, and how much, is being learnt — how fast and how well. These certainly are obvious truths, but to Maude they were, despite their fundamental importance, being almost universally ignored in the politics of the educational world in 1964. Only by their pursuit, Maude argued, could *excellence in education* be secured.

Maude was one of the Party's leading authorities on education, having been Chairman of the Conservative Education Committee in 1954–55 and 1963. In 1964 he was a member of the Conservative Teachers' Association National Advisory Committee (CTANAC). In *Good Learning*, he described the Conservative approach to education as not wanting to destroy any existing good institutions but to encourage all manner of experiments. Maude's exposition of the Conservative approach to education was firmly rooted in the belief that government should stimulate, not stifle, the wide variety of educational provision needed to meet the requirements of many different communities and individuals (*ibid.*, p. 88). Though it was by no means the archetypal expression of CE opinion, the book did contain an important declaration:

> It is right that the government should set standards that must be met: but the best results will be achieved with the maximum possible freedom for LEAs and voluntary bodies to work out their own systems in the most suitable ways. (*ibid*)

Maude believed that there should be a high degree of democratic local control of local education. This would not only enable local needs and problems to be met by distinctive *ad hoc* methods, but would also allow for a variety of local experiments from the results of which all might benefit.

In the book's concluding chapter ('The Right Way') Maude contrasted the Conservative government's record on education and Labour Party's plans for education. The book, of course, was penned by Maude and published before the Tories' election defeat. Thus, the tone of Maude's rhetoric is strongly partisan with its self-congratulation ('Conservative concern for education, and success in achieving great improvements, have been clearly demonstrated by results') (*ibid.*, p. 93) and scathing in its accusation ('attempts to belittle these achievements come strangely from the Labour Party, which has no educational reforms at all to its credit in the whole of its history') (*ibid*). According to Maude, twelve years of Conservative government had produced a rate of educational progress which amounted to nothing less than a 'social revolution' (*ibid*). He believed a Labour government might endanger the whole basis of educational advance because the Labour Party offered only a few stale, doctrinaire threats based on political prejudice rather than educational needs (*ibid.*, pp. 93–4). As Maude put it 'They would destroy what is best in our schools without putting anything better in its place'. (*ibid.*, p. 94). Freedom, variety, experiment and change were all essential to education and under Tory governments, argued Maude, they had had full play, with impressive results. He considered that 'it would be tragic if socialism strangled them' (*ibid*).

The CEs' fear of socialism as 'the enemy of educational progress' embodied in Maude' writings, requires our special attention. Not only did it run right through CE expressed opinion (in books, pamphlets, Party speeches etc.) during the whole of our period but it may well have prompted Maude's appeals to his Party in 1966 to develop its own philosophy: philosophy would tell Conservatives what it was they wanted to conserve. It was CEs inside the Conservative Party who, perhaps more than anybody else, appreciated the rising power of socialism as an intellectual force and the need for Conservatives to meet its challenge. But even as recently as 1971 one eminent Conservative intellectual would conclude:

> The Tory party has emotions but no doctrine . . . . The Conservative Party
> has maintained continuity and preserved its identity, but there has been no
> coherent ideological development. (Gilmour, 1971, p. 84)[8]

Though Maude's *Good Learning* did not, in any way, contain a refinement of CE principles it did herald the start of the CEs' campaign to preserve the traditional curriculum against aggressive mediocrity at a time when so-called 'progressive' teaching and learning was in the ascendant. In this context it is possible to agree with Gamble's assessment (1974) that, from 1964, Maude represented the forces of a *New Right* tendency (p. 87).[9] Certainly Maude was not alone in feeling that developments in education now dictated a need for realism in policy and a critical attack upon education's 'pseudo-experts' and 'liberal-minded educators'. Other CEs who now believed in the tradition of Burke, Disraeli and the gifted amateur, were similarly disposed towards identifying a philosophy for the formulation and conduct of a conservative educational policy. For example, from 1964, Rhodes Boyson moved to a *New Right* position on education having discovered a new 'iron-mood' in the nation, a preference for freedom and a contempt for tyranny.[10]

Although Gamble (1974, p. 264) has noted how the *New Right* gradually came, from 1964, to express a mood in the Party and secure a strong base in the constituency associations (the latter being a prerequisite for the formation of Party policy), he has explained its growing influence in terms of the failing leadership of the Right Progressives (such as Sir Edward Boyle) and the growing problems of the state, rather than in terms of its own particular coherence. This misses the point. What people like Maude and Boyson were seeking was not outside the framework of traditional Conservative principles.[11] But they wanted, and expected, the electorate to turn to the Conservatives for radical change and this meant formulating ideas for people to vote for. It meant producing policies which were sharp in focus and coherent in presentation. This required the Party to shift its emphasis and proclaim new priorities.

From 1964 Maude, Boyson and other Conservatives opposed to modernist, enlightened Toryism would meet with others to exchange ideas and begin to formulate proposals for a change of course in Party policy. These 'Right-mided People' would form, what Ralph Harris has called, the 'awkward squad'[12] — a distinct body of individuals inclined to oppose the post-war consensus because of its obstruction to principled and open debate. Maude's role would be to 'toughen-up' Tory education policy.[13] Though Maude was a friend of Sir Edward Boyle he felt him to be 'all wrong on education'.[14] Maude believed in the principle that 'learning is hard work', something which he thought the new egalitarian educationalists had overlooked.[15]

In defence of excellence

The Maude-line on education had the support of Gilbert Longden.[16] In 1965 — the year that fellow One Nation MP Edward Heath was elected Party leader, and Sir Edward Boyle was made Shadow Minister in charge of policy formation and Deputy Chairman of the ACP — Longden was elected Honorary Secretary of the CTANAC, an office he retained when the CTANAC became the NACE in 1966 and held the post until 1974. Longden, like Maude, was a preservationist: a defender of educational excellence. He had joined the CTANAC in 1962 where he had, again, met regularly with Maude (a close friend and joint *One Nation* founding member).

Longden's position on the CTANAC (NACE) was significant. He was both a Heathite (he supported Heath for the Tory leadership) and a personal friend of Sir Edward Boyle, but he did not share Boyle's line on comprehensivization.[17] Preservationist thinking on the CTANAC (NACE) was not yet a coherent rival philosophy to modernist, enlightened Toryism. Nevertheless, between 1965 and 1968 the preservationist voice was strengthened by the presence of Dr Kathleen Ollerenshaw,[18] Harry Greenway and Dr Rhodes Boyson. All three were to join forces with Longden and Maude in fighting ill-thought out comprehensive school schemes.

It was on the CTANAC (NACE) that Longden first met Greenway and Boyson.[19] He was conscious that they were both right-wing but he admired them because he believed they had 'the right approach to education'.[20] He supported their search for, and defence of, standards of excellence.[21]

On the CTANAC (NACE) Longden acted as the 'gatekeeper' of educational-right and educational centre-right opinion.[22] His role was important because it was his job to vet CTANAC (NACE) minutes prior to their forwarding to Boyle and Heath and, in a later period, to Thatcher, Stevas and Heath. Longden himself was now a member of the educational-right.[23] With Maude, Ollerenshaw, Greenway and Boyson, he would express the case for quality in education.[24]

Longden's own preservationist instincts were first formulated in a pamphlet *A Conservative Philosophy* (published privately by Longden in September 1947). This paper was dedicated to his supporters in the Parliamentary divisions of Watford and Morpeth,[25] and urged each of them to help in 'the resuscitation of the English character'.[26] Longden argued that there was only one fundamental issue that divided political opinion — man's relationship to the State (the issue of individual freedom, the reconciliation of the two, at first sight conflicting, concepts of order and liberty).

In *A Conservative Philosophy* Longden described Socialism as 'an alien and malignant virus which has to be defeated' (p. 4). He denied the socialists' claim that it was in man's best interests to be nursed, or if necessary dragooned, from the cradle to the grave as if he were still but semi-civilized (p. 6). This, for Longden, was to underestimate and insult civilized man and, in particular, the British character. It was not the prime duty of the state (acting through the comparatively few privileged officials of the Party in power) to be man's nursery-governess, his schoolmaster or his policeman (pp. 6–7). However, Longden did assert the commitment of Conservatives to 'change' (pp. 10–11). Here he took his lead from the briefly expressed policy bequeathed to Conservatives by Disraeli: the maintenance of the nation's institutions; the preservation of the Empire (now called the Commonwealth); and the elevation of the condition of the people. To Longden, and to Conservatives generally, Disraeli's three great aims were still the determined objects of the Party. The first two were to be regarded as the means to the achievement of the third. The elevation of the condition of the people implied improvement, which meant change. Conservatives did not oppose, in fact they had often initiated, enlightened and necessary change (p. 11). But like other preservationists (most particulary Maude) Longden wished to be satisfied that the objects of any given change were sound and that the methods of change were the most appropriate and effective ones (p. 11). Thus, it was the duty of Conservatives to conserve all that had been won (p. 11). Such an approach would, as we shall see, closely determine Longden's attitude towards secondary school reorganization.

Since Longden's adherence to Disraelian Conservatism (particularly the conservation of the institutional legacies of the past against whatever movement, group or party appeared to threaten them) was pivotal in shaping his own educational philosophy,[27] it was not unexpected that his view of education would prove to be at some variance with the official Tory line on education (as expressed by Heath and represented by Boyle). Evidence of this variance is to be found in personal commentaries by Longden, private correspondences between Longden and Boyle, and speeches by Longden to Party conferences.

The official Tory line on education, in 1965–66, was that whilst the Party believed there was room for a variety of systems of education, it was premature to attempt a reasoned judgment on comprehensive and other types of secondary education.[28] Consequently, the Party agreed with the Crowther Report (1959) that no good school should be lost whatever its classification, and therefore deplored reorganization for doctrinaire political reasons. The official Tory line on education also embraced a conviction that the grammar school, having proved its great worth through generations, had still an invaluable part to play in a modern British educational system; accepted that a comprehensive type of education might, in certain areas, be the most suitable form of secondary provision, and that any reorganized educational system should allow for co-existence of grammar and comprehensive schools (reorganized systems should provide for the continuance as separate entities of existing grammar schools of proved efficiency); and affirmed the belief that the direct grant and independent schools were an integral part of the national educational system and that nothing should be done to their detriment.[29]

Longden was in total sympathy with each of these principles and gave support to the Party's criticism of attempts to treat the education system as a medium for political action or of providing an opportunity to implement ideological theories. However, events and developments during 1965–66 caused Longden to question Boyle's representation of the official Tory line on education.

On 21 January 1965 the Tory opposition had moved a resolution urging the government to discourage LEAs from adopting schemes of reorganization at the expense of grammar and other existing schools of proven efficiency and value, and deploring any proposal to impose a comprehensive system upon LEAs. But the government tabled an amendment alleging that the raising of educational standards was impeded 'by the separation of children into different types of secondary schools' and approving 'reorganization on comprehensive lines which will provide all that is valuable in grammar school education for those children who now receive it and make it available to more children'. The Liberals voted against the Tory resolution and abstained on the amendment which was carried and the result was *Circular 10* of 12 July 1965, by which Crosland requested that all LEAs should prepare and submit, within twelve months, plans for comprehensive reorganization throughout the territory for which they were responsible. *Circular 10/65* was merely an expression of the Minister's wishes; if these were to become commands, legislation would be necessary.

At the January 1966 Northern Education Conference, Sir Edward Boyle was asked if he would withdraw this Circular when the Conservatives came back to office. He replied that he would continue to judge individual proposals of LEAs on their merits as he and his predecessors had always done. Shortly after, he made it clear that in any circular which he issued, he would substitute the sense of the Tory resolution for the socialist amendment; and that he repudiated the declared socialist objective of abolishing all selection. In a personal commentary[30] Longden welcomed Boyle's commitment to the view of the Party, which was to go slow and leave LEAs freedom to decide (in collaboration with their teachers and in accord with parents' wishes) what was best for the children in the light of local conditions, but deeply regretted that the Party was not campaigning more forcibly against the pace of secondary school change. What Longden desired was pragmatic adaptations to new social and economic conditions without sacrificing the best of the old traditions:

Conservatives are pragmatic, and want educational changes to come about organically: and we put excellence first. We do not condemn comprehensive schools out of hand. It would be foolish to do so for many are doing an excellent job. But we will not destroy existing schools which have proved their worth; we will not, on any account, abolish all selection; and far from preventing, I hope we will encourage parents to pay for, or contribute towards, their children's education in public and direct grant schools.[31]

In May 1966 Longden, who was now a member of both the Education Committee and the Policy Group of the Party, entered into a series of correspondences with Sir Edward Boyle and the Conservative members of the South-West Herts Divisional Executive. These show Longden's increasing concern about the direction of Tory education policy, the Shadow Minister's role in stating and representing Party education policy and the failure of the Central Office in educating Party supporters about Tory education strategy.

Following a meeting of the CTANAC, which, as we have seen, now had a strong preservationist representation, Longden informed Boyle:

They were, I am afraid, all very hot under the collar and do not think that the Parliamentary Party is pulling its weight . . . .As you will know, since Saturday's meeting, Circular 13/66 of 23 May has appeared in which LEAs are again required to show for each proposal in their secondary programme for 1968/69 'that it would be compatible with an intention of introducing a non-selective system' (para. 6(b)). This reinforces para. 5 of 10/66 in which Crosland warns LEAs that he will not approve any new secondary projects which would be incompatible with a comprehensive system. This seems to Conservative teachers to be alteration of the law by blackmail.[32]

According to Longden, the story repeated time after time by teachers from various parts of the country was that:

Conservative members of LEAs and Divisional Executives simply do not know what the Party's policy is; and that, if one of them attempts to state what he thinks it is, he is at once countered by some Socialist quoting you.[33]

Longden told Boyle that he had already put out one broadsheet in explanation and defence of Tory policy and that he had also written an article in *The Parent Teacher*, and was now circularising members of the Divisional Executive in South-West Hertfordshire.[34] He concluded, 'I think it is now time for the Central Office to take the lead in educating our supporters'.[35] Longden sent a copy of his letter to Heath and to Richard Hornby.[36]

The circular letter referred to by Longden, a copy of which was also sent to Boyle, outlined the proposals for reorganizing secondary education in Longden's own constituency. It was issued by Longden because, as he put it:

> the National Advisory Committee of the Conservative and Unionist Teachers' Association tell me, as its Honorary Secretary, that they are concerned that so few people interested in education seem to know what our Party policy is.[37]

Longden reminded members that, in Circular 10/65, Crosland had described the policy of the Labour Government as being 'the complete elimination of selection and separatism in secondary education'. In other words, said Longden,

> LEAs are to be blackmailed into discarding completely the tripartite system laid down by Parliament in the 1944 Education Act and replacing it universally by a new and, as yet, untried experiment. (*ibid.*)

Whilst Longden acknowledged that the tripartite system was not perfect and that Conservative ministers had encouraged alternative experiments such as comprehensive schools, he asserted 'no Minister has the right to amend an Act of Parliament by decree'. (*ibid.*)

Longden took some comfort from the appreciation that Crosland's circulars of 1965 and 1966 were only requests to conform to a socialist pattern of education, and that LEAs still had sufficient autonomy to refuse to comply with them if they thought that the educational needs of their children were being better catered for under their existing arrangements — with or without modification. This view had been reinforced in speeches by Boyle, who believed that not only had the Secretary of State no power to direct authorities to reorganize comprehensively but that there was nothing 'inevitable' or 'irresistable' about a bad or unrealistic plan. It was Boyle's belief that the 'irresistable' in history was all too often simply that which people had not bothered to resist, and that the right approach was to concentrate on reorganization in those parts where there was still insufficiently wide opportunity, and ensure that 'selection' never involved taking a final view of a child's potential ability, while doing as little as possible to disturb those existing institutions which were already doing a first-rate job.

Longden, too, believed that equality of opportunity was nowhere more important than in education. But he questioned Boyle's growing support for comprehensivization, and asked:

> Can we yet be sure that a universally imposed system of comprehensive schools — especially since the majority of them could not possibly be built for the purpose — would give all children equality of opportunity? (*ibid.*)

Taking a lead from the Crowther (1959) and Newsom (1963) Reports, which had both warned against sweeping away good selective schools for the sake of replacing them by a system which had yet to prove itself, Longden declared:

> The Herts., LEA in its Circular of October 1965 is satisfied that the rapid

development and success of our secondary schools ensures that no one today is deprived of the opportunity to progress to higher education. By all means let comprehensive schools co-exist with good grammar and secondary modern schools as they could easily do in our county. That would give a genuine measure of parental choice. (*ibid.*)

Here, Longden formulated an important modification to CE thinking on secondary school organization. Obviously aware of the rising support for comprehensive schools in the population, and recognizing the electoral dangers of too rigid a secondary education policy, Longden was now (somewhat defensively) prepared to accept the notion of the *comprehensive school* but only as an adjunct to the CEs' defence of parental choice. His preservationist instincts, however, remained unchanged. Although he acknowledged that everyone now agreed 11+ selection was unfair and wasteful of talent, and that it had, in fact, all but disappeared, he was concerned that much more wasteful of talent would be a system where there was no selection at any stage of a pupil's educational life — the declared object of *Circular 10/65*. In what may be seen as a deliberate attempt to remind the Shadow Minister of his Conservative duty to guard against educational mediocrity, Longden wrote:

It is estimated that, at present, not more than 25 per cent or so of our children can benefit from a grammar school or academic kind of education and it is vitally important that the intellects of these brighter children shall be encouraged and trained to their own and the Nation's best advantage; and almost certainly that is best done in separate establishments. (*ibid.*)

For Longden, perhaps the worst feature of the whole business of secondary school reorganization was that Crosland had admitted that the declared object of *Circular 10/65* was primarily a social one: that he did not claim that the reorganization that he advocated would provide a better education for any individual child. In the view of Longden, and CEs more generally, nothing could be more damaging to the nation and its children.

A Conservative approach to secondary school reorganization

Conservative Party policy on education was now largely non-partisan, promising to give primary education a high priority and, in the reorganization of secondary education, accepting the movement away from selection. However, as we have seen, some CEs were decidedly uneasy about the latter development. Following the Conservative Party's election defeat of 1966 the non-partisan approach to education was increasingly questioned by CEs, and, although the general direction of policy up to 1970 would be unaffected by their criticisms, some principal CE tenets were formulated by the central Party organization.

Probably the most pressing problem facing local Party organizations was the attitude that should be adopted towards plans for the reorganization of secondary schools. The Party considered that many of the schemes for reorganization were badly thought out; many of the schemes involved the breakdown of well-established, recognizably good, grammar or secondary modern schools. Yet it felt it important to adopt — and be seen to adopt — a positive, not a negative, approach to the changes proposed.[38]

It is important to understand that when the Conservative Party is in opposition much policy-making is done in the CRD, whilst presentation is largely in the hands of the CCO. In 1966, those inside the circle of non-Central Office advisers around Heath and the Shadow Cabinet were conscious that it was very easy to be perceived as adopting a negative, obstructing role — perhaps, in part, because the press expected the Party to react in that predictable way to the amalgamation of good, with less favoured schools. The CRD now affirmed that the Party should welcome — and be seen to welcome — change, provided that what was proposed fulfilled certain definite conditions, and that it enabled positive educational aims to be achieved (CRD, 1966 memorandum). In order to assess the attitude that should be adopted towards reorganization proposals, the CRD advised that the Party had first to agree on what the aims of education for children between the ages of 11 and 18 should be; only then could the means to the end — the pattern of school organization — be ideally inferred.

In its approach document *Putting Britain Right Ahead* (October 1965) the Party had enunciated the principle that all young people should have the opportunity to receive the kind of education that would enable each of them to travel along the education road as far as their ability and perseverance might carry them. This was a developed expression of the view of the 1944 Act that education should be provided in accordance with the age, ability and aptitude of young people. Whilst the CRD considered this to be eminently satisfactory as a guiding principle for the individual, it noted the omission of the problems that would be encountered in translating principle into practice. The CRD suggested the educational aims for the 11 to 18 group should include: a firm orientation towards an appreciation by all, of scientific endeavour, technical activity and the human environment within which these occurred (particularly industry); greater emphasis on artistic and creative achievement and less on deductive analysis; the discouragement of any system of education which promoted premature specialization and early choice of options; and the encouragement of as broad based an education as was possible. Not all of these aims would be endorsed by CEs. However, beside the educational aims, the CRD's formulation of two Tory aims which it considered to be appropriate to an analysis of organizational change, did meet the CEs' demands for quality in education. These were the 'pursuit of excellence', by which was meant the best secondary organizational system was one which was most capable of generating a climate in which children would learn, and be taught, most effectively; and the continuing attempts to increase, rather than diminish, the 'opportunities for individual choice', which related not only to the choice of school but also to the choice of subjects and areas of study within schools.

The CRD review attempted, in effect, to examine the scope for political action, to produce a different platform from which to question proposals put forward by local authorities in response to *Circular 10/65*. It concluded that if the reorganizations proposed were assessed on the basis of clearly established aims of secondary education, and the overriding Tory aims as expressed in terms of the 'pursuit of excellence' and the increasing 'opportunities for individual choice', this would not only help the Party in changing the traditional pattern of the dispute between the parties, but help significantly in reaching a carefully thought out solution to the educational problems of the local area.

The CRD's formulation of 'excellence' and 'choice' as an integral part of future Conservative education policy owed much to Anthony Greenland (Education Desk Officer, CRD, 1961–72). Himself a CE in the preservationist mould,[39] it was his role to transmit ideas for education policy from the CRD to Boyle and Heath. Boyle has recorded how Greenland briefed him 'quite admirably'.[40] Greenland's recollection of the relationship is that they each worked 'very closely together' and were both 'sympathetic to small local comprehensive experiments'.[41] The gradual fusion of preservationist thinking on education and enlightened Toryism inside the Party machine, had its origin in this personal bond, a bond strengthened by a mutual recognition of the need to get the Party 'to accept the reality of the move towards comprehensive education'.[42] Their task was not an easy one: whilst Boyle sat as Chairman on the Conservative Parliamentary Education Committee (PEC) his sometime critic — Longden — sat as Secretary. The divisions between the two (which were ideological rather than personal) were mediated by Greenland. It was Greenland's responsibility to attend NACE meetings with Longden but Greenland felt that the NACE was 'neither an important or influential body'.[43] Boyle's position regarding the NACE, and Longden's Honorary Secretaryship, appears to have been less dismissive. According to Greenland, Boyle viewed the NACE as 'a bit of a nuisance'.[44] Tensions were probably eased by Boyle's and Heath's agreement over the newly-formulated approach to secondary school reorganization.[45] Lord Vaizey has observed (1983, p. 102) that Boyle never embraced the fancier, vaguer visions of the Right. As we have seen, the CRD formulation was very much centre-right, adopting both preservationist and enlightened Tory aims.[46].

In the CRD Greenland worked alongside another defender of educational excellence — Brendon Sewill (Director of CRD, January 1965–September 1970). Sewill supported the ideas of the One Nation Group on education having read their book *One Nation*, and having been impressed by Maude's contributive essay.[47] His own principal concern in the sphere of education was 'to examine how education could assist the economic enterprise and achievement of the nation'.[48] Between 1965 and 1970 he did not see education as a major political issue though there was a worry over Boyle and comprehensivization.[49] Sewill's view of the NACE was more positive and supportive than that of either Greenland or Boyle. He has recalled 'the NACE did not worry us — they could look after themselves'.[50]

In 1965 Sewill had written a letter to Boyle (which Boyle found a useful analysis), saying that the problem with comprehensive schools was that they were too large, and that Tories should rather favour sixth-form colleges and middle schools to enable only 'academic' young people to enter sixth-forms.[51] The move over to comprehensive schooling was, for Sewill, the 'real issue' of the 1960s, and his letter to Boyle was an attempt to re-assert the case for excellence without the need to reintroduce selection, the case for which he considered had been lost in the public debate of the 1950s and early 1960s.[52] According to Sewill, it was because the 11 + had, by 1964, been publicly discredited that Heath had accepted the move to comprehensive schools, but only at a reasonable pace.[53] Sewill's preservationist impulse was strong and was not diminished by the onward march of Socialist doctrine or enlightened Toryism:

> Heath was no different to Macmillan and Home on the comprehensive schools issue. Boyle had to carry the Party's policy at the Annual Conferences. In my letter to Boyle I was appealing for smaller schools and segregation by age — not ability — to ensure that, despite the comprehensive school system, excellence would be encouraged.[54]

During Sewill's incumbency as Director of the CRD the issue of excellence and standards in education was not on the Shadow Cabinet agenda, and education was discussed purely in terms of its contribution to the economy.[55] Moreover, the preservationists were not making ground as quickly as they had hoped:

> Inside the Party the impact of the preservationists was, up until 1970, marginal. I remember that Kathleen Ollerenshaw was a member of Heath's education policy group but the group never reported on anything major.[56]

Part of the problem, of course, was Boyle. Boyle was not a traditional Tory politician; he was a radical social democrat and, like Crosland, he represented liberal social democracy and its ideals at work. Significantly, Boyle and Crosland were friends.[57] Boyle had already demonstrated his social democrat approach when, as Minister of Education in the Macmillan and Home governments, he had developed a new, liberal Tory education policy, one which he believed was free from political dogma and based on the principle of social justice. Whilst a policy of equal opportunity had been pursued, he had endeavoured to protect educational standards. Writing to Sewill's predecessor, Sir Michael Fraser (Director of CRD, 1951–1964), Boyle had remarked:

I understand that you and Eldon Griffiths would find it helpful to have a few suggestions on the philosophy of education and why our Party attaches such importance to expansion of the service.[58]

In his letter Boyle stressed that one argument for rising levels of educational expenditure was that it fitted in with the Conservative ideal of an *Opportunity State*. He also emphasised that the whole purpose of education and of growing wealthier as a nation, was to encourage the spread of humane values — cultural awareness, toleration and emotional maturity. It was precisely because Boyle's philosophy of education, despite the 1966 CRD formulation, continued to permeate the direction of Conservative education policy, that the preservationists continued their challenge to, what they saw as, the illegitimate demands of the enlightened Tories.

The case for a 'new look' in education

Between 1967 and 1970 the preservationists were to increase their calls for a restoration of traditional conservative education principles to counter the Socialists' ideal of a collectively enforced equality of condition in schooling. Boyle's failure to condemn comprehensive schemes outright brought on him heated criticism from preservationist Conservative MPs and rank-and-file Party members.

To understand the reaction of Boyle's critics, and the way their campaign developed, it is necessary to trace and examine Boyle's statements on comprehensivization: first, to appreciate his conception of a Tory policy for secondary education and, second, to appreciate the objections of some preservationists to the Party's *New Look* in education (see pp. 36–8).

Boyle's association with Crosland was not the sole explanation of his social democratic tendencies. In February 1965 Boyle had been made a patron of PEST (Pressure for Economic and Social Toryism) in succession to R. A. Butler. In 1954 he had been made President of the Birmingham Bow Group, an office he held until 1978. The Shadow Minister took his lead on secondary school reorganization from the 1958 White Paper *Secondary Education For All: A New Drive*, which had made it quite clear that Conservatives saw a place for the comprehensive school, or local patterns of schooling on comprehensive lines, within the overall national provision of secondary education. Lord Butler had told Boyle on a number of occasions that he never intended in his 1944 Act to establish a tripartite system of education which should remain rigid for all time.[59]

Boyle believed that there were two types of area, in particular, where some form of comprehensive organization might prove best: in relatively scattered rural districts of few large centres of population, and in new housing areas. He never accepted, or acted on, the view that every small market town could expect to maintain its own grammar school (maybe a very small one) unaltered and unreorganized. In Boyle's view, secondary schools did not, as a rule, want to be too large, but neither should they be too small, and this is why he thought a county like Anglesey was quite right to go for the comprehensive pattern. Boyle's point was that local authorities were to be free to choose, and that nobody should attempt to assert, as a matter of dogma, that whereas socialists were, in principle, in favour of comprehensive schools, Conservatives were equally committed against them. He considered that, what he and other Conservatives were opposed to, was the rapid and universal imposition of comprehensive school education (especially in the large cities) involving the loss of integrity of established schools of real excellence.

Such a view, as already shown, was not restricted to Tory educators alone. Prior to 1964 Labour Party supporters like Brian Cox and Rhodes Boyson had voiced a similar opinion. What the preservationists wanted was some positive indication from Boyle that his interpretation of the *New Look* would not put their conception of *educational excellence* in jeopardy.

Boyle's speeches between 1965 and 1967 gave the preservationists little comfort being, too often, guarded expressions of Tory concerns and Tory philosophy and suggesting that, whilst he was willing to deploy preservationist rhetoric, he was not wholly convinced by, or committed to, preservationist ideas.

For example, though he did speak at the 1965 Conservative Party Conference on the question of preserving and developing standards of educational excellence, he did so without due regard to the necessary logistics:

> If, as I hope, I become Secretary of State before too long, I will set my face firmly against proposals that level-down educational standards. I see Mr. Enoch Powell a few places to my right. He made a magnificent speech on this subject recently in which he pointed out the importance of fostering traditions of excellence. Traditions are much more closely bound up with institutions than many people realize. We as a Party, I hope and believe, understand institutions in a way that many of our opponents do not.[60]

Boyle's reference to Powell 'a few places to my right' could not have been more ironic for, as we shall shortly see, Powell was to be one of those Conservative MPs who would be canvassed by the founding Black Paper editors and who would give tacit support to *Black Paper* ideas inside the Party.

It was at the 1966 Conservative Party Conference that the theme of 'excellence in education' first received wide debate. Perhaps it was because of this that Boyle felt himself obliged to praise the preservationist Dr Kathleen Ollerenshaw for her 'superlative work in Manchester fighting one of the worst comprehensive schemes imposed by any big city'.[61] This was a reference by Boyle to Dr Ollerenshaw's campaign against, what she and the Party saw as, Labour's obsession with going comprehensive without regard to cost or circumstance. Boyle had supported her campaign as he believed Labour's obsession could put at risk the future of the nation's primary schools and, also, the success of the Tory Party's plans for raising the school leaving-age. Of Dr Ollerenshaw, he said 'there is no one in our Party who, on education matters, I admire so much as her — she is a magnificent fighter' (*ibid.*). He especially gave support to her contention that the Tory Party could not afford any dilution of sixth-form standards.

Besides Dr Ollerenshaw there were other CEs in the Party keen to champion educational excellence. John Selwyn Gummer, a future Vice-Chairman and Chairman of the Party, spoke on excellence as 'a likely casualty of Labour's secondary reorganization policy'. To this Boyle responded:

> Let me assure Mr. Gummer that I wholly agree with him about excellence.
> I am not one of those who regard selection by merit as a dirty word. Sooner
> or later in any education system there has got to be selection.[62]

It was not just younger Conservatives like Gummer who were questioning the strength and direction of the Party's policy for education to preserve educational excellence. Older Tories, like Maude, also had misgivings. In his public speeches Maude endeavoured to establish that the principles for which the Party stood on education were clear:

> The Party does not insist rigidly on selection for secondary schools at 11 +
> but it does firmly believe that selection at some age for different types of
> secondary schooling is essential, except where local conditions make it
> impossible to maintain separate schools of adequate size.[63]

But Maude was continuing to insist that the nation could not afford to lose or destroy a single good school. Conservative councils had to be prepared to defend their local grammar schools and direct grant schools by every means in their power against the socialist assault.

Longden, too, favoured the retention of some selection. Like Maude he appreciated that though the tripartite system now required some modification the case for the complete elimination of selection and separation had not been convincingly made by Crosland. Longden was a congenital Tory. As we have seen his instincts were for organic change and compromise. Longden would display these instincts in his responses to a series of developments inside and outside the Party, developments which would prompt him to further press the preservationist case.

The CRD was now advising Boyle to formulate the case for a *New Look* in education — 'the case for realism and for frankness'.[64] He was advised to emphasize the differences between Conservative and Labour policy on secondary reorganization:

> First, the difference between respect for local democracy, and the belief that
> nothing matters except the will of the central government; second, the
> difference between making academic use of scarce resources, and advocating

expensive schemes without having the money to pay for them; third, the difference betweeen a policy of trying to make educational sense in each area, and a policy of using the educational service as a means of imposing social uniformity (*ibid.*).

Memoranda compiled by Greenland was also being translated into a draft paper[65] for Boyle's use. Within this paper the main tenets of Conservative education policy were outlined. It described the economic and social arguments for educational advance, arguments concerned with the sort of society Conservatives wanted to see. The paper emphasized the Conservative commitment to the fight for education and applauded the efforts of earlier Conservative ministers (notably Lord Eccles) in establishing the principle of an annually increasing share of economic resources for the education service:

> The first thing to be said about Conservative policy for education is that Conservatives accept, not merely that more money should be spent each year on the education service, but also that it should receive a rising share of our total national wealth . . . .Mr. John Vaizey, no supporter of our Party, has recently stated that 'Britain now spends a higher proportion of national income on education probably than any other country in Europe'. This is, surely, a notable tribute to the efforts of past Conservative ministers. (*ibid.*)

But, of course, the preservationists did not, generally, extol the demands for 'more of everything'. Nor did they necessarily accede to the notion that more educational expenditure would raise educational standards. The Conservative plan for education, outlined in the CRD draft paper, extolled other aims which fell short of preservationist demands and expectations. In particular, the call to Conservatives to stress the importance of thinking about priorities for the education service as a whole, was too vague, whilst the proposition (whose authorship was Richard Hornby's) that Conservatives believed in 'putting first things first' (of which, incidentally, the paper gave no clear example) was precisely the issue still dividing the preservationists and the enlightened Tories.

The paper did, however, contain several statements of policy and commitment which were close to preservationist thinking. It emphasized that the fight to prevent the total abolition of separate grammar and secondary modern schools 'would be bitter and prolonged'; schools of 'proven worth' had to be 'protected'; the complete abolition of 'established schools of real quality' was bound to be 'educationally damaging'; no 'let up' in the quality of sixth-form education 'could be afforded'; the danger to sixth-form standards was 'one of the most serious risks inherent in the drive to eliminate all selective schools'; and, whilst the 'expansion of good comprehensive schools' would be supported, the Party would not sanction these everywhere and, above all, not 'on the cheap' (*ibid.*).

The Party's dilemma was to balance enlightened Tory calls for rather more social equality in education (the Heath-Boyle line) and the preservationist calls to protect the grammar schools (the Maude-Longden line).

In an effort to strengthen his own position, Longden now mustered the preservationist case in a private circular letter to Conservative members of all LEAs. In this letter Longden called attention to a correspondence in *The Times* of 3 June 1967 from the Vice-Chancellors of twenty-five universities, and to an article in the same edition by Walter James (editor of the *Times Educational Supplement*) both of which were highly critical of universal comprehensivization. The Vice-Chancellors had written to *The Times* as 'people concerned with the preservation and extension of individual excellence' and had expressed their concern about the attempted comprehensive revolution, particularly its effects on existing sixth-forms. They were alarmed lest some of the plans for secondary reorganization led to the denial of opportunities for the individual pupil of ability, particularly those from a poor or uneducated background. The VCs had considered that if the needs of the able minority were prejudiced at the school stage by hasty schemes of reorganization, by the diffusion of specialist staff, and by loss of morale in some sections of the teaching profession, serious difficulties were bound to arise. They feared that the result of 'universal comprehensiveness' would be a decline of academic standards. Walter James' article had explained why this teaching difficulty had arisen, and had called on newly-elected Conservative councils to signal a halt to comprehensive reorganization.

Longden wrote in his letter:

> I hope you will forgive me for bringing these opinions to your notice. I do not see how any but the most bigoted of Socialist dogmatists can fail to heed these authoritative warnings which only echo similar warnings from numerous educationists and which are borne out by actual experience in America and Russia, in which countries they are changing back to selection.[66]

Longden's intimation of the widening support amongst professional educationists for the preservationist case at a time when it was not Conservative policy to deny the need for some reorganization after twenty-three years of secondary education, nor to preserve the 11+, was a signal to preservationists to speak out again against the government's determination to obliterate the tripartite system of secondary education (which was agreed by all parties in 1944) and impose instead a universal comprehensive system. It was also, quite clearly, an attempt by Longden to encourage Conservative members of LEAs to reflect on any second thoughts they might have themselves about their own Party's policy for secondary reorganization.

The Conservative policy on education, summarized in a speech made by Heath to the Party's NACE on 18 June 1967, did not satisfy Longden's private desire for a restoration of selection and separatism in secondary education. The policy was overwhelmingly non-partisan stating that, in the reorganization of secondary education, the Party accepted the movement away from selection and the consequences that flowed from it. Though Heath expressed the Party's belief in streaming by ability within schools, he gave no suggestion of replacing the 11 + by selection at a later age. And while he expressed the traditional Conservative belief in keeping the grammar schools, he made the qualification that such schools would have to continue to adapt themselves to changing circumstances. It was Heath's plan to abolish the GCE 'O' level if the Tories were returned to office, and it was this which ultimately incensed the preservationists.

Longden's anxiety over the direction of Labour and Conservative policy on education led him to write a private letter to *The Sunday Times*. He noted:

> Where the Parties differ fundamentally is upon whether or not there should be selection at any stage.[67]

And:

> Most of us have long agreed that 11 is too early an age for teachers unerringly to discern a child's 'aptitude and ability' — though such decisions were not intended by the 1944 Act to be final and irrevocable (*ibid.*).

Longden stressed that whilst Conservatives accepted the trend of opinion against selection at 11 + they nevertheless thought there had to be selection (or grouping by ability) at some stage or other if the nation was to do justice to children's differing needs and abilities. Longden argued that once this fundamental principle was firmly grasped, the method by which it was implemented was a matter for legitimate discussion.

The preservationists in the Party had good reason to feel discontented. Not only had they been angered by some aspects of the Heath-Boyle line on education; they had also been disturbed by intelligence collected by the CRD concerning the activities of Marxist educationists whose aims appeared to include the destruction of the tripartite system of secondary schooling — particularly the elimination of streaming in schools. The CRD was especially concerned about the role of Professor Brian Simon, whom it considered to be a leading spirit of the educational left and the key figure in the Left's campaign to abolish educational selection in all its forms. The preservationists feared that this campaign threatened to reduce secondary schooling to an imbecilic level and create the kind of chaos that plagued Soviet schools in the 1920s. The CRD saw the set intent of the neo-Marxian levellers and egalitarians to be not just the destruction of grammar and secondary modern schools but also the direct grant, voluntary aided and independent schools.[68] It noted:

> ... the campaign for non-streaming is being carried on in the Institutes of Education and left-wing sympathizers are at large in these centres (*ibid.*).

Attacking, what it saw as, Labour's hopes to eliminate good schools all over the country, the CRD recorded:

> Unfortunately for them parents have reacted sharply against this totalitarian bullying and this threat of annihilation that hangs over so many schools. Unless continued resistance is kept up, the end result must be the coming into being of a series of neighbourhood comprehensive schools all functioning at the same low level of intellect and seeking to mould pupils into citizens of a dreary Animal Farm on a nationwide scale![69]

At the 1967 Conservative Party Conference Longden told delegates:

> I do not believe that our Party, is showing itself sufficiently aware of the disastrous consequences to the nation and its youth if the socialists are allowed to get away with their egalitarian policies for secondary education in both the State and private sectors.[70]

Longden argued that the nub and essence of Conservative opposition to the Labour levellers should not be the abolition of the 11 +, not the experiment of purpose-built comprehensive schools where there were no others, but the abolition of selection and its motive, the fear that anyone should be seen to be different — in short, 'compulsory mediocrity' (*ibid.*). He acknowledged, and welcomed, what the Party Leader and Sir Edward Boyle had said in their past speeches about the need to select, but suggested that too many Conservatives had still not got the message, and that too many LEAs were prepared to succumb to the Minister's blackmail and to sacrifice some very good schools on his ideological altar.

In his Conference speech Longden appealed to delegates to make more widely known the Party's support for the public schools and parental choice. He also made a particularly incisive comparison between the contrasting philosophies of socialism and conservatism:

> The philosophy of Socialism can be summed up in a nutshell: because everyone cannot go to the Ritz, no one shall go to the Ritz; and, if no one goes to the Ritz, the Ritz goes. Thus, the first casualty of egalitarianism is excellence; and socialism is the midwife of the second-rate.
>
> Our philosophy is the exact opposite. It teaches us not to destroy until we can replace with something better. It teaches us not to envy, but carefully to nurture excellence. Let us say so loudly and clearly from every rooftop in the land (*ibid.*).

Longden's judgment, delivered to a receptive but not wholly converted audience, would very shortly be preached by the *Black Paper* group — an association of CEs whose ideas would permeate the Conservative Party and significantly alter the character of Tory education policy.

Towards the Black Papers

At a NACE meeting of 7 October 1967, Dr Rhodes Boyson had been elected a Greater London Area Advisory Committee representative.[71] Boyson was now the new Headmaster of Highbury Grove School and a sponsor of the Comprehensive Schools Committee (CSC).[72] His admission to the Conservative Party, and rapid election to the NACE, put him in close proximity with not only his friend Harry Greenway but also fellow NACE preservationists Gilbert Longden, Angus Maude and Dr Kathleen Ollerenshaw.

Boyson's arrival on the NACE effectively gave Longden and Maude a major ally in their defence of the traditional educational style of secondary schooling. The Party was now concerned about developments in the London Borough of Ealing where it considered the Socialists were seeking to hurry into being a group of *sixth-form colleges* fed by junior schools that were non-selective. To CEs in the CRD and on the NACE, such so-called 'modern educational planning' merely illustrated the neo-Marxist educational line. Even Boyle was moved to state:

> Once again Harold Wilson's party, despite all their smokescreens, is shown
> as welded in reality to policies that are closely allied to the kind of
> extremism with which Harold was once associated.[73]

Significantly, one of Boyson's first responsibilities on the NACE was to monitor other examples of 'modern educational planning' — Boyson having alerted the NACE to the dangers of the Schools Council's suggested reform of the sixth-form curriculum.[74] Boyson was asked to keep a 'watching brief' on this matter as the Dainton Report was soon expected.[75]

These developments, just one year away from the start of a series of initiatives to contact and assemble contributors to the first Black Paper, suggest that factions inside the Conservative Party were now already mobilized to meet the 'egalitarian threat' which they saw to be posed by Labour's education plans. What these factions required to further their campaign was some statement of their case which would reach across the Party organisation and help bridge the divide between the preservationists and the enlightened Tories. Such a statement now appeared.

Angus Maude's *Education: Quality and Equality* (1968) — a formulation of the preservationist case which may be seen as the precursor to the first Black Paper — offered Conservatives a critique of egalitarian propositions in education, and signposted directions for Conservative educational reform. Maude's principal charge was that the Party had been too long experimenting with the organization of secondary education (this period of experiment having been sanctioned by Sir Edward Boyle when he was Minister of Education) and that it was now time for Conservatives to think a second time about which decisions were reversible and which were irreversible (*ibid.*, pp. 3 4). Here Maude's appeal to Conservatives to rethink the direction of Conservative education policy duplicated Longden's earlier request to Conservative members of LEAs.[76] The most important part of Maude's pamphlet was his exposition of the case for selection and, again, like Longden, he pursued the line that Conservatives had to stand quite firmly for the principle of selection, however it was done and at whatever age (Maude, 1968, p. 11). He charged the Boyle-Heath line on the 11+ and selection as being a 'weak and woolly approach', (*ibid.*, p. 12) and repeated Longden's claim that local authorities all over the country were doubting whether the Party itself knew what its policy on selection was (*ibid.*). Maude's proposition — 'Selection essential' — informed Conservatives that they should select for schools and select inside schools. Selection was something for which Conservatives had to fight and defend (*ibid.*). More selection was required not just to segregate intelligent children but to segregate, at least for a remedial period, those children who made it virtually impossible for other children to be properly educated in the schools in which they were (*ibid.*).

Maude's position on the GCE 'O' level exam ('it had raised academic standards but was now rigidifying the curriculum') was a move towards the view of the enlightened Tories. But he warned the Party that it should not condone and connive at the destruction of all that was best in the education system, nor allow the cry of 'social justice' to stampede it into what would be the worst injustice of all — the deliberate lowering of academic standards where these were now high (*ibid*, p. 15).

Maude's pamphlet was not a scholarly treatise. It was intended only 'to propose some guidelines for further thought and discussion'. What was significant was the timing of its publication and its sponsorship. When it appeared, Maude had already been dismissed by Heath from the Shadow Cabinet. Consequently, his attacks on the Boyle-Heath line on education were now becoming more regular. The pamphlet was published under the auspices of the CPC and whilst it was not an official Party pronouncement (it merely contained the personal views of the author) there can be little doubt that it also expressed the views of the CPC's new Director, Russell Lewis. The Party machine now had as Head of its political education centre (which had itself become an integral part of the Party organization in 1964) a founding member of the preservationist 61 Society. Lewis' contacts with Boyson were already established. Since 1963 Lewis had visited the IEA where he had become a friend of the preservationist Ralph Harris.[77]

By spring 1968 preservationist forces were located in key policy bases inside the Party: Maude, Longden, Ollerenshaw and Boyson on the NACE; Lewis at the CPC. Most significantly of all, Lewis was an opponent of universally imposed comprehensivization.[78] He would prove to be a key figure in the presentation of the preservationists' case to the Party's grass roots activists.

The political education of the Party into preservationist thinking, first seriously initiated by Maude's CPC pamphlet, was furthered by a series of symposia held at the Swinton Conservative College. Ramsden (1980, p. 274) has noted the importance of these meetings, especially for Shadow Ministers, allowing as they did for a reflective look at policy trends. The NACE held its own weekend conferences at Swinton. And it was within the *Swinton Journal* that several preservationists came in spring 1968 to discuss, with others, the subject of 'Intellectuals and Conservatism'. It was, in the course of the symposium that followed, that Russel Lewis met Gilbert Longden and John O'Sullivan.[79] Also in attendance were Angus Maude, Ralph Harris, Peter Utley, Arthur Seldon and Tibor Szamuely.

Maude had long argued that the Party lacked a philosophy. His view was shared by O'Sullivan, a central figure in the organization of the planned intellectual renaissance. O'Sullivan was a liberal conservative.[80] His meeting with Lewis, Maude and Longden brought closer together the views of the enlightened Tories and the preservationists. It was his idea to call the 'Intellectuals and Conservatism' symposium[81] believing, as he did, that certain fundamental qualities such as 'rigour', 'enterprise', 'choice', and 'achievement', had been lost and denied by socialist revisionism, and that in this situation intellectuals were more ready than at any other time since the war to listen to the Conservative Party and to examine the alternative view of society it represented (see O'Sullivan, 1968). O'Sullivan argued that as more and more matters of public and private life were, under Labour, being withdrawn from the market and from individual choice, Conservative and Liberal intellectuals were coming to see that the only alternative was to organize their protests, to secure mutual intellectual support by demonstrating as consistently as they could, that *liberté* was more important that *egalite* (*ibid.*). For matters of education Conservatives should increasingly 'respond to every ideological tenet of the socialist creed and grasp the principle that equality, as the prime aim of education, was false and would defeat the true purpose of free and independent thought' (*ibid.*).

The striking parallel between O'Sullivan's position on education and Maude's preservationist view — the former's *Swinton Journal* essay endorsing much of the latter's CPC pamphlet's criticism of educational egalitarianism — reveals some coalescence between enlightened Tory and preservationist intellectuals in 1968. O'Sullivan's selection of Tibor Szamuely (shortly to be a contributor to *Black Paper Two*) as the principal paper-presenter in the spring 1968 *Swinton Journal* symposium suggests that this coalescence was being deliberately harnessed to effect significant changes in Conservative philosophy.

Szamuely's paper *Intellectuals and Conservatism* (1968) pointed out the opportunity which existed for the Conservative Party to exploit the failing identification between intellectuals and the Left, and to accept that there could be an intellectual Right. Szamuely attacked a number of the doctrines of 'progressive' socialism, in particular, the contempt for tradition — the urge to destroy every traditional institution and custom (*ibid.*, p. 13). Significantly, he argued that the most stimulating political writing was to be found in those authors opposed to the 'progressive' orthodoxy — scholars like Professor Michael Oakeshott, Sir Karl Popper, Sir Isaiah Berlin, Warden

John Sparrow — while, at the same time, the genuinely creative approach to political theory of men like Enoch Powell, Quintin Hogg (later Lord Hailsham) or Angus Maude, was unmatched in the Labour Party hierarchy (*ibid.*, p. 6).[82]

Since the essence of the Conservative intellectual tradition had been its pragmatism, Szamuely argued that conservatism had never created a unified body of formulated principles; it had never established a doctrine, a dogma that could be defended with the self-righteous fervour of the exponents of modern ideologies (*ibid.*, pp. 6–7). Rather, it was an attitude to life and, true to its character, the Tory Party had long been seen as the natural repository of the national tradition (*ibid.*, p. 7). It was Szamuely's belief that between 1964 and 1968 there had been growing evidence indicating the disenchantment of a considerable part of the British intellectual elite with the Leftist ideologies that had held them in thrall for so long. Here, he noted the 'turn to the Right' by post-war Leftist novelists like Kingsley Amis and John Braine (*ibid.*, pp. 10–11).[83]

As Szamuely saw it the root of the problem for Conservatives lay in the absence of a genuine and intellectually satisfying alternative to 'progressivism'. It was, he argued, for the Conservative Party to counter Labour's 'new Jerusalem', to put forward a different prospect, to stress the crucial and precious role of tradition (*ibid.*, p. 13). Consequently, one of the main tasks of the true intellectual was the preservation of the nation's cultural heritage, with developing that heritage, with the search for new ideas, with the change necessary to keep the nation and the field of learning and culture in the forefront of an everchanging world: tradition and progress had to be combined (*ibid.*, p. 14).[84]

Thus, Szamuely's paper embraced not only some of the key tenets of future *Black Paper* philosophy but also reference to some of the imminent Black Paper authors themselves. According to O'Sullivan, the paper was 'rapturously received by those attending at Swinton'.[85]

Whilst the Swinton assembly had given the preservationists new heart, Boyle's concern for 'planned educational change' had led him increasingly to seek advice from the socialist economist of education, John Vaizey.[86] In June 1968 Vaizey was invited to address the NACE about the economic problems of education. Vaizey argued[87] that the education system had become more expensive and that the greater part of this increase had gone to the non-academic secondary children, as a result of the lengthening of school life and the improvement in the conditions in which they were taught. He noted a major switch of educational priorities up to 1965 towards secondary education, and concluded that the nation was now in for a period when the demands for education would considerably outstretch the financial resources that would be necessary to meet it, and that it would be in this context that much of the educational dicussion by Conservatives would take place over the coming years. Vaizey urged the Conservative Party to establish priorities and, having established priorities, to maintain them. He set before the NACE his own priorities for consideration:

primary schools, especially education priority areas (which Mrs Thatcher was to support as Education Secretary, 1970–74); the education of immigrant and other disadvantaged children; and making the comprehensive schools work.[88]

Among those present at the NACE meeting was Dr Boyson who, in May 1968, had been elected a member of the Waltham Forest Council on which he now served as Chairman of Establishments. Boyson had his own priorities that he was already putting before the NACE. He was much more concerned with restoring traditionalist patterns of education and teaching methods than with what he saw as vague notions of 'making the comprehensive schools work', schools which he found often inhibited the academic achievements of their pupils.

Boyson's priorities were, of course, the priorities of the first Black Paper editors who were now beginning to canvass the educational world for support in their preservationist *Fight for Education* campaign. As liberal-humanist teachers, Brian Cox and Tony Dyson had once supported the Labour Party and voted for the Wilson government in 1966. But in 1968 they each found themselves 'going in a conservative direction'.[89] They intended that their *Fight for Education* campaign would be educational, not political, and that it would not lead to the creation of a new dogma (Cox, 1984, p. 12).

Whatever their intention they did not initially win ready support. Though some arch-traditionalists in the media might have been expected to welcome the approaches of the Black Paper editors, some were not inclined to make a personal contribution. Walter James (*Times Educational Supplement*) was asked by Dyson to assist in the campaign. He told Dyson:

> I think I am in general sympathy with the attitude of your coming pamphlet, but I feel that I should not take part personally. I do write from time to time on education outside the TES, but on the whole I avoid controversy because it seems to involve the TES in my private views which I do not think is good. We shall, however, hope to give the pamphlet a good send off when it comes out.[90]

Such setbacks caused Cox and Dyson to temporarily suspend further canvassing until mid-November. In this interim period developments inside the Conservative Party were indicating a renewal of pressure from preservationists against aspects of Party policy on comprehensivization and Labour's plans to reform the traditional sixth-form.

At the 1968 Conservative Party Conference Maude challenged Boyle to acknowledge that the Party was still divided over the issue of secondary education, the grammar schools and reorganization. Maude was convinced that the Party had, for many years, been making soothing noises in the direction of equality of opportunity without working out very carefully what the concept meant, or how far it was possible or even desirable (Maude, 1968, p. 4). Boyle attempted to deflect the preservationist challenge by reminding delegates that the three previous conferences had already discussed at length the matters raised in Maude's question and suggesting that a larger share of time be devoted to other subjects.[91] On comprehensivization, Boyle assured delegates that the Party remained, as it always had, firmly opposed to legislative compulsion. He denied Maude's contention of a continuing Party divide over secondary school reorganization. He stated:

> May I be clear that we will not have botched up comprehensive schemes. I know at this moment that a number of Conservative authorities are reviewing schemes that were introduced by the socialists. Having said that, I really would question very much indeed going so far as Angus Maude and suggesting that Conservative controlled local authorities if they decide to reorganise can only do useless botched up jobs everywhere.

Boyle believed secondary school reorganization was a field where the Party had to go forward, backed all the time by practical experience, regardless of whether such a view was seen as insufficiently right-wing for some or left-wing for others. He wanted to widen opportunity without sacrificing standards of excellence. For Boyle, this was the sensible view educationally and what was educationally right would, in the long term, be politically right.

Boyle's unwillingness to oppose socialist dogmatism with an equal and opposite Conservative dogmatism (because he felt in education it was dogmatism itself which was wrong) failed to appease the preservationists. The Shadow Minister's Blackpool Conference speech effectively quickened the preservationists' resolve to organize extra-Party support for their case. If, as one observer has suggested, Maude was a 'plague for Boyle'[92] at the Party conferences, it would seem that he was not entirely successful in his mission.

Inside the NACE Boyson was now formulating the preservationists' 'right approach to education'. In November he submitted an article, 'The threat to the sixth', to Peter Baguley (Secretary, NACE) for publication in *Focus on Education*.[93] He informed Baguley:

> Enclosed please find article for your Education magazine. I've tried to make it controversial. This is a serious matter.[94]

Boyson was now prospective Conservative Parliamentary candidate for Eccles. His article was a response to, what he perceived to be, the attack by socialists upon the tight but liberal academic sixth-form curriculum — what Boyson termed 'the pride of English schools' (*ibid.*). It was also a warning of the threat to the continued existence of the sixth-form as it was traditionally understood. The core of Boyson's thesis was that the explosion in sixth-form numbers, the encouragement of new academic sixth-forms, the dearth of specialist stable staff and possibly the pop sociology of the age ('which had brought many leaders to doubt society's wisdom and purpose and to worship at the shrine of callow youth') had all threatened the sixth-form (*ibid.*).

It was the Conservative Party's attitude to the grammar schools which now caused the preservationists to act in earnest. Party promises to defend these schools had been vague. *Make Life Better*[95] had promised to maintain the academic standards of grammar schools but had suggested that these schools adapt themselves to changing circumstances. Heath had told the 1968 Party Conference that he and the Party would support the grammar schools to the hilt and ensure their healthy future. The preservationists were not convinced.

In November 1968 Cox and Dyson sent a letter and enclosure to all public and grammar school headmasters. The letter informed the headmasters of a pamphlet on education to be published by the CQS early in 1969. Cox and Dyson told them:

> If you sympathise with our aims, and can send comments or articles, we shall be most grateful. It seems important to defend traditional standards of education firmly and rationally, before the moment for doing this passes for good.[96]

Cox and Dyson had originally intended the Black Paper to deal only with universities, but as contributions and advice accumulated, they decided they had to include the schools.[97] The enclosure, *Back to Education*, began with what became the opening statement of the first Black Paper:

> Since the war revolutionary changes have taken place in English education — the introduction of free play methods in primary schools, comprehensive schemes, the expansion of higher education, the experimental courses at the new universities. There are powerful arguments in favour of such changes, but, particularly in the last year or two, many people have become increasingly unhappy about certain aspects of the general trend.[98]

The 'general trend' for which the preservationists had a particular distaste, was the egalitarian trend. In their enclosure Cox and Dyson accused politicans and Vice-Chancellors of imitating the fashion for disregarding *the teacher* as the exponent of the great achivement of past civilization, and drew attention to the dangers this posed to traditional high standards of English education. They claimed that at the post-11 stage there was a strong impetus to abolish streaming, and to treat with contempt the grammar school concepts of discipline and work; that there was 'a feeling about that excellence in education was undemocratic' (*ibid.*).

Cox and Dyson considered that these so-called 'liberal' views (the 'new fashionable hierarchy') flew in the face of human nature. They stated:

> Our purpose is to publish, about March next year, a polemical pamphlet attacking these recent developments, and insisting on the importance of the highest standards at all levels of education. (*ibid*)[99]

Their problem was to make clear that modern 'free' methods were themselves old-fashioned, an application of ideas well-known in the 1930s, and often only muddled products of an out-of-date romanticism.

The premise of the first Black Paper editors — that people in powerful administrative positions needed to know more about the facts in education — matched the view of other preservationists, notably Longden and Maude. Cox and Dyson set a deadline of Christmas for the submission of contributions, which could be 'information, facts, anecdotes, comments or short articles' (*ibid.*). The pamphlet was to receive maximum publicity (free copies to all MPs) and was to contain separate articles on all branches of education, and also more general pieces (in praise of examinations, etc.).

Response to the Cox-Dyson invitation was mixed. Tom Howarth (Headmaster, St. Paul's School), though sympathetic to the preservationist case, refused to contribute to the first Black Paper, as he considered it wrong to criticize the state education system from the privileged position of the independent sector.[100] Angus Maude, who had been sent a modified letter with the *Back to Education* enclosure, was delighted to help, and considered the proposed education pamphlet to be 'a most desirable exercise'.[101] Maude informed Cox that he would submit a piece on *The Egalitarian Threat* which would be an attack on ideology and its effects.[102] The essay was to be 'a highly reactionary piece . . . fairly rapidly condensed from part of a chapter in my next book'.[103] Cox and Dyson were sufficiently impressed by it to place it first in the pamphlet.[104]

Elsewhere Cox and Dyson were able to recruit the participation of several distinguished Conservative teachers. R. R. Pedley (Headmaster, St. Dunstan's College) replied to Cox:

> I am delighted to hear that you are producing a counter-blast to the nefarious activities of the levellers and saboteurs of national education. This is something that urgently needs to be done. Otherwise what appears to be a national death wish in education will be fulfilled. I have for a number of years been an inveterate protester against the current sabotage of educational standards.[105]

Likewise, Tibor Szamuely was happy to accept Cox's invitation. He wrote to Cox:

> Kingsley Amis has already told me about your project and I find the idea very interesting.[106]

The first Black Paper (*Fight for Education*) was launched with a press conference held at Brown's Hotel, London on 12 March 1969. One of the correspondents who attended was Stuart Maclure. According to Cox, Maclure proved to be the *Black Paper* group's strongest critic and opponent.[107] Maclure has recalled that he attacked the Black Papers 'very hard'[108] because he was 'strongly opposed to extremism in education'.[109] But the early Black Paper formulation of the preservationist case was not extreme. It argued against the 11 + but in favour of selection at 13. It did not argue against purpose-built 11–18 comprehensives but cautioned against neighbourhood schools with inadequate sixth-forms. It propositioned that inner-city comprehensives would inevitably mean a decline in educational opportunity for able working-class children. It advocated that teachers should put into practice the best of formal and informal methods and should not abdicate their authority as exponents of the best in the nation's liberal and humanist traditions.

Those writers who have analyzed the Black Papers, notably Hopkins and Wright, have failed to fully examine either the role of particular contributors to the organization of the *Fight for Education* campaign or its impact on the Conservative Party. For example, the role of Angus Maude has never been seen as one of major significance. And yet the personal correspondences between Cox and Maude testify his influence in developing *Black Paper* ideology and promoting that ideology inside and outside the Conservative Party. For example, the phrase 'counter-revolution' was coined in its educational context by Maude when he told Cox, 'I am getting quite excited by the whole project, and hoping that it may really launch a counter-revolution'.[110] Whilst this does not nullify Hopkins' assertion that the main figure-head of the Conservative *counter-revolution* in education was Dr Boyson (Hopkins, 1978, p. 79), it does suggest that Maude's role was far more central than writers have hitherto assumed. In fact, Maude acted as the main publicist in the *Fight for Education* campaign. Following a luncheon meeting held at The Reform Club on 6 February 1969 (where Cox, Dyson and Maude had discussed plans for publicizing their campaign) Maude obtained the support of *The Daily Telegraph* and *Sunday Telegraph* for reviews and advance publicity. Maude's circle of contacts now included James Cobban (Headmaster, Abingdon School and contributor to the first Black Paper) and Tom Howarth, but he was particularly keen to locate support within the universities and the colleges of education. To Cox, he remarked: 'So many professors of education are on the wrong side in this fight that it might be useful to have a good one with us.'[111] Though it was Cox's idea to establish a Campaign Committee (which included Cox, Dyson, Maude, Cobban and Howarth) to advance the ideas of the *Black Paper* group to a wider audience, it was Maude who led the search for new contributors and organized meetings to debate *Black Paper* ideas. As well as suggesting to Cox 'a large meeting to which interested parties could assemble to debate further the ideas of the Black Paper group' (*ibid.*), Maude was himself contacted by Party constituency agents to address meetings on the main themes of the *Fight for Education* pamphlet. One invitation came from Margaret Thatcher's own Finchley and Friern Barnet Conservative Association. Maude was asked to lead a discussion on the Black Paper at the constituency's meeting on 12 June 1969 and was congratulated 'on some very clear thinking on education'.[112] Invitations also came for Maude to speak to various teacher groups.[113]

On 22 April 1969 Cox informed Maude that it was the firm intention to do a second pamphlet in October. Maude considered that the most important thing now was:

> . . . to produce lots of hard evidence to support the general theses of *Fight for Education*, since our opponents have simply been saying that we have no evidence and it is not true.[114]

Maude was willing to contribute to *Black Paper Two* but still felt it essential to enrol more distinguished professors of education. He reminded Cox to get in touch with G. H. Bantock.[115] Maude's prompt to Cox to engage the support of Bantock (Maude had met Bantock at Swinton) would prove especially significant.

Professor Bantock had already canvassed preservationist ideas in Tory journals prior to Cox's contact.[116] Though he accepted Cox's invitation to contribute to *Black Paper Two* he was not prepared to endorse Cox's treatment of the primary schools believing that, carefully handled by skilled teachers, 'modern methods' had a good deal to contribute.[117] Bantock advised Cox:

> I want very much to see the case that you support put. In general on the universities I think it was put pretty well, it was not bad on the comprehensive school, but it was not really good enough on the primary schools. What we need is a sober and careful analytical presentation of the conservative case; and with this I would be willing to help in any way in which you thought I could.

Bantock was not the only preservationist seeking a 'sober and careful analytical presentation of the conservative case'. Boyson, too, counselled Cox and suggested the next Black Paper should contain 'a scrupulously fair analysis of the comprehensive schools issue'.[118] This was Boyson's first contact with the early Black Paper editors. Boyson felt he was well-qualified to provide such an analysis and requested a meeting to discuss his ideas.[119]

Between April and October 1969 (when preparations for the publication of *Black Paper Two* were being laid) the intra-Party impact of the *Fight for Education* campaign was accelerating. Whilst Wright (1977, p. 152) has argued the difficulty of trying to assess the impact of the Black Papers and suggested that evidence of their significance for Tory MP's has been scant, personal correspondences between individual Tory MPs and Dyson suggest the lines of *Black Paper* argument did receive some discussion and support within the Conservative Party (pp. 150–1). For example, Enoch Powell seen by Norton and Aughey (1981) as the 'ideological irritant to the Heath-style Conservatism', with his criticsm of the Party leadership's over-concern with being 'modern', 'dynamic' and 'progressive', expressed an interest in the work of the *Black Paper* group. He told Dyson he had read the first Black Paper with 'much appreciation', that it had 'had quite an impact' and that he would be 'returning to these subjects soon in public'.[120] As well as Powell, other Tory MPs were rallying to a Black Paperite position. Stephen Hastings (C. Mid-Bedfordshire), like Powell, had read the first Black Paper with its call for a return to *excellence in education*. He informed Dyson:

> May I say how very much impressed I was with the *Black Paper*. My congratulations to you and Professor Cox on undertaking this work of incontestable national importance. You may be interested to know that there is a lively debate in progress within the Conservative Party at Westminster on the *Black Paper* which I initiated myself. I think that you can take it that your work is having a most useful effect.[121]

Similarly, Ronald Bell, a former right-wing Vice-Chairman of the Conservative backbench Education Committee, when sent an advance copy of *Black Paper Two* shortly before the 1969 Party Conference was enthusiastic for a conservative restoration of those traditional high standards of English education that seemed to be in danger of being overthrown by 'new' and 'progressive' theories. He told Dyson: 'It is splendid stuff, every sentence of which badly needed to be written'.[122] Victor Goodhew (C. Albans Division, Herts), shortly to become Assistant Government Whip (June–October 1970), was pleased to receive a bound set of page-proofs of *Black Paper Two* before the Conference debate, which he saw as a most 'thoughtful gesture'.[123]

It was Maude's idea to get *Black Paper Two* published on 7 October 1969 — the first day of the Party Conference — for maximum Party impact.[124] He was convinced that the first Black Paper had had an immense effect throughout the country and that his Conservative colleagues, and even some Labour ones, had taken a lot of notice of it.[125] Upon receiving a copy of the revised draft introduction of *Black Paper Two* he had told Cox. 'I think it is most impressive — just what is needed to squash the progs!'[126] Cox's own view of *Black Paper Two* was that it was not so lively and witty as the first one but its inclusion of solid statistics would create an immense impression.[127] Both he and Dyson had followed Bantock's counsel but the test of their case now rested in the hands of the Party leadership.

Though Boyle had been prepared to accede to some of the softer demands of the preservationists by advising local authorities not to embark on schemes which fragmented sixth-forms, he had not countenanced some of the more extreme *Black Paper* ideology. At the 1969 Party Conference Boyle made a number of specific comments about the *Black Paper* school of educational thought. He hoped *Black Paper Two* would inspire not just verbal gunfire but genuine debate.[128] He found the paper to be 'a more formidable document than Black Paper One' (*ibid.*). But he also cautioned Conference against the paper's rhetorical flourishes and suggested that the Party could fight for quality in education without taking a sort of shrill and peevish tone which implied 'stop the modern world, I want to get off' (*ibid.*). Boyle concluded that it was time for the voice of moderation to have its say.[129]

Boyle's criticism of *Black Paper Two: The Crisis in Education* did not halt the Party's steady absorption of *Black Paper* ideas. We shall see in the next chapter that even before she replaced Sir Edward Boyle as Education spokesman, Margaret Thatcher was canvassed by Cox and Dyson, and that she gave positive support to their campaign immediately she became Education Secretary.[130]

For the preservationists themselves the period between October 1969 and June 1970 was one of considerable activity. The most significant development followed a suggestion made by Bantock to Cox that the *Black Paper* group should turn its attention to teacher training.[131] Bantock's counsel was timely. Several preservationists had expertise in the area of teacher training and the topic was of increasing concern to both the Labour government and Conservative opposition. This bipartisan interest was to allow the preservationists to state their case one more time before the 1970 General Election.

In March 1970 a number of Black Paper contributors submitted evidence to the House of Commons Select Committee on Education and Science enquiry into the provision of teacher training, in support of their claim that the impact of 'progressive' theory in education had led to a fall in teaching standards.[132] The *Black Paper* submission recommended that college lecturers themselves should be 'excellent' teachers and that the disciplines they taught should be 'relevant'; it emphasized the importance of 'tradition' in determining public standards of education; it called for more attention to be given to the quality, rather than quantity, of teachers; and, most significantly of all, it argued that any major change had to come through a national committee of some kind which might make clear what the standard of the profession should be.[133] Its view of poor teaching standards, and standards in the use of English language, would be restated by Stuart Froome on the Bullock Committee (see chapter 4).

The influence of preservationist thinking on the formation and formulation of Tory education policy in the period of Conservative opposition (1964–70) was both deep and substantive. It helped the Party to make up its mind on fundamental issues of policy — among them the extent of secondary school reorganization and on where priorities should lie within the education system. It cautioned against 'undue hurry to change established systems when they are manifestly good'. The essence of the preservationist case, as stated prior to the 1970 General Election, was that Labour's policy of universal comprehensivization threatened the very foundations of *structured learning* in schools.

The personal correspondences between the Black Paper authors show that amongst some preservationists there was an urgency to meet the new Shadow Education Minister to impress their 'sober and careful analytical presentation of the conservative case'. Despite their submission to the House of Commons Select Committee they had not been able to meet Mrs Thatcher personally. Bantock told Dyson:

> I too was sorry to miss Mrs Thatcher and hope I shall have a chance of meeting her sometime in the future.[134]

Notes

1 Dr Rhodes Boyson MP, to author, 20 February 1985. This perception, amongst others, caused Boyson to leave the Labour Party and join the Tories in 1964.

2 *Ibid.*

3 For example, Rhodes Boyson and Ralph Harris. Both Boyson and Harris would become Black Paper contributors in 1969. Boyson would start The Churchill Press (Constitutional Book Club) with Harris in 1970. Both Boyson and Harris were Christians and both were the products of grammar schools. Between 1947–49 Harris was Political Area Education Officer for the Conservative Party in the South-East Area, based at St. Stephen's Chambers, Westminster.

4 Butt cites as examples, an unpopular pay restraint policy, high public spending and the Robbins report (which advocated a massive and precipitate increase of expenditure on expanding university education) as well as the voguish vocabulary of 'classlessness' that had crept into Conservative rhetoric. In 1964 Butt was a journalist on *The Sunday Times*.

5 Minister of Education (July 1962–March 1964); Opposition Spokesman on education (February 1965–October 1969); Maude was Director of the CPC (1951–55) and, in 1965, a member of Heath's Policy Group on Future Economic Policy.

6 For a more recent restatement of the 'Maude-view', see Butt (1987). Butt argues that it was largely politicians of the social democratic and Labour persuasion who helped contribute the wreck that has been made of state education since the sixties. Both Maude and Butt would welcome Black Paperites and would work in partnership in establishing the Council for the Preservation of Educational Standards (1972) to restore objective standards to education. Both had backgrounds in journalism and understood 'the power of the pen', and the importance of pamphleteering, in changing opinions and revising educational attitudes.

7 The book was Maude's own personal statement written, and expressed, independently of the Conservative Party.

8 Interestingly, in March 1974, Gilmour was appointed by Heath to be Chairman of the Advisory Committee on Policy and the Conservative Research Department, and, in March 1975, Maude was made Chairman of the CRD in succession to Gilmour.

9 Gamble's observation that it was Maude and Powell (another representative of the 'New Right' tendency) who led the challenge in 1964 to Heath's leadership of the Party, indicates the extent of the disillusionment of the One Nation CEs with modernist, enlightened Toryism.

10 Dr Rhodes Boyson MP, to author, 20 February 1985. Boyson would follow Maude into the Black Paper group in 1969. Like Maude he would prove to be a vehement opponent of Heath-Gilmour liberal Tories.

11 For a rebuttal of the notion that the New Right in the Conservative Party constitutes a distinct style of conservative practice see Gash (1984).

12 Lord Harris, to author, 23 August 1985. The Black Papers would be one manifestation of the 'awkward squads' growing disillusionment with post-war educational orthodoxy.

13 Lord Maude, to author, 19 February 1986.

14 *Ibid.*

15 *Ibid.*

16 MP. S. W. Herts (1950–February 1974); Executive Committee member 1922 Committee (1965–74); Knighted in 1972; awarded an MBE in 1944.

17 Sir Gilbert Longden to author, 11 February 1986.

18 Member, Manchester City Council (1956–80); Leader of Conservative opposition (1977–79); Education Committee AMC (1968–71); Manchester Education Committee (1967–70); Member of Heath's education policy group (1966–69).

19 Sir Gilbert Longden to author, 11 February 1986.

20 *Ibid.*

21 *Ibid.* Longden and Boyson would both shortly become pro-education voucher men. Longden and Greenway would have a much closer working relationship, both becoming, at different times,

Chairmen of the all-party British Atlantic Committee, where they would help monitor the politicization of education.

22 *Ibid.*

23 *Ibid.*

24 Longden's influence would be strengthened by his own participation as a lecturer at the Swinton Conservative College where he would meet, and impress, two other CEs, Norman St John-Stevas and John Selwyn Gummer, both of whom were to become (from 1973) his personal friends and themselves champions of 'excellence in education'.

25 Longden had been adopted as Conservative Parliamentary candidate for Morpeth in 1938. After his defeat at Morpeth in the General Election of 1945 he had helped to form three Young Conservative branches in that division. In March 1947 he was adopted as the prospective Conservative candidate for Watford. His paper was written in order to express to Young Conservatives his views upon the principles of the Conservative Party.

26 Longden (1947) *A Conservative Philosophy*, p. 1.

27 Sir Gilbert Longden to author, 11 February 1986.

28 Here the Tory Opposition was endorsing one of the main recommendations of the *Newsom Report*.

29 Each of these tenets had been formulated in 'Statement on Secondary Education' prepared by the Education Sub-Committee of the Conservative Party National Advisory Committee on Local Government issued by the CCO Local Government Department, June 1965, *The Longden Papers*. On his copy of the statement Longden wrote 'Couldn't agree more'.

30 Longden (1966) 'Topical commentary: Comprehensive Schools', S. W. Herts Conservative and Unionist Association, February, *The Longden Papers*.

31 *Ibid.*

32 Letter from Gilbert Longden to Sir Edward Boyle, 25 May 1966, *The Longden Papers*.

33 *Ibid.*

34 *Ibid.*

35 *Ibid.*

36 Richard Hornby MP, Tonbridge (1956–74); Vice-Chairman, Conservative Education Committee (1965–68); Chairman, Conservative Party Study Group on Higher Education (1969); Member of the ACP (1965–68).

37 Circular letter from Gilbert Longden to members of the Divisional Executive, S. W. Herts, May 1966, *The Longden Papers*.

38 'An Approach To Secondary School Reorganisation', CRD memorandum, 5 December 1966, *The Longden Papers*.

39 Anthony Greenland, to author, 19 August 1986.

40 Boyle to Kogan, in Kogan (1971) p. 118.

41 Anthony Greenland, to author, 19 August 1986.

42 *Ibid.*

43 Anthony Greenland, to author, 18 February 1985.

44 Anthony Greenland, to author, 19 August 1986.

45 *Ibid.*

46 Anthony Greenland, to author, 18 February 1985.

47 Brendon Sewill, to author, 12 March 1986.

48 *Ibid.*

49 *Ibid.*

50 *Ibid.*

51 *Ibid.*

52 *Ibid.*

53 *Ibid.*

54 *Ibid.*

55 *Ibid.*

56 *Ibid.*

57 Anthony Greenland to author 19 August 1986. According to Susan Crosland, Boyle was 'one of the few Tories for whom Tony had any time'. See Crosland (1983, p. 143).

58 Letter from Sir Edward Boyle to Sir Michael Fraser, 26 February 1964, *The Boyle Papers*, MS. 660/22684. Eldon Griffiths had been a member of the CRD (1963–64). In 1964 he had been elected MP for Bury St. Edmunds.

59 Speech by Sir Edward Boyle at the meeting of the National Union of the Conservative and Unionist Associations Central Council, 6 March 1965, *The Boyle Papers*, MS. 660/22929.

60 Speech by Sir Edward Boyle to the Conservative Party Conference, 14 October 1965, *The Boyle Papers*, MS. 660/22930/2.

61 Speech by Sir Edward Boyle to the Conservative Party Conference, 12 October 1966, *The Boyle Papers*, MS. 660/22937/1.

62 *Ibid.* Boyle's statement on 'selection' would seem to suggest that he had not acceded to calls from some on the centre-left of the Party that policy should be guided by the findings of educational research even if many of its conclusions ran counter, as many of them did, to traditional Conservative thinking. The centre-left course had been outlined by Dr Keith Hampson and Simon Jenkins (both members of the CTANAC) in *Educating The Individual Child*, PEST Ed. Series 1. CPC, No. 337, February 1966.

63 Speech by Angus Maude, at the Mechanics' Institute, Bradford, 9 May 1967, *The Boyle Papers*, MS. 660/22632.

64 'Conservative policy on comprehensive education', AGLB/CRD/519/08, Letter No. 37, May 1967.

65 'Education — Conservative policy', AGLB/CRD/519/08, May 1967.

66 Letter from Gilbert Longden to Conservative members of LEAs, June 1967, *The Longden Papers*.

67 'Tory policy for secondary education', letter from Gilbert Longden to the Editor, *The Sunday Times*, 28 June 1967, *The Longden Papers*.

68 CRD memoranda, 'Two aspects of the current comprehensive battle', author not assigned (NDG), AGLB/CRD/519/08.

69 *Ibid.* One example of such 'resistance' came in June 1967 when a group of parents took action against the Enfield Council's plans to impose comprehensive reorganization, converting seven grammar and twenty-three secondary modern schools into fifteen 'comprehensives'. The parents' action was unsuccessful. One of the parent-plaintiffs was Ralph Harris who, in 1965–66, had lectured at the Swinton Conservative College and contributed to the journal *Focus on Education*, successor to *The Conservative Teacher*, and an important outlet for the views of the CEs.

70 'Speeches from the party conference', *Focus on Education*, October 1967, p. 25.

71 *NACE Minute Book, Vol. 2, 1965–1977*, p. 70, CPA. In 1967 the NACE had its headquarters in Conservative Central Office though NACE meetings continued to be held at The Royal Overseas League, Park Place, St James', Westminster.

72 CSC Newsletter, October, 1967, *The Longden Papers*. The CSC was a body established to monitor the development of the comprehensive principle in English education. Besides Boyson, other sponsors included Harold Elvin (Director, London Institute of Education), Brian Jackson (Director, ACE, Cambridge), Simon Jenkins (NACE and PEST), Dr Robin Pedley (Director, Exeter Institute of Education), Professor Brian Simon (Leicester School of Education), Professor Peter Townsend (University of Essex), Angus Wilson (novelist and lecturer, University of East Anglia) and Dr Michael Young (Chairman, ACE). Committee members included Caroline Benn and Guy Neave. Boyson's contact with the CSC and his position on the Conservative NACE allowed him to keep Gilbert Longden informed of developments regarding comprehensive schools.

73 Speech by Sir Edward Boyle to the 1967 Conservative Party Conference, *The Boyle Papers*, MS. 660/22938.

74 *NACE Minute Book, Vol. 2, 1965–1977*, pp. 77–88, CPA.

75 *Ibid.* Boyson assumed his responsibility for monitoring sixth-form curricula at the NACE meeting, 9 December 1967.

76 Maude's CPC pamphlet was the text of a lecture given at the 1967 CPC Summer School held at Christ Church, Oxford. Maude delivered his lecture after Longden had issued his own private circular.

77 Russell Lewis, to author, 22 August 1986.
78 *Ibid.*
79 John O'Sullivan was Junior Tutor, Swinton Conservative College (1965–67); Senior Tutor (1967–69); Assistant Editor, *Swinton Journal* (1967–68); Editor, *Swinton Journal* (1968–69); Prospective Parliamentary candidate, Gateshead West (1970); leader writer, *Daily Telegraph* (1970–71); London correspondent, Irish Radio and Television (1971–72); Parliamentary sketch writer and leader writer, *Daily Telegraph* (1972–77); Consultant, CPS (1974–75); Assistant Editor, *Daily Telegraph* (1977–79); Editor, *Policy Review*, Heritage Foundation, USA (1979–83); Fellow of the Institute of Politics, Harvard (1983); Associate Editor, *Daily Telegraph* (1983–84); Editorial page editor, *New York Post* (1984–86); Columnist, *The Times* (1985–86); Associate Editor, *The Times* (1986–87); and a Member of the Reform Club.
80 John O'Sullivan, to author, 24 September 1986.
81 *Ibid.*
82 Szamuely's citation of Powell, Hogg and Maude was important not just because these men were prominent Conservative thinkers but because they were also three of the principal CEs inside the Conservative Party. The mention of Warden John Sparrow (All Souls, Oxford) was equally significant. Sparrow would join Szamuely and Maude as contributors to *Black Paper Two*.
83 Szamuely believed the 'turn to the Right' was occasioned, in part, by the Labour government's vindictive demolition of the grammar schools and its crass, utilitarian attitude to education, scholarship and research which were mere subsidiary weapons of economic planning and the balance of payments. Kingsley Amis would be a contributor to *Black Paper Two*.
84 Interestingly, Szamuely's conceptualization of the 'intellectual task' parallels Maude's own usage of the term 'Conservative Educationalists'. Like Szamuely, other CEs would welcome change — but not 'change for change's sake'.
85 John O'Sullivan, to author, 24 September 1986.
86 Sir Edward Boyle corresponded with John Vaizey between 1962–79. Vaizey was a friend of Crosland.
87 Speech by John Vaizey to the Annual Conference of the NACE, Overseas House, Westminster, 22 June 1968, *The Boyle Papers*, MS. 660/22640/1.
88 Enoch Powell addressed the same NACE meeting and argued: 'the adoption of "growth" as the absorbing object of policy, and the belief that education is an indispensable ingredient of growth goes far to explain some of the characteristic phenomena and aberrations of our time in the field of education'.
89 Professor Cox, to author 21, February 1986.
90 Letter from James to Dyson, 29 August 1968, *The Cox Papers*. James was a friend of Robert Conquest, himself a contributor to the first two Black Papers.
91 Sir Edward Boyle to the 1968 Conservative Party Conference, *The Boyle Papers*, MS. 660/22939.
92 Stuart Maclure, to author, 13 January 1986. Maclure was education correspondent on *The Observer* (1964–69), a columnist on *The Spectator* (1967–69), and Editor, *Education* (1954–69). He succeeded Walter James as Editor of the *Times Educational Supplement* in 1969. Between 1965–67 Maclure was invited by Sir Edward Boyle to speak to the Party's education study group. Maclure's 1968 paper 'Learning beyond our means?' (CEP), which described how the financial climate for education had changed as a result of demographic factors, was known to Boyle and was used by the Party in its 1970 Election campaign. Maclure was now a member of the All Souls Group (founded 1941), a private 'ad hoc' group of figures drawn from the Ministry of Education, the schools and the press, which met three times a year to discuss educational issues. The group had no policy functions and did not have any common view.
93 *Focus on Education* had, since its launch in September 1965, carried the writings of several CEs, notably Kathleen Ollerenshaw 'Conservataives and secondary education' (winter 1965), Ralph Harris 'The impact of change on the individual' (summer 1966), Keith Hampson 'Provision for diversity — Restructuring of secondary education', and Gilbert Longden 'Tory policy for secondary education' (winter 1967).
94 Letter and draft article from Boyson to Baguley, 14 November 1968, CUTA/Focus on Education correspondences CCO/4/10/88/95–96. CPA.

95 *Make Life Better*, a policy document, 1968. This document was an official mid-term statement of Conservative policy. From it would grow the manifesto on which the 1970 General Election would be fought.

96 Letter from Cox and Dyson, November 1968, *The Cox Papers*.

97 Letter from Professor Cox to author, 15 May 1986.

98 'Back to education', *The Cox Papers*.

99 *Ibid*. Kathleen Ollerenshaw's *Re-think on Education*, CPC No. 432, March 1969, would carry a similar message. Cox met Ollerenshaw several times at local Manchester meetings but there was no Manchester group. Letter from Professor Cox to author, 15 April 1986.

100 Tom Howarth, to author, 5 March 1986. Before 1968 Howarth had written a series of letters to *The Times* expressing concern about standards of literacy, and Cox and Dyson may have read these prior to locating Howarth as a sympathizer. Howarth was a friend and contemporary of Maude (both had attended Rugby School together).

101 Letter from Maude to Cox, 19 December 1968, *The Cox Papers*.

102 Letter from Maude to Cox, 2 January 1969, *The Cox Papers*.

103 Letter from Maude to Cox, 3 January 1969, *The Cox Papers*. The book to which Maude referred was *The Common Problem*.

104 Letter from Cox to Maude, 9 January 1969, *The Cox Papers*.

105 Letter from Pedley to Cox, 11 November 1968, *The Cox Papers*. Pedley was formerly a teacher representative on the London Borough of Bexley Education Committee, a post he resigned from in protest against, what he saw as, the plans to destroy the education system there. He had joined the independent sector largely because he believed his former school (Chislehurst and Sidcup Grammar School) was to be destroyed in the interests of 'equality'. Pedley would join Maude and Howarth in the foundation of the CPES in 1972.

106 Letter from Szamuely to Cox, 5 December 1968, *The Cox Papers*.

107 Professor Cox to author, 15 August 1986. Whilst Walter James publicized the first two Black Papers, Maclure's reviews in *The Observer* were condemnatory and his opposition to 'Black Paper' ideology continued when he succeeded James as Editor of the *Times Educational Supplement*. For his review of the first Black Paper, see Maclure (1969).

108 Stuart Maclure to author, 13 January 1986.

109 *Ibid*.

110 Letter from Maude to Cox, 22 January 1969, *The Cox Papers*.

111 Letter from Maude to Cox, 24 Febuary 1969, *The Cox Papers*. In the event Professor William Walsh (Leeds) was successfully approached to join the 'Fight for Education' campaign.

112 Letter from R. Langstone (Secretary and Agent, Finchley and Friern Barnet Conservative Association) to Maude, 22 April 1969, *The Cox Papers*.

113 The Ayrshire Local Association of the Educational Institute of Scotland were the first to contact Maude in a letter dated 7 May 1969, inviting him to speak at its 28th Annual Series of Educational Addresses in Ayr on 31 October 1969.

114 Letter from Maude to Cox, 8 May 1969, *The Cox Papers*. To this end Maude suggested that Cox should contact the Hon. Mrs Nicholas Ridley, the wife of one of Maude's colleagues at the House of Commons who, anxious to help the Black Paper group with some research, had personal knowledge of education and was particularly keen on doing some work on colleges of education and the standards of training and students there. Nicholas Ridley, MP, had been PPS to Sir Edward Boyle (1962–64) and was on the neo-liberal wing of the Tory Party.

115 *Ibid*. Cox had, in fact, contacted Bantock by letter on 21 April 1969, telling him 'Your own contributions to thinking on education seem to me outstanding, and among the most important of the last decade'. Letter from Cox to Bantock, 21 April 1969, *The Cox Papers*.

116 See, in particular, Bantock's article (1968) 'The purpose of education', *Swinton Journal*, 14, 1, spring, pp. 16–23. This article, based on a talk given by Bantock at Swinton Conservative College, reminded Conservatives of the way in which education was concerned with individuals and, as the Party stood for excellence, why educational standards were more important than a bogus equality secured at their

expense. Bantock believed schools should pursue and cultivate the culture of literacy, not the culture of the mass media.

117 Letter from Bantock to Cox, 25 April 1969, *The Cox Papers*.

118 Letter from Boyson to Cox and Dyson, 15 April 1969, *The Cox Papers*. Boyson's concern about standards in comprehensive schools had already been expressed in an article 'Threat to tradition', in Smart (1968). In this, he had argued that it was time to see if comprehensives had 'fulfilled the academic promise on which we supported them' (p. 56), and concluded that, in the socially organised comprehensive school 'academic excellence is a minor or non-existent aim' (p. 63).

119 *Ibid*. Boyson's offer of support was accepted and his analysis appeared in *Black Paper Two* as 'The essential conditions for the success of a comprehensive school', which argued strongly the case of the academic comprehensive school.

120 Letter from Powell to Dyson, 21 March 1969, *The Cox Papers*. Powell, in fact, gave a speech in April on the need to build more grammar schools.

121 Letter from Hastings to Dyson, 24 April 1969, *The Cox Papers*.

122 Letter from Bell to Dyson, 7 October 1969, *The Cox Papers*.

123 Letter from Goodhew to Dyson, 9 October 1969, *The Cox Papers*.

124 Letter from Maude to Cox, 16 June 1969, *The Cox Papers*. The plan was to have copies available on the Party Conference bookstall. In the event *Black Paper Two* was published one week before the Party Conference.

125 Letter from Maude to Cox, 21 May 1969, *The Cox Papers*. In fact, Eldon Griffiths had brought to Maude's attention details of his own children's experiences of comprehensive education whilst they had been resident in America. They had returned to England and found themselves 'seriously behind their contemporaries in English schools'. Griffiths declined Maude's offer to contribute to *Black Paper Two* but his support for the 'Fight for Education' campaign was enlisted. Eldon Griffiths was a former CRD officer and speech writer to Macmillan and Home. He became a government Minister in 1970.

126 Letter from Maude to Cox, 20 August 1969, *The Cox Papers*. One of the central arguments of *Black Paper Two* was that, where informal methods were used exclusively, educational standards declined.

127 Letter from Cox to Maude, 22 August 1969, *The Cox Papers*.

128 Sir Edward Boyle to the 1969 Conservative Party Conference, *The Boyle Papers*, MS. 660/22942. On this occasion Boyle was not the target of any 'verbal gunfire' from Maude who had decided to cut the Party Conference to take a holiday.

129 *Ibid*. Here Boyle may well have been influenced in his view by Quintin Hogg's plea at the 1968 Party Conference for 'moderation in all things'. Viscount Hailsham was Minister of Education (14 January 1957–16 September 1957) and Secretary of State (1 April 1964–16 October 1964). For an account of his abhorrence of the efforts of Socialists to make the education machine a vehicle for social engineering, and his contempt for those who wished to force comprehensive schools as a single pattern for all secondary education, see Hailsham, Lord (1975), pp. 139–40.

130 Mrs Thatcher was one of those who attended the Selsdon Park Shadow Cabinet weekend (30–31 January 1970) to discuss policy ideas for the next Conservative government.

131 Letter from Bantock to Cox, 30 October 1969, *The Cox Papers*. Bantock himself submitted an essay, 'Conflicts of values in teacher education' (a revised version of an article previously published in *The Colston Papers* Vol. 20) for the third Black Paper on 1 June 1970.

132 The memorandum was submitted by Professor Bantock, Dr Boyson, Professor Cox and Anthony Dyson on 3 March 1970. Conservative members who heard their evidence included Ronald Bell, Richard Hornby, Gilbert Longden and William Van Straubenzee. Thus, both the liberal and right wings of the Party were made conversant with those common assumptions of the 'Black Paper' school — that 'there were major deficiencies in teacher education (e.g. colleges of education offering an anaemic and claustrophobic pastoralism instead of a rigorous and demanding intellectualism) resulting from an unwillingness to work out an acceptable and reasonable rationale in initial training, and poor standards in the use of English language' — which formed the basis of their general thesis that 'the unthinking, dogmatic assertion of orthodoxies and uncritical acceptance of "progressive" ideas had caused educationists to apply in too naive a way the thoughts of writers such as Rousseau,

Froebel and Dewey to the complex learning problems in modern society'. *Minutes of Evidence taken before The Select Committee on Education and Science*, 3 March 1970, p. 316.

133 *Ibid.*, pp. 338–9. These were points noted by The James Committee on Teacher Education (1971). They were among the personal priorities of Mrs Thatcher. Lord James of Rusholme was a preservationist and friend of Tom Howarth. Tom Howarth to author, 5 March 1986.

134 Letter from Bantock to Dyson, 28 April 1970, *The Cox Papers*.

Chapter 4

The preservationists and the Conservative Party, 1970–74

Introduction

In 1970 there was still considerable unease within the Conservative Party about the lack of any clear statement of education policy. Lord Coleraine (Richard Law), a former Conservative Minister of Education,[1] was of the opinion that the Party was intellectually confused in the field of education and that the Conservative leadership was 'repeating the prevailing shibboleths without debate of any kind' (Coleraine, 1970, p. 140). According to another Conservative (Rhodes James, 1972), Heath's approach had seemed, erroneously, to consist of 'proposing variations on the Labour policy rather than of proposing a separate policy' (p. 174). This was the impatient constituency to which the *Black Paper* group sought to appeal.

At the same time as Lord Butler was recording in his memoirs (1971) how the years, since 1944, had brought great quantitative growth and much qualitative improvement to education (p. 124), Ralph Harris and Dr Rhodes Boyson were launching the first publications from their Churchill Press/Constitutional Book Club[2] to help counter, what they saw as, the 'large class of soft liberals' who were undermining traditional values in education. Boyson's own edited volume — *Right Turn* (1970) — was published after the June 1970 General Election when fresh hopes were beginning to be focussed on the new Conservative government. Written by Boyson as 'a moral trumpet-call for the good society' the book argued for the restoration of free choice, personal responsibility and standards of excellence to their rightful place as central values in the life of the people. Boyson believed the Conservatives' election victory was 'the opportunity for the Right to come into its own' (*ibid*, p. 11). The question was, would Heath's *Quiet Revolution* give effect to the Right's education agenda?

Although they were still very much a minority body in 1970, the preservationists would, by 1974, strengthen their alliances within and without the Conservative Party. The number of people then involved was at most a few hundred, and the numbers changed but slowly. Size was less important than contacts. The one inescapable theme in virtually every interview with the preservationists conducted by the author is the vital importance participants placed on 'mutual links' and 'confidences'. The preservationists were now located on the left, centre and right of the Party (as well as outside the Party) and, whatever their individual differences over the direction of Conservatism, all were committed to the *soundness* of the conservative case for education.

The motive forces operating among the preservationists — mutual confidence and common calculation — were essential elements in sustaining opposition to Heath's particular brand of Tory progressivism, inspired by the Macmillan-Butler tradition. Under Heath's leadership the Conservative Party would continue to be seen as the vehicle of reform, progress and moderation.[3] But the preservationists feared Heath's *Quiet Revolution* would not give expression to their particular educational vision.

At the time of the 1970 General Election the Personal Assistant to Heath was Dr Keith Hampson.[4] Hampson was on the centre of the Party on education.[5] He had served as Vice-Chairman of the CTANAC (1964–66) and was conversant with preservationist thinking. According to Hampson, it was during the period of the Heath government that established opinions in education were challenged by the Black Papers and when the educational-right slowly became more mainstream, with Professor Brian Cox giving the Right 'intellectual weight'.[6] In Hampson's view, the educational-right groupings of this period were 'incestuous, feeding off each other'.[7]

An illustration of Hampson's thesis is to be found in the private correspondences between the early Black Paper editors and Margaret Thatcher which, again, highlight the importance of shared mutual confidence and common calculation in strengthening the comradeship between the preservationists. Following her appointment as Secretary of State for Education and Science on 20 June 1970, Professor Cox wrote to Mrs Thatcher expressing his congratulations and good wishes. In her reply from Curzon Street she said:

> I also regard myself as a moderate but anyone who believes as we do in excellence in education is liable to be called a right wing extremist.[8]

Mrs Thatcher's response led Professor Cox to further his contact and impress upon the new Secretary of State the conservative case for education. Writing to her in September 1970, he said:

> I have pleasure in enclosing the current issue of the *Critical Quarterly* which of course publishes the Black Papers. We think the article by Mr. Edmund Ions on 'Threats to academic freedom in Britain' is of major importance, and we shall be sending off prints of it to all education correspondents in about ten days time. With all good wishes.[9]

On the day she became Education Secretary Mrs Thatcher addressed the Annual Conference and Dinner of the NACE at the Hall of India, Overseas House,

Westminster, to which Angus Maude and Jill Knight also gave key-note speeches. The preservationists were now about to set before the Party a clear statement of education policy which, they hoped, would harness a spirit of reform and zeal for progress in the true Conservative tradition.

A turn away to the right

In October 1970 Gilbert Longden presented a paper on *Trends in Education* at Swinton Conservative College. Longden prefaced his paper with an Oxford dictionary definition — that a trend was 'a bend or turn away in a specified direction' — and noted: 'Mercifully the great event of 18 June has meant a turn away to the Right — in every sense of that word'.[10]

In opposition Heath had decided that the Conservatives should not be known as 'the Party of the 11 + '. The decision had been prompted by the many parental protests over the examination and the considerable pupil neurosis which had been found to be associated with those facing selection at the tender age of 11. When Longden delivered his paper many of the existing 1000 'comprehensive', or, as they were known in his own Hertfordshire constituency 'all-ability', schools had been started, and given support, by Tory ministers of education only on condition that streaming and/or setting (ie. some process of selection) were operated within such schools. To the preservationists, 'selection' was only another name for 'diagnosis of ability' and was essential if every child was to be given the opportunity to make the best of its talents. However, the demise of the 11 + in a number of local authorities suggested that the notion of *selective education* was not only unacceptable to many people but that comprehensive uniformity in the public sector was likely to escalate. It was for this reason that Longden called upon the Party to 'reassert its faith in selection and selective education' (*ibid.*). Like his NACE colleague, Dr Rhodes Boyson, he considered the competition provided by other kinds of school was necessary to the success of comprehensive schools, and that if the public and grammar schools did not continue to offer their own achievements, a comprehensive school might have to fight hard to keep academic standards alive.

Longden told his audience that arguments against streaming at school (particularly those advanced by the ACE) and the use of public examinations to measure standards of pupil achievement (what Edward Short had, in 1969, called 'the tyranny of examinations') were being led 'by a few doctrinaire sociologists who were gambling with the minds and futures of the nation's children' (*ibid.*). Longden's paper utilized other examples of Boysonian rhetoric. Thus, he saw the prevailing fashion to decry rules, discipline, streaming, marks and examinations as a 'non-system nicely calculated to augment the delinquent brigade' (*ibid.*). And in an obvious, direct reference to the *Black Paper* group, he said:

> We all owe an immense debt to the distinguished educationists, writers and
> others who are trying to open our eyes to these doubtful experiments (*ibid.*).

Though Heath may have wished to distance himself from *Black Paperite* ideology two
of his closest education policy formulators (Longden and Thatcher) were now ardent
converts.[11]

Mrs Thatcher herself had lost no time in countering the socialist policy for
education. One of the early acts of the new government had been to withdraw
Circulars 10/65 and *10/66* and replace them with *10/70*, which indicated that schemes
for secondary education need no longer follow comprehensive principles but instead
were to take general educational considerations into account, along with local needs
and wishes and the 'wise use of resources'. For some Conservatives, especially those
who readily associated comprehensive schooling with 'progressive' styles of teaching
and learning, the government's action had come none too soon. Within a few months
of their Party's election victory a number of Conservative MPs were in receipt of
complaints from constituents about perceived lax teaching standards. These were
passed to Curzon Street for the attention of ministers. Anthony Royle[12] conveyed one
constituent's compaint directly to Lord Belstead.[13] Belstead's reply, though guarded,
suggested a deep appreciation of the dilemma facing schools and teachers wishing to
adopt modern teaching methods whilst retaining publicly acceptable educational
standards:

> I find your constituent's (Miss V. E. Hoare) remarks on progressive
> methods too generalized for me to be able to comment on them in detail. I
> am sure, however, that teachers in general do not 'deliberately remove
> discipline and encourage contempt for authority'. It is true that many
> teachers encourage their pupils to do a great deal more work on their own
> than was the case a generation or two back, notably 'project' work . . . But
> such work does not mean abdication by the teacher of his own overall
> responsibility and involves a good deal of self-discipline on the part of the
> pupil if good results are to be achieved, as they so very often
> are . . . Obviously there will be exceptions, but these should not be taken as
> representing the whole body of pupils, nor should the behaviour of pupils
> be linked, without individual examination, with the methods employed in
> their education.[14]

Belstead's assurances to Royle of the possible benefits of some 'modern' teaching
approaches suggest that the official DES view now (despite Mrs Thatcher's unofficial
correspondences with the Black Paper editors) was to allow the 'progressive'
education experiment to continue, though ministers would keep under review any
obvious decline in standards or individual malpractice. That one of Mrs Thatcher's
junior ministers should have responded in such a liberal fashion to a mounting public

concern about schooling standards indicates the divisions of opinion still prevailing within the Conservative government's political executive as to the proper direction for education.[15]

Despite such divisions of opinion, a gradual turn away to the Right was effected by changing relations within the CRD, by the proliferation of educational-right thinking in the *Swinton Journal*, and by the efforts of individual CCO personnel who recognized the potential political capital of such thought for the winning of future elections. We shall see below how these developments were paralleled by a persistent, external lobbying of the Party, by new groupings of preservationists fundamentally committed to the restoration of traditional educational values and practice.

One result of Sir Edward Boyle's withdrawal from politics early in 1970 was a change in relations within the CRD that critically altered the direction and shaping of education policy formation. The position of CRD Education Desk Officer — held by Anthony Greenland since 1961 — was now under the direct supervision of Charles Bellairs.[16] Bellairs was a man of the Right and, from 1970, a close working colleague, friend and supporter of both Mrs Thatcher and Sir Keith Joseph (then Secretary of State for Social Services).[17] Whilst Greenland had been one of Boyle's closest associates, his alliance with Boyle during the period of Conservative opposition had, according to one CRD officer interviewed, discouraged any rightward direction of schools policy.[18] The same CRD officer believed that Boyle's departure from the political stage left Bellairs as the dominating figure in the transmission of education briefings to Mrs Thatcher.[19] According to Bellairs, the situation in the early 1970s saw fewer differences on education policy as such and that problems arose from differences of emphases.[20]

The proliferation of educational-right thinking in the *Swinton Journal* was now especially significant. The journal, described in its editorial as a 'forum for a wide-ranging debate on the nature of modern conservatism', had been established in 1951, four years after the foundation of the Swinton Conservative College at Masham, near Ripon, West Yorkshire. As we saw in chapter 3, the Swinton College courses, weekends, symposia, and *Swinton Journal*, had each helped build up a Conservative education movement. Swinton's first Principal, Sir Reginald Northam, had earlier observed (1939, p. 167) that the problem of education was something more than one of organization, of curriculum and of method. More than anything else he believed that the best in the nation's past (which was borne of spiritual values inculcated by traditional learning and teaching) would be the guide to the future and that the people would become imbued afresh with 'the right outlook' (*ibid*, p. 1). Northam wished that Conservatives would conserve what was best in the education system but realized that the best could only be preserved by being enhanced and enriched, and that it would often be necessary to reform in order to preserve (*ibid*, p. 167). Thus, as one of the earliest CEs, Northam was instrumental in setting out that grounding philosophy of education to which the preservationists adhered with such conviction.[21]

Between 1970 and 1974 the *Swinton Journal* carried numerous essays by people of the Right seeking to fashion a conservative educational policy in line with Conservative philosophy. Three essays, in particular, made a challenge to the Conservative Party's progressive-wing led by Heath: John O'Sullivan's *The Direction of Conservatism* (Vol 16, no. 1, pp. 30–6), Ronald Bell's *The Content of Education* (Vol 18, no. 4, pp. 11–18) and Tom Howarth's *The Future of Our Schools: A Conservative View* (Vol 19, no. 3, pp. 3–7).

O'Sullivan's essay urged caution regarding facile blueprints for the 'New Tory Jerusalem' and castigated those Conservatives who had lined up on both sides of the argument about the relative merits of comprehensive schools and the tripartite system. In his view neither scheme was based upon Conservative assumptions. Thus, he argued, Conservatives were in the anomalous position of disagreeing among themselves about two educational reforms which, whatever their incidental advantages, were inherently and essentially socialist. He suggested Conservatives should seek an alternative choice and examine schemes that would truly conserve individual parental freedom and choice in education, promote competition between schools and encourage decentralized initiative (perhaps through a system of education vouchers). O'Sullivan's position owed much to the influence of Arthur and Marjorie Seldon.[22] Like them, he believed in *excellence in education* but claimed that it could not be secured by a state school system alone.[23] Though his essay was not written with any specific design for effecting policy changes in the Party in 1970, he was conscious of its potential significance to the *Swinton Circle* generally.[24] O'Sullivan had written his essay after he had just finished his employment at Swinton, at a time when Heath was using the College as a base for making new policy.[25] O'Sullivan could not say if his essay was ever discussed by Heath.[26]

Bell's essay was the product of one Conservative MP's engagement in some fundamental rethinking about the role of education in a modern, mass, consumer society. Bell believed in the fierce struggle of conflicting ideas and was happy to see education a battleground. Having served as Vice-Chairman of the Conservative backbench Education Committee, his rightward voice was respected, if not yet widely supported, in the Party. Bell argued that if the state was to be in control of virtually all education then the normal safeguard of conflict and diversity would be absent and there would be increasing prescription of the content of education. He believed this would pose very great problems for those on the Right who did not want education to be basically political indoctrination. Like other preservationists, Bell's concern was to urge Conservatives to seek ways of preventing education being the plaything of Left-wing politicians.

For Bell, there had been more 'change for change's sake' in education than in most other aspects of British life. Theories had been allowed to dominate the schooling debate. Thus, his essay called upon the Party to defend the general standard of basic literacy against mediocrity at a time when 'astringency of judgment is so rare and thinking in fashion is so widespread' and to give children certainty and security when 'everything formerly accepted is called into question'. Bell's essay — resonant of *Black Paperite* philosophy — attacked moves to suppress streaming and abolish fixed criteria like examinations, both of which were, in his view, symptomatic of the desire of the 'equalitarian levellers' and the 'interventionist levellers' to pursue social engineering aims. Bell was convinced that when people intervened in the interests of levelling they were not preoccupied with excellence but with averages. It was for this reason that he recommended that the Party had no alternative but to enter the politics of curriculum content, and indeed of teaching methods also, not because either was a good thing to do but because the other side were doing it. He believed it was better to have a balance of political struggle than for there to be a monopoly of influence upon the minds of children.

Howarth's essay made a direct appeal for a return to traditional teaching and learning. It posed the question 'What positive education in values could be reasonably looked for in the modern secularized school?' Howarth believed this question was the centre of the problem facing a Conservative theory of education. He considered that it was the 'obvious' in learning that was in urgent need of restatement. Thus, instruction should include the transmission of the best in the nation's cultural tradition and not what was arbitrarily deemed to be 'relevant'. Howarth had long been an opponent of mammoth comprehensive schools and his essay poured scorn on Lord Boyle for failing to resist, from 1964, the gathering momentum of many Conservative working voters moving into the comprehensive lobby. He called upon Mrs Thatcher to continue to oppose some of the more lethal reorganization plans and to carry on the fight to preserve good schools, and appealed to the Party to move away from a more or less defensive posture in education.[27]

These Swinton essays may be seen as indicative of what Powell had sensed to be 'signs of the worm turning'.[28] The *Black Paper* group, and its parliamentary supporters in the Conservative Party, had good reason to rejoice. Not only was the *Swinton Journal* carrying their 'Fight for Education' message but, within the CCO itself, key figures were allowing that message to be transmitted to Party activists in the regions. It was Russell Lewis — the Director of the CPC and himself an enthusiast for the growing rightward turn in the education debate — who sponsored the publication of Rhodes Boyson's two CPC pamphlets *Battle Lines For Education* (1973) and *Parental Choice* (1975).[29] Two of the founding members of the 61 Society were now working closely together to secure wider agreement in the Party on, what they saw as, the imperative conservative case for education. According to Lewis' deputy, the two CPC pamphlets were written in a framework with which Lewis identified and sympathized, and, on each occasion it was Boyson who came to the Central Office to ask Lewis to publish his ideas which, Boyson believed, would help the Party win elections.[30] There appears to have been two reasons for Lewis' patronage of Boyson. First, he believed that Heath wanted to keep *Black Paperite* thinking at a distance.[31]

Lewis, of course, was warmly sympathetic to *Black Paper* ideas (Lewis, 1975, p. 57).[32] Secondly, he thought that the spirit of the *Black Paper* authors was not shared in the Education Ministry (*ibid*, pp. 69–70).[33] But, whether by design or coincidence, Lewis clearly used his position in the CPC and his friendship with Boyson, to help spread that spirit within the Party.

The absorption of the 'Black Paper' spirit into the Party

Though the preservationists were not successful in turning Tory education policy in a sharply right direction during the period of the Heath government, their ideas did attract increasing Party support and interest.

The incorporation of *Black Paper* plans for education (largely, but not wholly, a return to the old ways) into Party thinking and policy dates from Mrs Thatcher's speech to the Annual Conference of the Association of Education Committees (AEC) at Scarborough on 28 October 1970. In her address she told delegates 'We must avoid becoming preoccupied with systems and structures to the detriment of the actual content of education'.[34] The declared intention of the Education Secretary — to see that schools and their pupils should have access to specialized knowledge, to liberal-minded teaching and to general education of high quality — closely matched the aims of the *Black Paper* group. Her observation that 'schools are for children, and it is what goes on inside them that matters' (*ibid.*) echoed the concern of the preservationists, that the Party should ensure that schools concentrated on achieving those educational objectives which were necessary both to national survival and to personal fulfilment for the individual.

Mrs Thatcher's position on education had been informed not just by her private correspondences with Professor Brian Cox and Tony Dyson, but also by her contacts with the NACE, which was now playing a much more decisive role in the formation of Conservative education policy. At a meeting held on 11 July 1970 the NACE had discussed its future role under a Conservative government and decided to hold a meeting at Swinton to confer with DES ministers.[35] The NACE had further agreed to the principle of establishing a small consultative group which would be prepared, at any time, to meet ministers at the DES. The preservationist voice on the NACE was now in the ascendant. Gilbert Longden was playing an active part in getting the NACE to further accept the thinking of the *Black Paper* group. For example, at a NACE meeting held on 5 December 1970 Professors Bantock, Beloff and Cox were each supported by Longden as possible speakers at the 1971 NACE Annual Conference and Dinner. Longden also welcomed the name of Angus Maude as a speaker for the 1971 Swinton Weekend Conference. Maude, who was now Chairman of the Party's backbench Education Committee, was selected to speak on the theme 'Priorities in Education'. Longden was taking a lead in other areas too. On 10 August 1971 Peter

Baguley, at Longden's request, circulated NACE members with copies of the first issue of the newly-formed Professional Association of Teachers' journal *The Professional Teacher*, which had been sent to him by Longden. NACE members were asked to give comments on it to Longden. The desire of the preservationists to canvass support within the Party for a more traditional sense of teacher professionalism was further illustrated by Harry Greenway's offer to serve on the NACE study group on teacher training in September 1971.

The direct product of the work of the NACE, which was now embracing certain *Black Paper* themes and engaging the services of several prominent *Black Paper* writers, was a series of policy statements for education which would later form the basis of a draft manifesto for the 1974 General Election.[36] One of these statements described the main aims of Conservative education policy to be:

> To widen opportunities for children, to raise standards of provision in the education service and to give greater choice to parents and pupils between educational institutions as well as choice of curriculum within them.[37]

In other times these aims may have been regarded as nothing more than platitudes. But, in 1971, they were astutely judged objectives, built on populist ideas inspired by the *Black Papers*.

By early 1972 the mood of *Black Paper* thinking was occupying the attention of not only Mrs Thatcher and the CNACE[38] but also of House of Commons research officers, who were informing the Party of the activities of the recently formed Council for the Preservation of Educational Standards (CPES). The following letter, sent to Sir Gilbert Longden, bears testimony to the way in which formal sections of the Conservative Party were now being afforded information about the views of new *Black Paper* groupings:

> I enclose press comment on the conference of the CPES at Cambridge during the first week of January. As you can see, reactions to the conference have been extremely mixed! I spoke to Dr Rhodes Boyson in order to get further details. As yet the Council (which has been renamed the National Council for Educational Standards) is in embryo. It grew in the 'minds of like-minded men' to use Dr Boyson's words — and the main supporters are those people who have contributed to the Black Papers on education. The Cambridge Conference was the first meeting held, and about seventy people attended. The Council is now in the process of setting up a headquarters and will be extending its membership. Its aims will be broadly concerned with the maintenance of standards and values in all branches of education and Dr Boyson considers the article in The Daily Telegraph as the fullest statement of their aims yet published (I have marked the passage he mentioned). I'm afraid this is as much as he was able to tell me. He has

promised to send me any documents and reports of the Council issues, and I will certainly pass the information on to you.[39]

That the Party should have been alerted in this way to the moves by some preservationists to seek a restoration of traditional schooling, illustrates the closed nature of Conservative education policy formation. Certainly the news of the work of the CPES, and Boyson's participation in its organization, may well have strengthened Longden's own resolve to continue the fight for education.[40]

The founding members of the CPES included Professors Brian Cox and Jacques Barzun, Anthony Dyson, Dr Rhodes Boyson, Tom Howarth and Angus Maude. The decision to rename the Council the 'NCES' was taken upon the advice of Ronald Butt, a man who has been described as 'an important figure in the early stages of the counter-revolution'.[41] Butt had attended the Pembroke College meeting in a personal capacity. He did not consider himself to be a lobbyist.[42] But he sympathized strongly with the cause of Cox and Dyson in their Black Papers and had written in his column in *The Times*. Thus:

> The fact that I had a family of my own at independent schools, where they were able largely to escape the educational fashions damaging the opportunities of many children in the public sector, only made me all the more convinced of the need for a return to proper educational standards in the interests of the children. I suggested to the Cambridge meeting that it should change its name and drop the word 'Preservation' because it might have implied a rather narrow concern whereas we were all interested in the far wider issue of state schooling provision and educational change (*ibid.*).

The letter sent by the House of Commons researcher to Sir Gilbert Longden drew his attention to an article by Dr Boyson which attempted to establish evidence of a return to faith in traditional schooling (Boyson, 1972b). In his article Boyson had sought to highlight the disparity between what appeared to be, rising public support for the critique of schooling offered by the *Black Papers* and, the official Conservative Party posture reflected by Mrs Thatcher's address to the 1972 North of England Education Conference. Boyson claimed that it was symptomatic that the CPES assembly had opened on 1 January — since it pointed to the future — whereas the Leeds conference ignored the rising discontent with state school education, and continued to mouth many of the very nostrums that had brought the education service to its present perilous condition. Boyson believed increasing numbers of people were supportive of the traditionalist approach to education: that schooling should be schooling, not social engineering or child minding. As Boyson put it:

> The Cambridge conference, with little or no doctrine, came near to reaching agreement on what should be the aims of schooling in this country — universal literacy and numeracy; opportunities for all children to reach

their full potential; encouragement of the academically most gifted to add to
the stock of learning; and the need to pass on the concepts and traditions of
Greek-Jewish-Christian tradition (*ibid.*).

The above extract from Boyson's article was the very passage marked by the
House of Commons researcher for Sir Gilbert Longden's attention. Clearly, it was felt
by the researcher that Longden should be informed of the thinking of the CPES,
namely, that schools should pass on traditions ('the memory of the race' as Boyson
described it) without which nothing would be achieved, and that traditionalist aims
could best be obtained in an ordered school framework where teachers did not abdicate
to pupil impulse. Since the thinking of the CPES here mirrored the thinking of the
Black Paper group, the spirit of the latter was, in effect, conveyed to Longden. There is
no record of Longden's response to the House of Commons communication.
However, the CEs' insistence on good discipline, high educational standards and
traditional teaching methods (the preservation of the grammar-school ethos) had long
had Longden's full support and there seems no reason to doubt that he would have
received the news of Boyson's extra-Party activities with nothing less than a close
interest.

Because of other commitments Professor Cox had been unable to attend the
Cambridge conference. Consequently, Tony Dyson had performed the central
organizing role in establishing the CPES. Following the Pembroke College meeting
Professor Cox informed Professor Bantock:

> I am sorry that I did not meet you at Cambridge. As Tony probably told
> you, I was in charge of 450 sixth-formers at a CQS conference here in
> Manchester — no small undertaking. I thought the publicity was excellent.
> From 1 January 1973 the *Critical Quarterly* will be published from
> Manchester University Press. We are extending our coverage to include
> general cultural matters, particularly education and sociology. I feel that the
> campaign in education must be fought on different levels, and that a
> magazine of high academic reputation is essential.[43]

Professor Bantock's reply suggests that a certain jubilation was now in evidence
amongst the preservationists. He told Cox:

> I, too, was sorry not to see you in Cambridge. I thought the Conference
> was a great success, and the publicity we have had has been surprisingly
> favourable in view of the usual reaction to anything which even smacks of
> conservatism.[44]

Both Cox and Bantock were correct in their perceptions of the media coverage of
the Cambridge meeting. However, one critical note was, not unexpectedly, struck by
the National Union of Teachers (NUT) which believed the CPES to be:

> an august body of Black Paperites, committed to the return of eleven-plus

selection, but lacking credibility as a result of its limited experience of state education.[45]

Preservationist opinion in 1972 required from the Conservative government a return to belief in educational standards and in real parental choice, not huge building programmes and a competition with the Labour Party as to which could spend most state money (Boyson, 1972b). Boyson, at least, was confident that the tide had been turned in time to save national schooling and culture, though he was conscious that the battle would still move back and forth (*ibid.*).

For the demands and expectations of the preservationists to be met and realized it was necessary for them to strengthen their position in the Conservative Party. In 1972 a series of Party changes augured well for the future success of their ideas.

The Party moves towards the preservationist path

Although the Conserative government had rejected Labour's example of imposing systems of education — those authorities that wished to pursue comprehensive systems, and whose schemes were acceptable, were allowed to continue with them, and local authorities that did so included those that were Labour and Conservative controlled — many preservationists were still disturbed by the haste of reorganization and the failure to allow schools to evolve in their own time.

By mid-1972 there was still no clear Conservative education policy. The government was certainly pursuing themes and priorities but these did not constitute an overall strategy. However, during the summer and autumn of 1972, two changes of personnel within the Conservative Party occurred which can be seen as marking the end of the enlightened Tory approach to education and heralding the beginning of a new epoch in Conservative thinking on schooling. In turn these changes would lead to the formation of an educational policy based upon preservationist principles.

The first of these changes — Lord Boyle's retirement from political life — had important implications for the prospect of a preservationist Conservative educational policy. In June 1972 Lord Boyle (the newly appointed Vice-Chancellor of the University of Leeds) informed Sir Richard Webster (Director of Organization, Conservative and Unionist Central Office):

> I have now resigned from the Advisory Committee on Policy and I am no longer taking the Party Whip in the House of Lords. I do not wish to attend any more Party conferences since I feel I am no longer eligible.[46]

Lord Boyle's departure from one of the Party's key policy formation bodies meant that the Heath-Boyle line on education was now effectively curtailed.

The second change — the appointment in November 1972 by Heath of the liberal Norman St John-Stevas as Parliamentary Under-Secretary of State for Education —

initially promised a reinforcement of support for the enlightened Tory approach. But, as Stevas has recorded in his review of his life in politics (1984) education was one of the few issues on which he was right-wing (p. 16). Though he was never a right-wing Conservative (*ibid.*) Stevas was a preservationist and his views on education were very close to those of Longden and Maude. As Stevas has recorded:

> I was sceptical about the advantages claimed for comprehensive education, believed in the upholding of high standards, the preservation of the grammar schools and the affording of opportunities to the bright child of modest background through the network of direct grant schools. (*ibid*)[47]

Preservation was also supported by Professor Brian Cox, who had now joined the Conservative Party and would shortly join the N.W. Area Regional Group of the CNACE. Thus, towards the end of 1972 a growing Tory preservationist base was represented at the Department of Education (Mrs Thatcher and Norman St John-Stevas)[48] as well as on the voluntary side of the Party.[49]

The CNACE was now linked with the right-wing National Education Association (NEA).[50] Maynard Potts (NEA Chairman and CNACE member) had been in regular correspondence with Sir Gilbert Longden over the issue of political bias in schools[51], and this contact may well have influenced the moves by the CNACE to get area committees to monitor cases of such educational malpractice. This, and the other main thrust of the CNACE — reminding LEAs that Conservative education policy included proposals which suited local needs consistent with the retention of highly successful schools in their present form[52] — suggest that the preservationist drive was now a positive force in the regions.

It will be remembered that at the beginning of 1972 Boyson had called on the Conservative government to show a return to belief in educational standards. In December 1972 the Government published a White Paper entitled *Education: A Framework for Expansion* (Cmnd. 5174) which detailed its broad educational plans for the next decade in every part of the education service, except adult and further education. Although no specific reference was made to improvements in the quality of education there were plans for more teachers and better staffing standards, as well as improvements in teacher training. The latter issue had, as we saw in chapter 3, been the subject of a *Black Paper* representation to a House of Commons Select Committee in 1970.

Shortly after the publication of the government's proposals Mrs Thatcher delivered a speech to the Association of Metropolitan Authorities in which she reflected the *Black Paper* view of education's malaise. She told the AMA:

> There is no point in just expanding education when there is also a great deal of need for improvement.[53]

The Education Secretary's words, possible prompted by her own reading of the

Black Papers, were an indication of her intent to look more closely at the inner-workings of schools.

In its response to the government's plans the Party's PEC noted that:

> As a principle the presentation in a White Paper of a ten-year strategy for the education service is to be welcomed, not only because we recognize the need for longer term planning but also because we believe broad policy decisions in education involving major expenditure deserve clearly focused presentation and not low profile pronouncements over a period of time. Necessarily the paper does not examine all sectors in equal depth and is primarily concerned with matters of scale, organisation and cost. Rightly it does not seek to spell out in precise detail every aspect of policy. The education service is seen in the White Paper as a partnership between central, local government and those with a professional interest in education, requiring continuous decision-making. This approach we support.[54].

Whilst the PEC commentary on the White Paper was generally approving (though it did express some concern about the raising of the school leaving age and the need for careful monitoring of difficulties which might arise with the arrival of more reluctant 16-year-olds in the schools) and had concluded with a declaration that the Committee would do all it could to support and promote it in educational circles, the attitude of the Council for Educational Advance (CEA) was decidedly critical. The motion on the White Paper as adopted by the CEA at its Annual General Meeting on 5 March 1973 read:

> This AGM of the CEA regrets that in its White Paper, the government has failed to lay the basis for an adequate education service in the next decade. In particular the Council deplores the proposal to devote a diminishing proportion of the nation's income to education as a threat to educational opportunity and an obstacle to the expansion and reform of the education system, and cannot regard as adequate any programme for expansion which fails to provide for the completion of the reform of secondary education and the educational needs of the 16–19 age group.[55]

On 9 March 1973 the Secretary of the CEA wrote to Mrs Thatcher conveying the Council's resolution. In her reply the Secretary of State gave her comments on the points the CEA had raised. She denied that education's share of public expenditure would fall between 1973-77, and emphasized that the new initiatives announced in the Education White Paper would extend and expand the education service.[56] On the Government's policy on the organization of secondary education, she told the CEA:

> I have made it clear that I believe that it would be wrong to impose a uniform pattern of secondary education from the centre.[57]

Here Mrs Thatcher was pursuing the same path as the NCES, which was now seeking to expose socialist educational philosophy as 'social manipulation' and 'a denial of the pursuit of excellence'.[58]

However, it would be an over-simplification to say that, in 1973, support amongst Conservatives for the preservationist line on education was total. Among the doubters were the High Tory journalist (and apologist for the political right) Peregrine Worsthorne, and the Conservative Junior Minister Timothy Raison. Though Worsthorne believed in preserving the British class structure and considered that the genius of British politics was to be found in its civilized (hereditary) class (see Worsthorne, 1971), he was not attracted to the crusading polemics of the *Black Papers*.[59] Whilst he welcomed the *Black Papers'* defence of the English grammar school, he did not support the Black Paperites' pamphleteering style which he found to be too aggressive and incompatible with true Toryism.[60] Raison also had reservations. He was appointed by Heath as Parliamentary Under-Secretary of State for Education (Schools) in December 1973, a post he held until the February 1974 General Election. A former editor of *Crossbow* and *New Society*, Raison had been a co-opted member of the ILEA Education Committee (1967–70) and a member of Richmond-upon-Thames Council (1967–70). He had supported Richmond's switch to comprehensive education. His educational experience (as a member of the Plowden Committee on primary schools and the ILEA) prior to his election as an MP in 1970, allowed him to view educational developments with a certain degree of expertise. Though Raison was a liberal-minded educator (he had been pro-Boyle and had worked on the ILEA with Christopher Chataway, himself a Junior Minister to Boyle when the Party was last in office) he had, in 1971, introduced a Ten Minute Rule Bill advocating limited contracts for headteachers — an idea that the educational-right would later pursue as part of its campaign for greater teacher accountability (see, for example, Honey, 1981, pp 24–8). But this hard-line on the issue of teacher tenure was not prompted by the Black Papers:

> One of my special interests in education had always been the professionalizat-ion of teachers and the establishment of a General Teaching Council. The *Black Papers* introduced some interesting ideas into the education debate. Where we agreed was on the switch of emphasis to quality in education.[61]

Because of his remarkably short period at the DES and his subsequent transfer to other areas of political responsibility, it is not possible to fully assess Raison's role as a CE.[62] But both he and Stevas represented a changing Tory Party now, more than ever before, committed to *excellence in education*.

The government ideal for education and society — to create a rich diversity of choices to be steadily made available to more and more citizens — had been notified by the Secretary of State in her speech to the 1973 Conservative Party Conference. At Blackpool she signposted a number of ways in which parents could be given some choice of school:

First, authorities have power to pay full or part fees to an independent school if that would be better for a particular pupil . . . .Secondly, authorities can take up free places in direct grant schools. Authorities can also retain those schools to which entry is based not on income or background, but on grounds of academic ability — the grammar schools . . . .Where there are only comprehensive schools in an area it is vital for parents to have a choice between them . . . .It is also vital that the voluntary aided schools continue.[63]

Like the preservationists, Mrs Thatcher considered a too rigid education system to be the enemy of advance. Consequently her emphasis now was upon the need for flexibility and on promoting the scope for schools of excellence.

The high profile given by the government to the theme of 'parental choice' was the direct outcome of recommendations made by a second CNACE Working Party on the subject chaired by Harry Greenway. The Working Party's draft report on *Parental Choice* had been submitted to the National Union, and discussed by Greenway, at the CNACE Swinton Weekend Conference (27–29 April 1973). Among its recommendations were that encouragement be given by the DES to LEAs to adopt schemes of transfer to secondary education which would give parents maximum possible choice of school within the pattern established in the area; and that where comprehensive schemes were introduced, or where they were already running, parents be given fuller information about each school in written form.[64]

Vigorous preservationist activity during 1972–73 had contributed significantly to the Tory Party's radical approach towards education. Two NCES members and *Black Paperites* — Stuart Froome (Head of St. Judes' C. of E. School, Englefield Green) and Professor Brian Cox — had sat on the Bullock Committee of Enquiry into the Teaching of Reading and the Use of the English Language. Mrs Thatcher had set up the Committee in the spring of 1972. Her invitations to Froome and Cox were yet another instance, and measure, of her regard for those who held to the notion of *excellence in education*. Froome had published a Note of Dissent to the Bullock Report on the basis that, in his view, it had not made enough of the deficiencies of the schools in respect of children's written expression, and was clearly reluctant to attribute any deterioration which had taken place since 1944, to the adoption of free, unsystematic English teaching methods. He believed the Committee of Enquiry had had an unrivalled opportunity to state boldly and unequivocally that it was not satisfied with the way children's writing was being taught in schools, and that a return to a more structured teaching procedure involving systematic training in the traditional accomplishments of spelling, punctuation and grammatical sentence construction was required. Froome considered it was a great opportunity missed (see, for example, Froome, 1977, pp 29–33).

Professor Cox appears to have played a more central role in the submission of evidence to the Bullock Committee. Not only had he collated and summarized the evidence submitted by the NCES, he had also separately submitted evidence of his own. The NCES submission (which had been made in January 1973) contained evidence provided by schools in the maintained and private sectors given in response to a circular letter issued by Cox to NCES members, asking those with relevant experience (who wished to do so) to pass on their views on English teaching and literacy standards as these appeared to them in 1972. All respondents had expressed a concern over a decline in literacy, although there had been no unanimity on the causes.[65] A considerable degree of alarm had been expressed at the seemingly low standards of teacher training colleges. Others had written to say that they had felt that the stimulus of competition had disappeared from the English education system. The NCES submission noted:

> The 11 +, which was a goal for all the system, and could have been improved, has not been replaced with anything but national confusion (*ibid.*).

Professor Cox's own submission had argued that fashionable assumptions about the teaching of reading and English (adhered to by many teachers, college of education lecturers and even some professors of education) were quite often in direct contradiction to the findings of proper research.[66] The pursuance by some teachers of a *value-free* concept of culture (a popular culture) had, according to Cox, been one cause of the dilution of English teaching and the reaction against spelling and grammar. He had informed the Bullock Committee that an explicit grammar was an acceptance of order and that the 'new revolutionaries' deliberately rejected such structuring of experience.

Cox's submission had symbolized the preservationist view: that the structuring of experience provided by the traditional style of schooling was essential, both to the preservation of individual humanity and the nation's common culture. It had also contained a recommendation that, as the conflicting ideologies involved in the teaching of English were little understood by parents, schools should be required to clarify their policies and parents given more freedom in choice of schools. In the next chapter we shall see how the Tory Party in opposition drew upon this advised course of action in formulating its 'Parents' Charter', a statement of objectives which would include a call for greater curricula information to parents and wider parental choice of school.

Other preservationist activities during 1972–73 had included an NCES delegation, led by Sir Desmond Lee (an NCES sponsor), to see Sir Alan Bullock at the DES in June 1973. Shortly after this meeting Lee had told Bullock:

> I hope we didn't seem to be too wild a set of back-woodsmen. I think the value of our evidence was to show the concern felt about a serious problem by those of a particular way of thinking.[67]

Those of 'a particular way of thinking' included, of course, Dr Boyson (NCES

Chairman) who had been using his position as a columnist on *The Daily Telegraph* (where Russell Lewis was also a journalist) to promulgate preservationist ideas and alert Conservatives to the Labour Party's plans for a new education programme, which again threatened abolition of selection by ability for different kinds of schools for pupils up to 18 (Boyson, 1973b). Boyson believed Labour had now reached the view that state comprehensive schools could not compete with direct-grant or independent schools, which had to be abolished. He feared that Labour was making preparations to open sixth-forms to all — the academically gifted, the average, the dull and the illiterate. He argued that collectivism could only be defeated by freedom of choice for a majority of the people; and, that whilst choice and freedom were divisive, the Labour Party's nightmare of a totalitarian collectivist philosophy of all alike ('like a Maoist crowd scene') could only be defeated by 'a genuine free libertarian philosophy on the Right, both political and educational' (*ibid.*). Without this Boyson was convinced Conservatives would, in ten years' time, be giving evidence to commissions discussing the collapse of the nation's culture.

One issue on which there was a convergence of thought — uniting preservationists and Conservative education ministers — was Labour's plans to move to more teacher-based examinations. Each believed that, the fury of egalitarians in their search for Utopia, would lessen equality of opportunity. Each considered school-based examinations were worth no more than the worth of the school. The university-board-examined GCE had to be preserved. Consequently, the preservationists and the Conservative Party had, during 1973, continued to monitor the Schools Council for the Curriculum and Examinations.[68] Though Kogan (1975) has noted the attempts by the DES, when Mrs Thatcher was Secretary of State, to cut the Schools Council budgets, he did not examine the motivation behind its strategy (p. 143). The proceedings of the CNACE show a strong Conservative distrust of the teacher-dominated Schools Council. For example, at its meeting on 6 October 1973 the CNACE had received a letter from Alderman Straw asking the CNACE to discuss a Schools Council Project document on 'Property'.[69] The CNACE agreed that the said document contained extreme bias against property-owners and that the Chairman write to Mrs Thatcher and Norman St John-Stevas bringing the document to their attention.[70] Such instances of Conservative suspicion may well have contributed to DES action on the Schools Council.

Better education and the February 1974 general election

The Conservative Party's absorption of preservationist thinking on education reached its zenith on 11 January 1974 when the CNACE forwarded to Mrs Thatcher its draft manifesto *Opportunity and Choice in Education*. Largely formulated by Dr Rhodes

Boyson, Harry Greenway and Sir Gilbert Longden, it declared that 'concern for quality will be the key-note'.[71] As well as circumscribing the role of central government in education (Whitehall was to satisfy itself that appropriate frameworks were provided within which LEAs could adopt and promote the highest standards of attainment) the draft manifesto also advised priorities ('the need to take into account parental wishes on choice of school should be the first consideration to which LEAs should respond').

The CNACE draft manifesto formed the basis of the education section of the Party's election manifesto in February 1974. Headed 'Better Education', it asserted that the Party was concerned to provide not merely more education but better education, which, besides being a matter of resources, was also a matter of standards and of attitudes.[72] By suggesting that LEAs should 'allow genuine scope for parental choice' (*ibid.*) the Party effectively endorsed one of the cardinal aims of the preservationists and set the framework for its future education policy.

It has been suggested to the author that Mrs Thatcher had now come to more openly embrace the views of the educational-right as a result of the sexism of the Cabinet structure.[73] But, as we saw in chapter 3, the Secretary of State was already (privately, if not publicly) on the right of the Party before her incumbency at the Department of Education and Science. And, anyway, though education policy would have been determined by Mrs Thatcher, Party policy was determined by the Party leader. The question, therefore, is why had Heath (in 1974) acceded to the preservationist scenario?

Responsibility for the initial oversight of education policy formation, prior to the February 1974 General Election, rested with Timothy Bainbridge (Education Desk Officer, CRD, November 1973–February 1974). Bainbridge had joined the CRD in September 1972 whereupon he had been asked by James Douglas (Director of CRD) to take up the *Spicer-Meyer* exercise.[74] In his report on this exercise Bainbridge had advised against any resumption of the practice of making use of outside (i.e. non-Party) specialist advice in policy formulation.[75] He had felt that, the Party's policy-making process was ill-adapted to the incorporation of such advice.[76]

It was, in fact, Bainbridge's predecessor Ian Deslandes (Education Desk Officer, CRD, June 1972–October 1973) who had written the education chapter of the Party's 1974 Campaign Guide.[77] Bainbridge's own reading of this chapter led him to conclude that education would not be a major issue at the February 1974 General Election.[78] Indeed, apart from an expressed concern over reading standards, the Party's 'Plans For The Future' largely embraced what might be described as improvements to the mechanics of schooling (more and better trained teachers, better staffing standards, and a secondary school building improvement programme) rather than radical initiatives to improve the quality of education via curriculum change.[79] Bainbridge believed that Conservatives, in 1974, were nervous of any state involvement in the school curriculum.[80] Aside from the continuing debate over public versus private education it was essentially expenditure issues (like school buildings, school milk and school transport) which formed the Party's educational agenda.[81]

Thus, within the Party, Bainbridge witnessed little evidence of radical changes taking place in the debate over the strategy and tactics most appropriate to deliver the 'Better Education' promised in the election manifesto. What he did witness was a Party muddling through, caught by a turn of events that had thrown it into some confusion:

> In my dealings with Mrs Thatcher I was conscious that the ideas of the *Black Papers* were around. But education, and particularly the matter of educational standards, were still dormant issues for the Party as a whole. They were a very minor concern of the CRD Home Affairs Section. The industrial situation, the three-day week and power strikes were the real questions of the day. Though Mrs Thatcher was embracing the concerns and general direction of the *Black Paper* group she had still to accept their remedies. The educational orthodoxy of the Party had not been radically altered.[82]

All of this seems to confirm Ramsden's conclusion that, despite the manifesto's appeal for the defence of democracy, the Conservative Party drifted towards a crisis election without proposals that were of crisis proportions and that, insofar as it made serious mistakes in the February 1974 campaign, it was in its strategy rather than its tactics (Ramsden, 1980, pp. 302–3). Heath may well have agreed to the preservationist scenario for education believing it to offer the best bulwark of democracy. Certainly in its manifesto formulation it appeared to be infused by a spirit of moderation and voter-directed level-headedness. But its most striking feature was its dullness. The February 1974 manifesto emerged from a Party uncertain of its approach to the crisis facing the nation (*ibid.*, pp. 301-3). In particular, the Conservative Party had failed to construct a radical programme to resolve the crisis in education. After the loss of office, Conservative educational policy-making would have to be based on a new stock of ideas.

Notes

1 Minister of Education (25 May 1945–2 August 1945). Lord Coleraine would become a co-founder (with Diana Spearman) of the Salisbury Group in 1977.

2 The Churchill Press/Constitutional Book Club (1969–79) carried the writings of a number of preservationists, including John Sparrow, Tibor Szamuely, Russell Lewis and Anthony Dyson, as well as Harris and Boyson.

3 It was at the 1970 Conservative Party Conference that Heath set out his theme of 'radical change in a free society', in which the British would come to appreciate that no one would stand between them and the results of their own free choice, and that to achieve this choice the Party would have to bring about 'a change so radical, a revolution so quiet, and yet so total, that it will go far beyond the programme for a Parliament to which we are committed and on which we have already embarked'.

4 Personal Assistant to Edward Heath (1966 General Election and in his House of Commons Office, 1968); Lecturer in American History, University of Edinburgh (1968–74); Personal Assistant to William Van Straubenzee, DES, (1970–72).

5 Dr Keith Hampson MP to author, 18 December 1985.

6 *Ibid*. Some measure of the impact of the Black Papers can be gauged by the Left's response — a series of Red Papers edited by Professor Cornford (Professor of Politics, University of Edinburgh 1968–76) and sanctioned by the outer policy circle of the Labour Party. In 1975–76 Professor Cox became a member of Dr Hampson's House of Commons Advisory Committee on Higher Education.

7 *Ibid*.

8 Letter from Margaret Thatcher to Professor Cox, 3 August 1970, *The Cox Papers*. In a House of Commons debate on 8 July 1970 Mrs Thatcher had stated 'I believe that there is still a place for certain selective schools of excellence. I believe it is wrong to exclude this from our future plans'.

9 Letter from Professor Cox to Margaret Thatcher, 14 September 1970, *The Cox Papers*. It should be noted that Mrs Thatcher had first corresponded with the 'Black Paper' group shortly after she had been appointed Shadow Education Minister by Heath in October 1969. Tony Dyson had written to her in November 1969 canvassing her support to oppose Edward Short's comprehensive school reform. Though Dyson had requested a meeting with her, Mrs Thatcher had declined. She told him: 'I think it will be as well to see Mr. Short's bill before we decide in what terms it will be opposed'. Letter from Mrs Thatcher to Anthony Dyson, 1 December 1969, *The Cox Papers*. In the event the Bill to make comprehensivization compulsory in 1970 never reached the statute book.

10 'Trends in education', paper given by Gilbert Longden at Swinton Conservative College, 20 October 1970, *The Longden Papers*.

11 It was significant that Mrs Thatcher had told the 1970 Conservative Party Conference that she hoped that one theme for the 1970s in education would be an increasing concentration on 'quality'.

12 In 1981 Sir Anthony Royle became a Vice-Chairman of the Conservative Party.

13 Parliamentary Under-Secretary of State, DES (1970–73).

14 Letter from Lord Belstead to Anthony Royle, 17 December 1970, *The Cox Papers*.

15 Junior ministers are not 'Ministers of the Crown' because, formally, they are appointed by their Secretary of State or Minister, not by the monarch on the advice of the Prime Minister. In practice they are selected by the PM. This might explain Lord Belstead's liberal approach to modern educational methods which was clearly at variance with Mrs. Thatcher's private view. For an account of the history and role of Junior Ministers, see Theakston (1987).

16 Head of Home Affairs Section, CRD, (1963–77); Consultant Director, CRD (1977–86).

17 Charles Bellairs to author, 19 August 1986.

18 Tony Hutt to author, 19 August 1986. Hutt was the CRD local government desk officer (1971–74) and (1975–84).

19 *Ibid*.

20 Charles Bellairs to author, 19 August 1986. Bellairs felt that with the departure of Boyle there was a change of emphasis to much more parental choice and involvement (brought about by Mrs Thatcher) and it was left to him, in cooperation with Anthony Greenland, to ensure that this policy was fully reflected in Party publications.

21 Both Angus Maude and Gilbert Longden visited Swinton Conservative College where they met Sir Reginald Northam. His influence over thier own educational philosophy must be assumed.

22 O'Sullivan was now a close friend of Arthur and Marjorie Seldon. John O'Sullivan to author, 24 September 1986.

23 John O'Sullivan to author, 24 September 1986.

24 Swinton Circle groups met regionally to debate themes in Conservative philosophy. A London Swinton Circle group had met since 1965, holding monthly meetings at the National Book League, Albemarle Street, Westminster. Two of its members were Dr Rhodes Boyson and T.E. Utley who had met in 1968, and who had both been drawn together by a mutual belief that socialist collectivism had denied parental choice in education and that variety, competition and freedom were the corollary means of strengthening society. They had each come to the conclusion that Conservatives should make the doctrinal decision to change State provision, from the direct provision of education in kind,

to the provision of subsidies to parents. T. E. Utley, to author, 11 December 1985. Both Boyson and Utley were contributors to the *Swinton Journal*. See Utley (1968) and Boyson (1971).

25 Heath had set up his own discussion group on education at Swinton in 1966.

26 John O'Sullivan to author, 24 September 1986. From 1970 O'Sullivan's disposition towards vouchers quickened. In 1973 he contributed articles on the American Alum Rock voucher experiment for *The Daily Telegraph*, and, in 1974, began attending the Seldon's 'Thatched Cottage' parties for non-conformists where voucher proposals were to be formulated. From 1974 he joined a variety of Conservative groupings (including the Selsdon Group, the CPS, the CPG and the Salisbury Group) enabling him to contribute further to the debate on the direction of Party policy. In 1987 he joined the Prime Minister's Policy Unit.

27 In an earlier writing Howarth had argued that only by educationists and politicians moving away in their thinking from the ideal and the abstract to seek a path of reconciliation, common sense and realism, might progress be made. See Howarth (1969). Howarth was High Master, St. Paul's School, Barnes (1962–73). In 1969 he was Chairman of the Headmasters' Conference. He first met Boyson in 1970 when they were invited by the Imperial College Students' Union to debate the comprehensive education principle. They were united by a common sympathy towards education vouchers. Together they attended the inaugural meeting, in 1972, of the CPES. Tom Howarth to author, 5 March 1986.

28 Letter from Powell to Dyson, 26 November 1970, *The Cox Papers*. Powell's comment was written after he had received his copy of *Black Paper Three* from Dyson.

29 Russell Lewis to author, 22 August 1986. In common with other CPC publications Boyson's pamphlets were a personal contribution to discussion and not official Party pronouncements.

30 David Knapp to author, 8 September 1986. Knapp was Deputy Director, CPC (1962–75). He succeeded Lewis as Director in 1975. In 1979 he became an Assistant Director, CRD.

31 Russell Lewis to author, 22 August 1986.

32 Lewis had found the Black Papers 'though often polemical in tone — extremely reasonable'.

33 It is unlikely that Lewis knew of Mrs Thatcher's private admiration for, and support of, the opinions of the 'Black Paper' group.

34 *Notes on Current Politics*, No. 2, CRD, 25 January 1971, p. 22.

35 *NACE Minute Book 1970–74*, CPA.

36 The CNACE draft manifesto 'Opportunity and choice in education', January 1974, would incorporate contributions from, amongst others, Dr Rhodes Boyson, Harry Greenway and Sir Gilbert Longden.

37 'A policy statement for education', NACE, 1971. Under the section 'Higher standards' the NACE declared: 'We seek to improve the quality of facilities and teaching throughout the education service and we are concerned that schools be of such a size and so organized as to avoid loss of pupil identity and promote effective self-discipline'. Under the section 'Greater Choice' it stated: 'We would requst all LEAs to operate schemes that allow parents to have every possible choice between individual schools for their child, within the maintained sector'.

38 From 5 December 1971 the NACE was known as the CNACE (Conservative National Advisory Committee on Education).

39 Letter from Kay Andrews (Scientific Section, Research Division, House of Commons Library) to Sir Gilbert Longden, 27 January 1972, *The Longden Papers*.

40 Though Longden offered his resignation as an MP in 1972 he did not leave the House of Commons until the February 1974 General Election.

41 Letter from Tom Howarth to author, 7 March 1986.

42 Ronald Butt to author, 27 August 1986.

43 Letter from Cox to Bantock, 11 January 1972, *The Cox Papers*.

44 Letter from Bantock to Cox, 13 January 1972, *The Cox Papers*.

45 See, 'Who are these preservationists?', *The Teacher*, 7 January 1972.

46 Letter from Lord Boyle to Sir Richard Webster, 29 June 1972, *The Boyle Papers*, MS. 660/22944.

47 In 1948 Stevas had visited Swinton College and helped draw up a report of Conservative principles. This report (reproduced in Part Four of *The Two Cities*) with its stress on the importance of moral

values, of tradition, and of the necessity to maintain national institutions, is the earliest expression of Stevas' preservationist instincts.

48 Both Thatcher and Stevas, despite their differences of Conservative complexion, were loyal to politics in its conservative manifestation and united in the fight to maintain the grammar schools.

49 As a Conservative with more than a passing interest in education, Professor Cox would carry the preservationist case further into the Party through a series of addresses to Area Regional Groups of the CNACE and CPC Conferences.

50 The NEA was founded in 1965 by Councillor Audrey Cooper as a voluntary non-political body representing parents throughout the country. Its twin aims have been "to preserve what is best in, and to further the development of, a full range of schools and to maintain a freedom of choice between a variety of schools for a variety of children both in the state system and the private sector". It has campaigned against those who have sought uniformity in education by suppressing excellence and disguising failure.

51 *NACE Minute Book*, 1970–74, CPA.

52 *NACE Minute Book*, 1970–74, CPA.

53 Speech by Margaret Thatcher to the AMA, Manchester, 29 December 1972, CPA.

54 PEC Comments on Cmnd 5174 *Education: A Framework for Expansion*, AGLB/CCO4/10/95, CPA.

55 Text of motion as adopted by the CEA at its AGM, 5 March 1973, AGLB/CCO4/10/95, CPA.

56 The Conservative government's assessment of the cost of education, and its plans for making economies by improving efficiency within the education service, were largely based on calculations worked out by the preservationist Dr Kathleen Ollerenshaw. In 1971 Dr Ollerenshaw had been made a DBE for her services to education. One of her papers entitled 'Education and Finance' (IMTA, 1969) had been circulated and discussed within the NACE in 1970. In 1973 Dr Ollerenshaw was a guest speaker at the CNACE Annual Conference and Dinner which was attended by the Secretary of State. For the text of her speech, see Ollerenshaw, Dame K. (1973).

57 Letter from Mrs Thatcher to the Secretary of the CEA, 2 April 1973, AGLB/CCO4/10/95, CPA.

58 In April 1973 Professor Cox made a series of BBC Radio broadcasts for the programme 'A Word in Edgeways', in which he sought to 'widen the anti-progressive lobby and draw public attention to the dangers to schooling of the left-of-centre educational philosophy'. Professor Cox to author, 21 February 1986.

59 Peregrine Worsthorne to author, 4 February 1986.

60 *Ibid.* In 1975 Worsthorne became a member of the Conservative Philosophy Group (CPG), a high Tory forum attended by Mrs Thatcher. For an account of Worsthorne's educational philosophy, see Worsthorne (1987) particularly the essay 'Oxbridge, Dimwits and Misfits', in which he describes the damaging effects of egalitarian admission policies on university education standards.

61 Timothy Raison MP to author, 4 March 1986.

62 After he left the DES, and before he was appointed Opposition Spokesman on the Environment (1975–76), Raison became a Senior Fellow at the Centre for Studies in Social Policy. One of the products of his fellowship was his pamphlet (1976) *The Act and the Partnership*, Doughty Street Paper No. 3, London, Bedford Square Press, in which he declared "Education does seem to me to have become too swayed by fashion, and in particular the commitment to child-centredness to have led (at its worst) to an excessive emphasis on simply holding the interest of children without too much regard for the value of what is being taught" (p. 45).

63 Speech by Mrs Thatcher to the Conservative Party Conference, 12 October 1973.

64 CNACE draft report 'Parental choice', April, 1973, CPA.

65 Evidence submitted by the NCES to the Bullock Committee of Enquiry, January 1973, *The Cox Papers*.

66 Evidence submitted by Professor C. B. Cox to Committee of Enquiry into reading and the Use of English, January 1973, *The Cox Papers*.

67 Letter from Sir Desmond Lee to Sir Alan Bullock, 20 June 1973, *The Cox Papers*. Lee himself had no rooted objection to informal teaching methods, but he did feel that they had been too often abused and that the lack of literacy could only be crippling to children in society. Where Lee differed from Cox was on the question of the training colleges. He did not feel so pessimistic about the standards in

these colleges as Cox did. Lee had spent fourteen years as Chairman of the Executive Committee of King Alfred's College, Westminster and had himself done some teaching for the Cambridge B.Ed. In all this he had been 'largely impressed by what he had seen'.

68 The Party's earlier monitoring may have been assisted by Dr Ollerenshaw (Member, Schools Council, 1968–71). Her dual position on the CNACE probably helped Dr Boyson maintain his 'watching brief' on the Schools Council's plans to reform the sixth-form curriculum.

69 *NACE Minute Book, 1970–74*, CPA.

70 *Ibid.* The same meeting also heard details of alleged left-wing political bias in Open University teaching and publications, an issue which had first been brought to the attention of Sir Gilbert Longden in a letter on 1 February 1972 from Geoffrey Finsberg MP, following complaints from a constituent.

71 'Opportunity and choice in education', CNACE draft manifesto, January 1974, CPA. Inputs to this document were also made by Ronald Butt who, although not a formal member of the CNACE, addressed its Area Education Committee Evening Conference on 8 November 1973 at Smith Square, which had been called to discuss the finalized version of the draft manifesto.

72 *The Conservative Manifesto 1974*, February, CCO, p. 21.

73 Chris Price to author, 6 March 1986. According to Price, Mrs Thatcher was 'patronized by the Heathites who hoped to beat her into submission'.

74 The 'Spicer-Meyer' exercise was an attempt to make more systematic use of non-Party specialist advice in policy formulation. In 1966–70 Sir Anthony Meyer (who had lost his Eton and Slough seat in the 1966 General Election) and Michael Spicer set in hand an updating of the Party's files, kept in the Conservative Research Department, of experts and academics outside the Party organization who might be willing to make a personal contribution to Conservative thinking. Meyer also founded and edited a short-lived journal of Conservative thought entitled *Solon*. Meyer became an MP again in 1970, and Spicer was elected to the house of Commons in 1974.

75 Timothy Bainbridge to author, 7 October 1986.

76 *Ibid.*

77 Though published by Central Office in March 1974 the text of the Campaign Guide was used by Conservative candidates in the February 1974 General Election campaign. The text was written in the late summer and early autumn of 1973.

78 Timothy Bainbridge to author, 7 October 1986.

79 See *The Campaign Guide, 1974*, CCO, pp. 308–310.

80 Timothy Bainbridge to author, 7 October 1986.

81 *Ibid.*

82 *Ibid.*

Chapter 5

'Now we have lots to do': Towards a new Party leader and the staging of an educational counter-revolution, 1974–76

Introduction

Though education did not become a major party issue for Conservatives until the 1979 election campaign it was the arrival of a new Party leader in 1975 which effectively allowed the preservationists' educational *counter-revolution* to be staged. Under Mrs Thatcher's leadership Conservative education policy formation would not be so readily based on the One Nation wisdom of Butler, Macmillan and Heath. Instead she favoured a radical break, away from the progressive education movement of the 1960s and towards the eclipse of *the ethic of the undermass* (an ethic underpinned by the devaluation of basic curriculum subjects and respect for the accumulated understanding of the past).

The preservationist constituency that had contributed to the February 1974 Conservative Manifesto *Firm Action for a Fair Britain* had won a notable advance with the Party's commitment to move the education debate away from the kind of school which children attended and concentrate on the kind of education they received.[1] And yet, in March 1974, little more than three years after winning a General Election and embarking upon a 'Quiet Revolution' to transform the face of British society, the Conservative Party found itself in opposition. If it is true, as Behrens (1980) suggests (p. 1) that many Conservatives regarded Heath as quite the most radical politician of his day, then it is equally clear that some preservationists had found him to be less than convincing on education.[2] In *Firm Action for a Fair Britain* Heath had identified 'the menace of unrestrained inflation'[3] as the gravest threat to the national well-being. But, as we saw in chapters 3 and 4, in the view of many on the Right, it was the undermining of traditional values and customs by a rampant egalitarianism which posed the greatest danger to national progress. Herein lay the incipient ideological rift between the liberal and right-wings of the Tory Party. Whilst both wings were in agreement with 'A Britain united in moderation and a society in which there was change without revolution',[4] they were not agreed on the role that education should play in the realization of such a Conservative vision. The preservationists on the Right wished to effect a cultural revaluation of society and sought to attempt this transformation through the obvious means of schooling.[5] That their 'Better Education' proposals had not heralded such a transformation is probably explained by Heath's own preference 'to err on the side of caution and to promise too little rather than too much'.[6] I hope to show in this chapter, and in chapter 6, how the burgeoning Tory right-wing came to command an increasing influence over the making and direction of a conservative educational policy — a shift which would permit the preservationists' notion of *excellence in education* to take the centre stage.

The changing environmental context of the Conservative education policy debate

In order to understand how the preservationists finally got their way it is necessary to give attention to the changing environmental context of the Conservative education policy debate. According to Patten (1980, pp. 17–18), policy work in the immediate aftermath of the defeat in February 1974 was largely governed by the circumstances of that election and the imminence of another campaign so that, between February and the October election, there was no time for the sort of broad, elaborate and detailed policy-making which had taken place in earlier periods. Similarly, Ramsden (1980) has argued that all policy-making after the loss of office was affected to a degree by the Party's bewilderment at its defeat (p. 305). Back in Opposition, from March 1974, education became a much more substantive matter on the Conservative benches both as a result of a rearrangement in personnel and a growing knowledge that the Party had singularly failed (in the February election) to represent the public disquiet over state schooling.

The months between March and June 1974 were dominated by a power struggle between William Van Straubenzee and Norman St John-Stevas[7] who succeeded him as Opposition Spokesman on Education. The question still at issue was the Party's attitude to comprehensive education and whether it would be possible for Conservatives to go along with its extension while still preserving the idea of *parental choice*.[8] There was now a tide running against comprehensivization on the Conservative benches, and many MPs thought the Party ought to be taking more account of the opinion among worried parents which they had encountered on the doorsteps whilst campaigning for the February 1974 election.[9] Stevas was very concerned about falling standards in state schools and linked this with the idea of greater parental involvement in the schools (parent governors, published reports of schools' progress and results, etc) as well as with the idea of trying to offer parents a choice between comprehensive schools.[10] Stevas offered a coherent range of policies with which most of the active Conservative backbenchers in the education field agreed. It was important to get an educational policy sorted out quickly and it was probably for this reason that Straubenzee was replaced by Stevas as Opposition Spokesman in June 1974.

The CRD Desk Officer with responsibility for education between March and November 1974 was Caroline Harvey. During this time the making of education policy was less a question of coming up with something radically new, than of choosing between available options or, of giving existing ideas a different emphasis.[11] Her impressions concur with Stevas' (1984) recollection of the events of June–September 1974:

> It was clear that an election would not be long delayed, and I entered on an
> intense period of activity, restating Conservative education policy in a series
> of speeches. I travelled from one end of the country to the other stressing
> the issues of parental rights, freedom and high standards, as well as the need
> for variety and choice of school. (p. 48)

The antecedent to this campaign was the CNACE Conference (19–21 April 1974). This was the first CNACE Conference to be held after the Party's election defeat. It was attended by both Stevas and Rhodes Boyson (now MP for Brent North).[12] The topic discussed was 'Assessment and threatened standards?'[13] Many preservationists in the Party now believed that academic standards had been sacrificed on the altar of *equality*; that much of the British educational scene had been a victim of experiment and expansion (certain doctrines such as comprehensive education and child-centred learning had been imported from the USA where the teaching of formal grammar was eschewed in favour of self-expression); that literacy had lost its place as the central business of schooling; and that parental options had been restricted. The blame for much of this rested, so the preservationists argued, with the dogmatic views and opinions of left-wing educationists and the Labour Party's aim of achieving equality in schooling rather than educational advance.[14]

Both the CNACE Swinton Weekend Conference and Stevas' campaign took place in a period of uncertainty. Not only was Heath's leadership in question (Ramsden, 1980, p. 304), the Party was also engaged in a debate about what to conserve — what one political analyst has labelled 'the search for true Conservatism' (Behrens, 1980, p. 3). Set against this background the preservationists' contribution to the development and discussion of Conservative education policy in the spring and summer of 1974 was both substantial and timely.

The character of Conservative education policy debate changed at a particularly significant juncture. Whilst the Conservative Party was now venturing to develop its educational philosophy and policy, and put forward ideas of its own, the new Labour government had found itself without either a clear schools plan or a fully prepared Education Secretary. Reg Prentice[15] had been 'sent to education' by Harold Wilson.[16] Recalling his time at the DES Prentice has said:

> We had very little education policy. What there was meant very little to me. I appointed Maurice Peston as my Special Adviser. We had to create Labour's education policy as far as it went. I also contacted Terry Pitt of the Labour Research Department to send me on Labour's education policies. The Party's schools policy was devised by myself and Peston, Ernie Armstrong and William Pile. I came into office when the most pressing issue was teachers' pay. My whole priority was teachers' status. I also wanted to advance the role of HMI and so I appointed Sheila Browne as its Head. She was pro-comprehensive. I was a pragmatic social reformer and I tried to seek moderation at the DES.[17]

Though Prentice did achieve a close continuity between his policies and those of his predecessor Mrs Thatcher — for example, he followed her expansion of nursery and special education, and his record on approving comprehensive school schemes was statistically about the same as hers — he has considered his main failing to have been his unwillingness to engage in any 'philosophizing about education'.[18] Evidence of this failing can be found in Prentice's response to the publication of *Black Paper 1975*. Asked in the House what his policy was towards the proposals contained in the *Black Paper*,[19] he replied 'I welcome discussion on educational issues but I have not found the *Black Paper* helpful or constructive'.[20] Questioned as to whether his Department had a case to answer which was not answered by the scorn it had poured on the authors of the *Black Paper* to date, Prentice retorted:

> The answer to the criticisms levelled at the comprehensive system is to be found in the experience of the comprehensive schools themselves, which have provided such a successful service to our children for many years.[21]

Although Prentice believed the *Black Paper's* call for national tests a 7, 11 and 14 to have been a dogmatic proposal, taking no account whatever of the fact that individual children developed at different rates, he was unwilling to acknowledge the degree of public discontent with the education service that existed. Pressed by Dr Boyson to agree that, since practically all newspapers and periodicals had reviewed and talked about the *Black Paper* at length, there was massive discontent, and, for a government which talked about participation, a participatory discussion and analysis of what the *Black Paper* said might be to the advantage of the government and the nation's children Prentice replied:

> I have already said that I welcome discussion on these matters. The interest that the *Black Paper* has attracted is a sympton of the fact that very large

numbers of people are intensely interested in education, and the whole House would welcome that. What I find at fault is that the *Black Paper* gets the whole problem out of perspective. It takes no account of the tremendous achievements of the majority of our teachers who do devoted work of a very high standard, which is rising year by year. So far as it identifies real problems, the solutions that the *Black Paper* proposes are totally irrelevant to those problems.[22]

The socialist appproach to education in 1974/75, the object of the preservationists' reconstituted offensive, was largely formulated by Ernest Armstrong.[23] A former primary school headteacher, Armstrong came to the DES believing education to be the key to the 'Good Society' (Armstrong, 1987, p.4). He was an advocate of *neighbourhood schools*. Though his priority was teacher morale his short incumbency as Junior Schools Minister was almost wholly devoted to the school building programme. But Armstrong's desire to shape schools as effective educational units (as secure, tolerant and friendly community schools) without specialization and segregation, was so ideologically distant from the Conservative approach to education (which now argued support for selective secondary schooling) (Stevas, 1974), that it probably hastened the Tory Party's resolve to counter the socialists' possession of the educational initiative.

The Preservationists and the 'Conservative Opportunity' in Education

By the time of the October 1974 General Election Conservatives had concluded that the Labour Party was incapacitated by its own doctrine from doing anything effective to help improve education. The approach of Prentice and Armstrong to national schooling was seen by Conservatives to be not only negative and destructive, but also combined with a complacency about what was wrong with education. Ironically, it was Labour's election victory which heralded the *Conservative Opportunity* — that five-year period of Tory Opposition in which the Conservative Party finally came to fashion a conservative educational policy.

The preservationists now considered that the trend of public opinion was in favour of taking a long, close look at what was actually happening in the nation's schools as opposed to placing trust in the version of events supplied by so-called 'education experts'. Via the Black Papers the preservationists had helped to reflect the public climate of disquiet over state education. But the *Conservative Opportunity* was not wholly of the preservationists' making. By 1974 Wilson was no longer as interested in the exercise of power as in the past, and had been determined, in his own words, to 'play as a sweeper in the defence rather than a striker in attack' (Donoughue, 1987, p. 48). Though Labour would become the natural party of government it would be at the expense of every last drop of radicalism. Significantly, education did not appear on Labour's Cabinet agenda throughout the first year of office (*ibid.*).[24] This was the very period in which the Conservative Party was to see the election of a new leader and a new stage of policy work (formulated and overseen by preservationists) that would give education a much higher profile than hitherto.

The Conservative Party has had a long tradition of political opportunism (Griggs, 1980).[25] Between 1974 and 1976 the Tories began to make much of the running on educational issues, capturing the attention of the media (and therefore the public) and also capturing, at times, the language of their opponents and exploiting it to good political effect. Hence, the cries of *falling standards* in primary schools, support for selective education in the guise of *parental choice* and the steady campaign to introduce vouchers in the name of *freedom* in schooling. That the Conservative Party was able to pose as the champion of high standards in education and as the party most concerned about the fate of intelligent working-class children was due, it would seem, to three main factors: the working out by the Centre for Policy Studies (CPS) of a new Tory radicalism based on nineteenth-century free-market anti-statism; the adoption and exploitation by their education spokesmen of the *best words* (freedom, parental choice, maintenance of standards, etc); and the emergence of Dr Rhodes Boyson, Tory populist *par excellence*, who was able to foster the real concern of many parents by presenting a grim picture of contemporary education.[26]

In chapter 4 we saw that it was, above all, in the years of the Heath government when the seeds of the new intellectual fashions were sown. By October 1974 the tide had turned towards Conservative ideas. Among those who believed the failure of the Heath government after the miners' strike and the three-day week marked the end of the post-war consensus were Margaret Thatcher and Sir Keith Joseph (see Kavanagh, 1987, ch.3). They believed Heath had failed because he had not given true Conservative principles a try. They had been appalled not only by Heath's failure to challenge the corporatist consensus but also by his persistence in justifying his failure to do so even after the Party's election defeat. Thatcher's friendship with Joseph (her mentor in the late 1970s) was a reflection of her wish to develop a new philosophy of Conservatism. Together they were ready to develop a rival think-tank to the CRD.[27] Ironically, the CPS was established by Sir Keith Joseph in August 1974, with the permission of Heath. Joseph became its Chairman, Mrs Thatcher its President, and Alfred Sherman became its first Director. The CRD reflected the policy outlook of the leadership, and it was this which Joseph wished to question (*ibid.* p. 89). Ramsden's (1980) comment that 'the existence of the CPS removed the CRD's absolute monopoly of research advice to shadow ministers' (pp 310–11), is important for the present study not just because the CPS was an organization independent of the Conservative Party which could think the unthinkable (for example, the virtues of free markets) but because it also established a variety of study groups whose aim was to develop new ideas and policies. One of these — the Education Study Group

(CPSESG)[28] — would be comprised of a number of CEs committed to challenging the ideas of the educational 'experts' of the left, and turning what was seen as the one-time politically unthinkable into the everyday commonsense wisdom of tomorrow. For these CEs, such rethinking was vital if the nation was to preserve and enhance what was best in its educational and cultural heritage to meet the challenges of the future.

The second factor enabling the Conservative Party to pose as the champion of high standards in education was the adoption and exploitation by their education spokesmen of, what might be termed, the *best words* (see Griggs, 1980). One of these — *freedom* — was championed by the CPS, whilst the phrase *parental choice* had been formulated by the CNACE. A policy initiative on education vouchers[29] would win increasing support inside the Conservative Party as a result of the lobbying of Marjorie Seldon.[30] In 1974 she was one of a growing body of CEs (which now included Caroline Cox and Dr John Marks, both former members of the Labour Party[31]) sharing certain beliefs and values which stemmed from a coherent intellectual and political position. They believed, for example, in greater freedom and more choice in the education system. They also believed the education debate to have been dominated by an emphasis on equality (including equality of outcome) which had been at the cost of freedom and the development of different abilities and interests of individuals. In their view the result had been the growth of socialist policies which had led to a drastic reduction in freedom of choice and, especially in many secondary schools and some colleges, a levelling-down or homogenization in the quality of education. They looked to the Conservative Party to initiate a 'brave new dawn' in educational policies.

In the month that Sir Keith Joseph founded the CPS, Marjorie Seldon was promoting the idea of the education voucher.[32] As Chairman of the Sevenoaks Branch of the National Council of Women of Great Britain, she had, in February 1974, prepared a motion on the voucher for presentation to the NCW Annual Conference at Worthing in October 1974. But even at this time, public acceptance of the 'politically unthinkable' was difficult. As Seldon has recalled, 'I had to persuade the NCW at Worthing to take on the education voucher resolution'.[33]

In August 1974 Seldon's resolution was finally chosen for the Worthing Conference. This prompted her to organize, in September 1974, a 'voucher party' at her home (The Thatched Cottage, Godden Green).[34] Among those who attended were Dr Rhodes Boyson (CNACE), John Barnes (CNACE and Kent Education Committee), John Grugeon (Kent County Council), Ruth Garwood-Scott and Linda Whetstone (NCW). The latter two figures were to become key members in Marjorie Sheldon's FEVER lobby. Seldon called the 'voucher party' in order to assist the voucher idea by additional Tory support.[35] Despite this initiative her voucher resolution was narrowly defeated at the NCW Conference. This failure prompted Seldon to establish FEVER (the Friends of the Education Voucher Experiment in Representative Regions) in December 1974, to turn the academic/intellectual campaign for the education voucher into a populist campaign.[36]

Prior to Mrs Thatcher's accession to the leadership, support within the Conservative Party for vouchers was mixed. Those who were attracted to the voucher idea included Sir Gilbert Longden, Dr Rhodes Boyson, William Shelton, John Barnes, Ronald Bell, Peter Utley and Professor Antony Flew. Opponents of the voucher included Edward Heath, Anthony Barber, Norman St John-Stevas, Harry Greenway, Professor Brian Cox, Angus Maude, William Van Straubenzee and Dr Kathleen Ollerenshaw.

The main block to the progress of the education voucher principle within the Party at this time appears to have been Anthony Barber.[37] In 1972 Barber had been sent an eighteen-page document *The Crisis in Education — A Voucher System to Improve Response to Parental Needs and Enhance Equality of Opportunity for Scholars*[38] by a grass roots Party activist, Lieutenant Commander H. N. Paulley. Paulley's paper, one of the most detailed CE statements put before Conservative Party policy formulators, levelled charges of declining educational standards, damaging changes in the educational environment, poor teacher quality, inadequate responses to parental needs and restricted choice in education caused by the advent of the *neighbourhood school*. It argued the case of vouchers as 'the most effective safeguard for the education of children' (Paulley, 1972, p. 11). Specifically, the paper argued: education had been 'progressing' backwards (the reading standard of 11-year-olds was lower in 1972 than it was in 1964) (*ibid.*, p. 3); egalitarian sociologists and educationalists had been responsible for rejecting the didactic method of teaching which had proved successful since the earliest days of education (*ibid.*); gradually and insidiously a new direction (the child-orientated revolution) had been given to British education, particularly in the primary and junior sectors (*ibid.*); the logical end of a neighbourhood school policy (whether parents' children attended a good or inferior school) would depend on whether the parents lived in a smart or poor locality (*ibid.*, p. 10); and, if the State were to withdraw from its existing role and confine its function to guarantor of the availability of education of specified minimum standard, then response to parental needs, equality of opportunity, educational standards and the use of scarce national resources would all be enhanced (*ibid.*, p. 5). The paper chided the Conservative Party for lacking the will to develop a policy on education. It recommended the institution of a system of education vouchers as an effective counter-argument to Labour's own egalitarian plans (*ibid.*, pp. 15–18).

In the event Barber did not accept Paulley's gloomy assertion of education 'progressing' backwards or his recommendations for introducing a voucher system. Barber told Paulley that both he and Mrs Thatcher had looked very carefully at the possibility of introducing such a system during the extensive policy review carried out by the Party when it was last in opposition but had concluded that, although the idea of voucher schemes was in many ways attractive, any such system would also involve a number of very considerable disadvantages.[39] One of the 'very considerable disadvantages' to which Barber referred in this reply to Paulley was the widespread disruption that would inevitably be caused by the introduction of a voucher scheme. Interestingly, the attitude of the entrenched State sector administration towards any form of voucher scheme, however modest and however much an ally of poor children, had been expressed by Dr Ollerenshaw when she said:

> No educationalist, experienced in trying to make a State service work in the best interest of all children, could countenance the disruption which would be the inevitable result.[40]

However, for a number of CEs, until some such radical change as the voucher system was attempted, there could be little prospect of any fresh dynamic in the organization of British education. One of this number was Dr Rhodes Boyson, and it was his emergence in 1974/75 which played a significant part in giving effect to the *Conservative Opportunity* in education.

Since his election to the NACE in 1967 Boyson had become one of the most dominant and persuasive voices in Tory education debate. As a successful headmaster, a historian, and now a prominent Member of Parliament, he was listened to with respect even by those who did not share his views (see Griggs, 1980). One MP who sat opposite Boyson in the House believes him to have been 'a man with an eye to the political chance — an opportunist'.[41]

Prior to his own election as an MP, Boyson had begun to promote the 'real' concern of many parents about the state of British education in a series of books and newspaper articles.[42] Tory press support for the various CE views was an important factor in Boyson's emergence, but as well as this circumstance other influences were to contribute to Boyson's rise. Following Sir Gilbert Longden's retirement from Parliamentary life, the office of Honorary Secretary to the CNACE had fallen to William Shelton. Mrs Thatcher's accession to the Party leadership, and Shelton's appointment as her PPS, would allow Boyson to proceed to the CNACE Honorary Secretaryship and reach an important position of influence over Conservative education policy formation. If it was by a mere coincidence, rather than design, that all three Honorary Secretaries of the CNACE between 1965 and 1976 should have been *defenders of excellence*, then the CEs were indeed fortunate that the nomination of candidates should have gone so much their way.

Thatcher as Party leader and the promotion of the 'defenders of excellence'

Mrs Thatcher became leader of the Conservative Party in February 1975, six years after the CEs' radical backlash in education politics had been launched. I have already shown that Mrs Thatcher was sympathetic to this reaction, and we have just seen how Dr Boyson — something of a symbol in the Party of the backlash — gained a significant base of influence over the making of Conservative education policy following her leadership victory. I shall now examine the significance of her election for the direction of Conservative education policy in the period 1975/76. Only in this way can we better understand how the various CE views were strengthened and represented in the Party as a prerequisite to their incorporation into the policy formation process.

According to two biographers of Mrs Thatcher (Wapshott and Brock, 1983), the rightward shift which her election as leader announced, was supported neither by the large majority of Conservative MPs, the Conservative peers, nor the Conservative Party workers (p. 106). But, of course, by CEs it was endorsed, even welcomed. Some, as we shall see below, would themselves be appointed by Mrs Thatcher to play key roles in articulating her vision of Conservatism. For her, the art of political leadership was the timing of an idea (*ibid.*, p. 154).[43] We saw in chapter 4 how Mrs Thatcher had, in 1970, expressed her support for the notion of *excellence in education* but had then felt it to be regarded by too many, as a 'right-wing extremist' view. Now, in 1975, events such as the William Tyndale Junior School affair and Labour's threatened withdrawal of charitable status from the independent schools, meant that the time was opportune to further exploit the idea of *excellence in education*.

In March 1975 Mrs Thatcher made Angus Maude Chairman of the CRD (in succession to Ian Gilmour) and a Deputy Chairman of the Party, and Sir Keith Joseph was appointed Chairman of the ACP (again in succession to Gilmour) taking special responsibility for the development of Party policy. Both Maude and Joseph were of the Radical Right. Both were senior Shadow Cabinet figures, close to the Party leader. They were each *defenders of excellence*.[44] According to another member of the Radical Right, they were all realists.[45] Christopher Patten, the Director of the CRD, was also an *excellence in education* man and, like Joseph, an admirer of Maude's thinking (see chapter 6). These CEs, and others, now located as they were in significant policy formation positions — Boyson (CNACE and Vice-Chairman, Conservative Education Committee 1975–76), Maude and Patten (CRD) and Joseph (ACP) — would be instrumental in determining and articulating the Conservative education programme adopted by the Party between 1976 and 1979 (see chapters 6 and 7).

Mrs Thatcher's promotion of the *defenders of excellence* came at a time of increasing public disquiet over education.[46] It also occurred at a moment when the CEs' critique of schooling was finally beginning to impress the Tory ranks more generally.[47] In 1973 Ronald Butt had charged the Conservative government of being 'bored or embarrassed by arguments about educational doctrine' (Butt, 1973) and had concluded that, while sending its own children privately to schools which maintained highly literate educational standards, it had paid:

> convenient obeisance to the views of the so-called progressive educational
> establishment so far as the nation's schools were concerned. (*ibid.*)

In his article Butt had absolved Mrs Thatcher from his criticism by pointing out that she had, almost alone in the Party, awoken to the dangers posed by the 'Educationists

Party' — that small but vocal and active coterie establishment (the purveyors of educational fashion), often pretty unrepresentative of people who actually teach and even more unrepresentative of parents (*ibid.*). It is an interesting reflection both upon the way in which the ground of educational discussion had moved to the right and the role of the CEs in mobilizing public opinion behind the shift, that just two years after Butt had called on more top Conservatives to wake up to the egalitarian threat, Mrs Thatcher had set in train (by her promotion of the *defenders of excellence*) signs of a real resistance to the doctrines of the educational establishment. Indeed she had appointed to the Chairmanship of the CRD that very same Black Paperite who had dared to suggest:

> There are certain standards of quality which are essential to the survival of civilisation, and they cannot be achieved and preserved except by rigorous and applied effort. The utmost toughness is required, somewhere at least in the educational system, if standards are to be maintained. No society can abandon all toughness in its educational system without, in the end, becoming soft itself . . . It is necessary now to get very tough with the egalitarians, who would abolish or lower standards out of sympathy with those who fail to measure up to them. We must reject the chimera of equality and proclaim the ideal of quality. (Maude, 1969b, p. 8)

Such thinking was now firmly in accord with that of Margaret Thatcher, Sir Keith Joseph and Norman St John-Stevas. All three were concerned by the apparent collapse of secular and learned authority in British society and its effects on schools. It was by no means accidental therefore that, between 1975 and 1976, the formation of Conservative education policy should have been based on a will to defeat the egalitarian lobby — long seen by the CEs as the principle cause of the decline in the authority of learning — and a determination to restore the principle that schools were for schooling and for the teaching of literacy/numeracy, the passing on of skills and the raising of job prospects. We shall now see how these dual objectives were formulated by the central and voluntary Party organization into a prototype conservative educational policy, a policy which would seek to enfranchise parents through parental choice and which would reflect some hardening of attitude of Conservative groups against comprehensive schools.

The Party's educational policy review

During the autumn of 1975 Mrs Thatcher launched an educational policy review to develop ideas and formulate proposals to put before the electorate at the next election. The formal preparation of a conservative educational policy based on preservationist thinking would take three years and engage the minds of CEs in both the CRD and

CPC, as well as CEs serving on the CNACE. The reason for the Party leader's call for the review, beside the obvious need to get in position and ready to use a clear programme for action, may well have been the realization that education would become a major political issue and that the Party conflict on education was growing sharper. It may be argued that it was Labour's campaign against the direct-grant schools in 1975 which occasioned the Tory Party to finally set in train its own 'Fight For Education'. The direct-grant schools system was abolished by the Labour Government on 27 October 1975. Thereafter the Tory Party embarked upon a fight to save the remaining grammar schools. (For a description of how the Party set about championing these 'excellent schools', see Stevas, 1984, p. 49).

If the climate was right for undertaking the educational policy review this was largely because of the Conservatives' failure to win from the Labour Party a concordat on the subject of education. Therefore, Conservatives had to find a way of recovering the educational initiative from Labour. This was the problem which had to be addressed if the Tory opposition was to effectively counteract Labour's continuing emphasis on social engineering to promote a theoretical concept of equality.

The educational policy review was overseen by Norman St John-Stevas (Chief Opposition Spokesman on Education, 1974–78). As a member of the Shadow Cabinet (the most central of the policy organs of the Party in opposition) and Chairman of the Conservative Education Committee, Stevas was well-placed for the task of seeking a *conservative solution* to the education question. But Stevas did not work alone in managing the Party's endeavour to displace the socialists' grip on the education debate and socialist influence over educational practice. He received considerable assistance from the CRD and, to a lesser degree, from the CPC and the CNACE.

Before tracing the first instalment of the educational policy review (1975/76) and the contribution made by the CEs to its progress, a preliminary note needs to be made about the key personnel advising Stevas. The CRD, described by Ramsden (1980) as 'the Party's civil servant on policy matters' (p. 2) now had a new education desk officer — John Ranelagh (CRD Education Desk Officer, April 1975–April 1977). Unlike his predecessor, Tony Hutt, Ranelagh was a man of the Right and his appointment, in the wake of Maude's own arrival at the CRD, was to prove of special significance. As will be shown below (see also chapters 6 and 7) it was as a result of the work of Ranelagh and Stuart Sexton (Education Adviser to the Conservative Opposition, 1975–79) that a *conservative solution* was found and formulated into Tory education policy for the 1979 election. Besides Ranelagh and Sexton, Stevas was also assisted by Dr Boyson. Boyson was now Stevas' immediate deputy on the Conservative Education Committee. His link with Stevas was further strengthened by his election (on 4 October 1975) to the Honorary Secretaryship of the CNACE. Interestingly, Boyson's election paralleled the start of Stevas' educational policy review — the Party's signal of its own *Fight For Education* campaign. Six months earlier Boyson's co-edited *Black Paper 1975* had been published — the fourth instalment in the original preservationist *Fight For Education* campaign. The real significance of these developments lay not so much in the fact that both campaigns shared a common objective — to oppose a radical critique to the prevailing educational orthodoxy — as in their convergence at a particularly momentus time in the Party's history.

The first instalment of the educational policy review focused on the issues of 'standards' and 'freedom' (ie. parental choice and parental rights). Here much groundwork had already been done. Besides Stevas' *Standards and Freedom CPC* pamphlet (September 1974) the CNACE had, at the suggestion of John Barnes, agreed on 4 December 1974 to the setting up of a working party on 'standards' to work in parallel with those on examinations. Barnes now sat on the CNACE with Boyson. His contribution is interesting since it illustrates Salter and Tapper's remark that policy-making in Opposition is quite different from that in government and provides different opportunities for intellectuals to make an impact (Salter and Tapper, 1985, p. 162). As an academic political scientist (LSE) and Conservative councillor, Barnes had first been elected to the NACE as Vice-Chairman of the South-East Area on 4 October 1969.[48] He had already made contributions to the *Swinton Journal* where he had voiced criticism at the inadequacy of the machinery of government, suggesting that the quality of its information was poor, and the questions it sought to decide were often wrongly formulated (Barnes, 1968, pp. 36–40). On 7 December 1974 Barnes had (together with Professor Bottomley of the University of Bradford) helped to establish a CNACE working party on the 'Finance of the Education Service', and on 22 February 1975 he had introduced to a CNACE meeting a paper on *The Transference of the Payment of Teachers' Salaries to Central Government*. The latter had been forwarded to Sir Keith Joseph, Timothy Raison, Norman St John-Stevas, the National Union Executive Committee and the PEC. It is important to appreciate here the exact lines of influence between CNACE deliberations and the PEC. Salter and Tapper (1985) have noted that unlike the Labour Party, the Conservative Party does not have a formal democratic machinery of policy-making to which intellectuals can make inputs at different points, and that there is no set hierarchy of committees through which ideas must journey in order to evolve into policies (p. 160). The Conservative PEC is just one of several policy committees for the Tory backbenchers. The CNACE, on the other hand, is located on the voluntary side of the Party though it is accountable to the Party's National Union.[49] The real link is the Chairman of the PEC who is an ex-officio member of the CNACE. The CNACE is an advisory body made up of grass roots activist people (LEA personnel, teachers, local councillors and retired educational administrators) and any formal resolutions are passed to the National Union Executive Committee of the Party. Because it is not an executive body, the CNACE cannot enforce aspects of education policy. But, as we have seen (chapters 2–4), it has influenced the general plan of action adopted by the Party.

Barnes' initiative on the issue of standards was the product of his own educational background.[50] As editor (1960–62) of the Cambridge University Conservative Association's magazine *New Radical*, Barnes had written articles on the defence of the grammar school. On leaving Cambridge and joining the LSE in 1964 he had been, in his own words, 'sucked into policy groups'.[51] At this time Barnes was already concerned about educational standards in the secondary school curriculum and the need to obtain greater parental involvement.[52] This was, of course, the concern shared by many other CEs throughout the sixties but it was not until after Barnes' arrival on the NACE in 1969 that the 'standards' issue was moved up on to the Party's policy-making agenda. Of the people who actually made Conservative education policy in 1975/76, Barnes has observed:

> Policy-making in education was made by a group of individuals who knew each other. We were a loose-nexus of persons, linked by friendship and association. In the Tory Party there is an outer and inner-circle advising policy. The outer-circle numbers, at any one-time, between 2-5000 people and the inner-circle between 150-200 people. The two circles may, at a particular time, cross-fertilize ideas as they did in 1974–75 when I, Rhodes (Boyson), John Grugeon and Alistair Lawton, met Sir Keith Joseph at the Seldon's Thatched Cottage voucher party. In 1975–76 these people, whether of the Market-Right or Paternalistic-Right, were seeking a more activist parental body, and they were agreed that, to achieve that end, the Party had to redirect public attention to the decline in schooling standards.[53]

Barnes' reflection upon how the idea of an *activist parental body* helped prompt the Tory concern for educational standards in 1975/76, is important because the same idea was then being actively canvassed by the Black Papers.[54]

The one CE who gave Stevas the most direct assistance in encouraging the notion of an *activist parental body* was Robert Vigars.[55] Throughout the first instalment of the educational policy review he was in close contact with Stevas, advising him of the progress of the Conservatives' campaign to fight for the preservation of London's remaining grammar schools. The organization and direction of this campaign had been Vigars' immediate task following his election as Leader of the Opposition on the ILEA. Vigars was a centre-right Tory and a friend of Leon Brittan (for whom he had canvassed in North Kensington in the 1966 and 1970 elections).[56] Of special relevance to the Conservatives' campaign was the fact that Vigars was a qualified solicitor. It was now commonplace for the Party to draw upon legalistic minds in its pursuit of the preservation of good schools, the raising of educational standards and the protection of the autonomy of LEAs and governing bodies.[57]

Initially, Vigars had found himself acting in a vacuum as a result of the Party's lack of a coherent, intellectual policy on education to challenge Labour's threats to abolish selective schools.[58] This, as Vigars has conceded, had meant that the Party had been, for too long, just compromising — drifting along.[59] As he has observed to the author:

> I wanted to see an intellectual approach to educational politics, and I wanted to get a national conservative policy on the defence of the grammar schools. I was in broad sympathy with Stevas, more so than with Boyson. We had meetings over protecting the grammar schools and educational standards generally. We both supported the Church schools and the voluntary school movement. I was a pragmatist in technique, in knowing how to influence people. It was my idea to target *The Evening Standard*, which was becoming increasingly sympathetic to the conservative case on education, with letters about the need to protect London's grammar schools. I felt that *The Standard* was our best means of getting our views across and it proved very receptive to our case for the need to get a more rigorous curriculum in London's secondary schools.[60]

The cohesion of the Conservative Party on the issues of 'standards' and 'freedom' followed upon the three and a half years of Mrs Thatcher's occupancy of the DES, a period in which she had used a particular educational language — stressing the need for 'quality' and 'achievement', accepting a variegated educational structure as good in itself, and believing in a society which rewarded effort and self-reliance. Despite this, and whatever her private liking for grammar schools, it was Mrs Thatcher who did more to make England comprehensive than anyone else.[61] Tony Hutt has suggested that the Party's performance in the defence of the grammar schools was exemplified by its soft approach towards comprehensivization in the period 1970–74.[62] Whoever's fault it was the fact remains that within two years of opposition the Conservative Party, realizing the disillusionment of its grass roots support, had moved to a more negative attitude to the comprehensive/neighbourhood/non-selective school. The defence of existing selective schools and the encouragement to build new selective schools was now on the agenda.

The significance of the overlap between the Black Paper *Fight For Education* campaign and the launch of the Conservative Party's own *Fight For Education* initiative (and the links and similarities between the two enterprises) have already been touched upon. If Dr Rhodes Boyson was a prime mover in both campaigns, then Professor Brian Cox was an equally stalwart supporter.[63] He had long looked for a conservative restoration of educational standards to the nation's schools but had been told several months before the start of Stevas' educational policy review that, though changes in the preservationists favour looked imminent, their ideas were in danger of becoming orthodox:

> It seems our views are gradually becoming acceptable or even respectable, which is something we shall have to watch.[64]

Whilst the first instalment of the educational policy review derived much of its broad framework from the ideas of the preservationists, it did not benefit from the direct participation of Boyson's 61 Society collaborator Russell Lewis. Lewis had been dismissed by Heath from his post as Director of the CPC in January 1975. The reason for his dismissal remains unclear. Lewis believes it was his actions as a founding member of the Selsdon Group which caused Heath to terminate his appointment.[65] A close working associate of Lewis has suggested the dismissal arose as a result of Lewis' anti-Heath writings in *The Daily Telegraph*.[66] Either way, Lewis' dismissal was never made public. His eight years as head of the CPC had seen the slow absorption of pre-servationist ideas into mainstream Party thinking. As we saw in chapter 4, Lewis had been a principal architect of this development. It is therefore surprising that Mrs Thatcher did not recall Lewis to the CPC on her election as Party leader.[67]

Lewis' departure from the central Party organization was a particular loss to those CEs who had hoped to see the inclusion of the voucher principle within the educational policy review. Prior to his dismissal Lewis had grown tired of Heath's anit-voucher position.[68] Up until the change in the Party leadership hardly anyone in the Party had seriously discussed the voucher.[69] Heath and Whitelaw had insisted upon calling vouchers 'coupons' and had shown no real understanding of the voucher principle.[70] It was a disappointment to Lewis that though he and other CEs had linked together for the opportunity to be positive and to get things done, they had not (in 1975) won the case for the education voucher within the Conservative Party.[71]

Though the first instalment of the educational policy review did not address the voucher issue the topic had not been entirely forgotten. By a strange irony the anti-voucher Stevas had, in September 1975, appointed (with the approval of Chris Patten) the pro-voucher Stuart Sexton as his Education Adviser.[72] We shall see in chapters 6 and 7 how Sexton's alliance with Boyson led to voucher experiments becoming official Conservative education policy.

Before examining the specific assistance given by the CRD to the initial stage of the educational policy review we should first understand the nature of the input provided by the CNACE. Here it was significant that the call for a 'new' Conservative policy on secondary education was first made by Professor Brian Cox.[73] Cox considered the most urgent need was for measures to redress the decline in language, maths and science teaching in comprehensive schools; the provision of a diversity of 13/14–18 comprehensives offering different opportunities; restoration of the direct grant schools and the provision of more places to children from low-income homes; and the development by LEAs of 'back-to-basics' schools with firm discipline and structured courses deliberately planned to help school-leavers to acquire skills needed for jobs. The Cox *scenario* was firmly based on a belief that it was wrong for the Con-servative Party to continue hankering for the 11 +: the Party had to move forward to diversification in comprehensive schools and work out practical plans to achieve this.[74]

Inside the CRD John Ranelagh was in charge of the collation of ideas for education policy formulation. As Secretary to the Conservative Education Committee he was in direct contact with both Stevas and Boyson. He, more than any other person, was responsible for the crystallization of CE thought.[75] Ranelagh has opined:

> The educational policy review was the start of the Party's intellectual campaign against Labour's ruinous education programme. We simply had to find an educational philosophy to fight Labour. The William Tyndale affair helped focus our thoughts on developing the idea of *excellence in education*. Myself, Stevas and Boyson arrived at the idea together, and we agreed that we should concentrate on promoting a cultural literacy for the nation's schools.[76]

Between November 1975 and January 1976 Ranelagh formulated the first early proposals for a *conservative solution*. In their published form these appeared, not unexpectedly, under the twin banners of 'standards' and 'parental choice and involvement'.[77] The proposals included the reintroduction of national standards in the 3Rs (which had been abandoned by Labour in 1966); a strengthening of the schools inspectorate to ensure that these standards were made effective in classrooms; greater emphasis on religious education and school discipline; and the discouragement of the practice of using children as guinea-pigs for the purpose of trying out new teaching methods.[78]

One particular worry to Ranelagh, Stevas and Boyson had been the announcement by the Schools Council, in October 1975, of its proposal to replace the CSE and GCE 'O' level exams by a common 16+ examination. They were concerned because, in their view, such a reform would not easily stem the falling general standards of literacy and numeracy caused by the collage of temporary relevance replacing a firm grounding in a common culture. Stevas urged the widest possible discussion, particularly with employers, before the reform's acceptance.[79]

By February 1976 the educational policy review had led to the formulation of an important principle, one which henceforward would largely determine the Conservatives' approach to education:

> It is not so much the kind of school but what is taught in the classroom that interests parents, who are much more concerned about standards than systems.[80]

Ranelagh's analysis, perfectly attuned to the inchoate public disquiet over schooling, was made at just that juncture when the Conservative Party was mounting its opposition to Labour's Education Bill requiring LEAs to prepare plans for reorganizing secondary education on completely comprehensive lines. According to the Queen's Speech (20 November 1975), the object of the Bill was 'the abolition of selection in secondary education'. To the educational-right this was absurd, unless it was intended to prohibit any form of ability-grouping which, in the vast majority of schools, was considered essential in the interests of good teaching. Ranelagh feared that such a move was being attempted in the cause of achieving, what socialists called, 'social integration':

> It could well be that the next step will be the *busing* of children to schools miles from their homes in order to achieve what Labour regards as the correct social mix in each school.[81]

The CRD's line on comprehensivization was not an isolated or minority view. It had already been represented in the educational press by centre-right/centre educationalists. Stuart Maclure had contended[82] that there was good evidence that the full, unadulterated, comprehensive gospel was not held by many in the educational world, and by few except ardent party ideologists anywhere. Dr Harry Judge had struck a similar note with his admission[83] that it was idle to pretend that there survived, in secondary schools, in LEAs, even in the hearts of bruised sociologists, any powerful conviction that the existing phase of comprehensive planning would bring great educational improvement, or even be worth doing at all.

Thus, the first instalment of the educational policy review was conducted within the context of an increasingly supportive body of lay and professional opinion, both of which seemed eager for a conservative response to the challenge of the comprehensive school. Just one year after the educational policy review had been begun the Conservative Party's first major articulation of a *new conservatism* in education appeared. The timing of its appearance — indeed its very incorporation in a strategy document entitled *The Right Approach*[84] — signified the direction in which the Conservatives' educational *counter-revolution* was being staged.

The right approach

It was the Conservative Party's misfortune that James Callaghan delivered his Ruskin College speech before the publication of its own statement of educational aims. As Stevas has recalled:

> In October 1976 the Prime Minister, Mr Callaghan, launched a campaign for raising educational standards. We had been in the course of preparing our own campaign, but we were not quick enough off the mark and were pipped at the post by Mr Callaghan's initiative. (Stevas, 1984, p. 51)

Stevas had good reason to feel cheated. The Party's new strategy document spoke of 'a return to commonsense'[85] and under the section 'standards in education' (authored jointly by Christopher Patten, Angus Maude and John Ranelagh) were enunciated a number of objectives which Callaghan had himself canvassed (for example, raising literacy/numeracy standards and preparing young people for working life). This section of the document drew upon Neville Bennett's study on teaching methods to underline 'the common-sense conclusions which Conservatives had spelt out again and again on educational standards'.[86]

Significantly, *The Right Approach* was the first document in which the Party made a correlation between educational standards and the quality of teaching. The same link had been made a year earlier by Dr Boyson (1975). By the time of the publication of *The Right Approach*, Boyson had been promoted to the position of Junior Opposition Spokesman on Education.

The aim of Conservative education policy now was to restore the balance between 'the pursuit of excellence' and 'the widening of opportunity'. At a time when the education service was experiencing a cooler financial climate that it had known for many years, Conservatives thought it should still be possible, given a rigorous concentration on priorities, to attain both these objectives.

The Conservatives' immediate response to Callaghan's Ruskin College speech was a four-page critique, penned by Ranelagh, to demonstrate Labour's inability to offer specific proposals to restore falling academic standards.[87] At the centre of Ranelagh's critique was a strong condemnation of, what he saw as, Callaghan's cursory approach to the whole issue of educational standards:

> Perhaps the most disconcerting feature of Mr Callaghan's speech was his proud boast that he intended to initiate a national debate on education. Ever since the late 1960s there has been growing evidence of a serious decline in academic standards, and the resulting concern has led to continuous public discussion. It is strange that the Prime Minister should have been unaware of this.[88]

Ranelagh briefed Party members and education Opposition spokesmen on four socialist policy directions likely to restrain the Conservative Party's own programme to raise educational standards: Labour's commitment to establishing a comprehensive system of education from the nursery schools up to and beyond school leaving age; its reluctance to support examinations on the grounds that they reinforced social divisions; its plan to allow the Secretary of State to change the curriculum, not for academic reasons but in order to promote 'democratic values'; and its aim of eliminating all forms of education independent of the state.[89] These approaches, argued Ranelagh, had to be resisted. Whilst Callaghan had now publicly acknowledged that a serious problem over schooling standards existed, it was the Conservatives who could legitimately claim credit for creating the political pressures which left him little choice.[90]

On the day before Callaghan's Ruskin College speech, Stevas had addressed an open letter to the Prime Minister welcoming reports of his interest in education and drawing his attention to the main proposals which Conservatives had been consistently advocating as necessary to improve standards. Stevas suggested to Callaghan that against a background of financial stringency, it was not a question of how much more education should be provided that was important but whether the country was receiving value for what it had already got. Stevas told Callaghan:

> These are questions which ought to be discussed intelligently and objectively . . . .If you and your colleagues now genuinely wish to initiate a new non-political era in British educational history, you will have the full support of the Conservative Party.[91]

According to Ranelagh, there was little in Callaghan's speech or in subsequent ministerial statements of the Government's determination to press the Education Bill through Parliament, to suggest that Labour was really contemplating a change of course.[92] Consequently, the Conservative Party's *Fight For Education* campaign would continue.

Notes

1　*The Conservative Manifesto 1974*, February, CCO, p.22.
2　In particular, Sir Gilbert Longden.
3　*The Conservative Manifesto 1974*, February, CCO, p.7.
4　*Ibid.*
5　Perhaps it was Mrs Thatcher's own experience as a minister that eventually prompted her to attempt this transformation not through education but by an indirect assault using the Manpower Services Commission.
6　*The Conservative Manifesto 1974*, February, CCO, p.7.
7　In March 1974 Stevas was appointed Vice-Chairman of the Conservative Education Committee, and in May 1974 Opposition Spokesman on the Arts, a post he retained on being appointed Opposition Spokesman on Education in June 1974. Straubenzee was Opposition Spokesman on Education (February–June 1974). Previously he had been a Joint Parliamentary Under-Secretary of State, DES (1970–72).
8　Private information.
9　Private information.
10　Private information.
11　Private information.
12　Boyson's ascendant voice over the Party's education debate was marked by his invitation to be the principal speaker at the CNACE Annual Dinner at the House of Commons, 22 June 1974.
13　This topic had already engaged Boyson for a number of years and his views had been formulated in numerous writings. See in particular Boyson (1972a) and (1973a).
14　See, for example, Norman St John-Stevas, *Standards And Freedom*, CPC No. 557, September 1974. This pamphlet holds a special significance in the history of CE thought. Not only was it sponsored by Russell Lewis (now a fervent Thatcher supporter) it was also informed by the thinking of William Shelton MP (Honorary Secretary CNACE, 5 March 1974–3 October 1975) the man who, with Airey Neave, organized Mrs Thatcher's campaign for the Party leadership. Stevas' tract, heavily weighted with Boysonian rhetoric, contained a 'Parents' Charter' and called on Tories to take up the offensive against the socialist approach to education. According to Shelton, the Conservative Party was now moving towards the notion of 'excellence in education' in reaction to the 1960s/1970s trend of anti-authoritarianism. William Shelton MP to author, 24 April 1986.

15 Minister of State, DES (1964–66); Shadow Employment Secretary (1972–74); Secretary of State, DES (5 March 1974–10 June 1975).

16 Upon Labour's election victory in February 1974 Prentice's post at Employment was vetoed by Harold Wilson and Jack Jones as a result of his public criticism of the Party's support for the 'Pentonville Five'.

17 Reg Prentice MP to author, 11 June 1986. It was during the Wlilson government (1974–76) that Labour ministers began appointing large numbers of special advisers. The Callaghan government (1976–79), as a result of fierce Tory opposition, reduced the number of these political apparatchiks from twenty-nine to twenty-four. During the first Thatcher government (1979–83) there were fourteen special advisers. In 1986 the number had increased to twenty-eight.

18 Reg Prentice MP to author, 11 June 1986. It was only from 1977, following his conversation to the Conservative Party, that Prentice began to formulate his own educational philosophy. During his time at the DES he had associated most with Maurice Peston and Anne Sofer, both of whom were then on the right of the Labour Party. In 1977 Prentice met Patrick Cormack MP, a man of the Tory centre-left. In 1986 they both joined the Council for Independent Education.

19 McCrindle to Prentice, *Oral Answers to Questions*, House of Commons, 6 May 1975, p.1190.

20 Prentice to McCrindle, *Oral Answers*, p.1190.

21 *Ibid*.

22 Prentice to Boyson, *Oral Answers*, p.1190.

23 Education Junior Minister (Schools), DES (1974–75); MP N. W. Durham (1964–87); Chairman, Sunderland Education Authority (1958–64).

24 Donoughue also notes that Education, in 1974, was not viewed as an important post either by Labour politicians or by senior civil servants, and that it was 'left vacant until the last minute'.

25 For example, Disraeli's well known 'dishing of the Whigs' in 1867, after the Tories had resisted the extension of the franchise for some time; and the introduction of Free Elementary education in 1891 although, again, Salisbury and other leading Conservatives had united with the religious societies to oppose such a measure throughout the two previous decades. For this insight I am indebted to Dr Clive Griggs of Brighton Polytechnic. See C. Griggs, 'The Language of Education', paper presented to the History Workshop Conference, 1980.

26 The Labour movement was slow to respond to the Tory challenge and when it did so it was in terms of defence rather than direct challenge to the substance of Tory criticism. There was considerable confusion among people of the Left. For example, many considered the term 'Progressive' in education to be synonymous with 'Progressive' in politics. In theory Labour supported comprehensive schooling, but failed to provide the legislation to end selection or to give sufficient financial support to enable comprehenive schools to be purpose-built (and thereby avoid the very real problems that split sites created). See C. Griggs, 'The Language of Education', paper presented to the History Workshop Conference, 1980.

27 There is an interesting parallel here with the Labour Party. It was after the failure of the Callaghan government and the social services cuts of 1976–78, that many Labour Party members made up their minds that what was required was 'real socialism', not the socialist gospel according to Harold Wilson, James Callaghan and Denis Healey.

28 For a description of the foundation, membership and work of the CPSESG and its influence over Conservative Party education policy formation, see chapter 8 of this volume.

29 The principle of education vouchers was first introduced into Conservative Party thinking in 1959 by Brendon Sewill. See Sewill (1959).

30 Founder of Friends of the Education Voucher Experiment in Representative Regions (FEVER); member of the CPSESG; member of National Council of Women (GB) Education Committee; married to free-market economist and author Arthur Seldon.

31 Caroline Cox joined the Conservative Party in 1974. Dr Marks joined the Conservative Party in 1977.

32 Marjorie Seldon began campaigning for education vouchers in 1966. Her first article (with Arthur Seldon) on the subject was in the Liberal Party's magazine *New Outlook*. Between 1966–74 she wrote widely (in letters and features in *The Times, The Financial Times, The Daily Telegraph, The Sunday*

Times, The Observer, NCES Bulletin, and many others) to persuade the general public of the benefits of the voucher system to tax-payers and parents.

33 Marjorie Seldon to author, 6 June 1985.
34 *Ibid.*
35 *Ibid.*
36 *Ibid.*
37 Chancellor of the Exchequer (1970–74); Chairman of the Conservative Party (1967–1970); Chairman, ACP (1970–74); MP Doncaster (1951–64), Altrincham and Sale (1965–74).
38 Copies were also sent to, amongst others, Edward Heath, Lord Carrington (Chairman of the Conservative Party), Margaret Thatcher, James Prior (Deputy Chairman, Conservative Party), Sir Michael Fraser (Deputy Chairman, Conservative Party), John Selwyn Gummer (Vice-Chairman, Conservative Party), Russell Lewis (Director, CPC) and Sir Gilbert Longden (Honorary Secretary NACE).
39 Copy of letter from Anthony Barber MP, to Lieutenant Commander H. N. Paulley, 30 January 1973, *The Longden Papers.*
40 Letter to *The Daily Telegraph*, June 1967.
41 Chris Price to author, 6 March 1986. Price was Labour MP, Lewisham West (1974–83), PPS to Frederick Mulley (1975–76) and Chairman of the Commons Education Select Committee (1979–83).
42 Principally his own Churchill Press publications and *Daily Telegraph* column, as well as leader articles in *The Times.*
43 Significantly, it was Norman St John-Stevas who first brought to Mrs Thatcher the news of her election triumph. Her sober reaction was, 'Now we have lots of work to do'. Quoted in Lewis (1975), p. 122.
44 Joseph had first declared his belief in 'excellence in education' in an article in *Crossbow*, in which he argued 'We must spend more yet on very highly qualified teachers . . . .Education is not only essential to us as traders. It is vital for the individual soul. Many hooligans today are the victims of purposeless-ness . . . they need access to good education — to give them the mental resources to enjoy their freedom. Without education the welfare state will become the Boredom State'. See Joseph, Sir K. (1959), pp. 28–34.
45 Dr Rhodes Boyson MP to author, 20 February 1985.
46 For a Marxist assessment of how, in 1975/76, the panic over falling standards and working-class illiteracy successfully turned the tide in the education sphere towards themes and goals established by the forces of the right, and how the sphere of education was successfully colonized by the radical-right, see Hall and Jacques (1983), pp. 19–39.
47 For an account of how the Party gradually came, in 1975, to rally round a more instructive, common-sense approach to social welfare issues, see Joseph, Sir K. (1987, pp. 26–31).
48 *NACE Minute Book 1965–77* Vol. 2, p.118, CPA.
49 The CNACE operates at the same level as the other arms of the voluntary wing of the Party, such as the National Committee of Trade Unionists, the Womens' National Committee, the Young Conservatives and the Federation of Conservative Students.
50 Barnes was born into a middle-class family in Newquay, Cornwall. His father had been a school-master at a direct grant school. He himself was educated at a direct grant grammar school in Plymouth, and then at Gonville and Caius College, Cambridge, where he became a politics don (1961–64). Among his student contemporaries at Cambridge were Edward Norman and John Selwyn Gummer. John Barnes to author, 22 March 1985.
51 John Barnes, to author, 22 March 1985. Barnes was invited by Sir Edward Boyle to serve on the machinery of government policy group in 1965. Shortly after, he was asked to lead a CPC study group on local government. In 1964, 1966 and 1970 he stood as the Conservative Parliamentary candidate for Walsall.
52 *Ibid.*
53 *Ibid.*
54 The need for the Conservatives to assimilate more tangibly the notion of 'greater parental partici-

pation' in order to counteract the motives of Labour's social and political engineers in parliament, had been foretold by Ronald Butt in the fourth Black Paper. See Butt (1975), pp.42–5.

55 Leader of the Opposition, ILEA (1974–79); Member: Kensington Borough Council (1955–59); LCC and GLC Kensington (formerly South Kensington) (1955–86); Chairman, Environmental Planning Committee, GLC (1967–71); Chairman, Strategic Planning Committee (1971–73); Chairman, GLC (1979–80); contributor to *Black Paper 1977*.

56 Robert Vigars to author, 3 November 1986.

57 For example, Leon Brittan had co-authored (with Norman St John-Stevas) a CPC pamphlet, *How To Save Your Schools* (CPC. No. 573, July 1975). In 1975 Brittan was Chairman of the Legal Sub-committee of the Conservative PEC. Brittan had been called to the Bar in 1962. In 1960 he had been Chairman of the Cambridge University Conservative Association, where he had met John Barnes. As a preservationist, Brittan had attended the 1973 Conference of the NCES.

58 Robert Vigars to author, 3 November 1986.

59 *Ibid.*

60 *Ibid.* It is also important to note that Vigars used *The Evening Standard* to publicize the Conservatives' disquiet over the William Tyndale Junior School and was himself a member of the panel which took disciplinary proceedings against the Tyndale teachers. For a detailed critique of how the educational-right was able to deliver its bad news on 'progressive' teachers and schooling through the reporting of education in the press, see CCCS Education Group (1981), chapters 9 and 10.

61 Mrs Thatcher personally approved 91 per cent of the 3600 secondary reorganization proposals put before her during her years as Education Secretary. She abolished more grammar schools than anyone else before, or since, and, during her term of office, England went from having one-third of its children educated in comprehensives to an irreversible two-thirds.

62 Tony Hutt to author, 19 August 1986. Hutt was the CRD Education Desk Officer (November 1974-April 1975). Prior to this appointment he had worked for Stevas in his capacity as CRD Desk Officer for Local Government, Housing and the Arts.

63 Professor Cox was now giving direct assistance to the Conservative Party as a member of its Higher Education Committee, which met in the House of Commons room of Dr Keith Hampson. This Committee was chaired by Leon Brittan.

64 Letter from Stuart Froome to Cox, 13 March 1975, *The Cox Papers*. Froome contributed an essay 'Reading and the school handicap score' to *Black Paper 1975*.

65 Russell Lewis to author, 22 August 1986. The Selsdon Group was established in 1973 to emphasize the case for the free-market. The Group took its name from the Selsdon Park Hotel where the Conservative Shadow Cabinet had, in 1970, drawn up plans for government which were eventually abandoned by Heath. The Group's founder, Stephen Sherbourne, was an associate of John Barnes and Assistant Director of the CRD (1974–75). In 1983 Sherbourne was appointed Political Secretary to Mrs Thatcher.

66 David Knapp to author, 8 September 1986. Knapp succeeded Lewis as Director of the CPC. Between 1972 and 1974 Lewis contributed a number of articles to the *Daily Telegraph* criticizing Conservative economic policies. Other possible factors which may have contributed to Lewis' dismissal, included his pro-Thatcher sympathies (he had been instrumental in encouraging Mrs Thatcher to attend IEA Hobart lunches) and his association with the pro-voucher Alfred Sherman and Arthur and Marjorie Seldon. Each of these put Lewis' position at the CPC in some difficulty.

67 The mystery of Lewis' ostracism is deepened by the fact that he gave full support to Mrs Thatcher's candidacy for the Tory leadership. Additionally his 1954 Bow Group paper 'Industry and the pro-perty-owning democracy' would appear to have been a forerunner to the new Party leader's own political philosophy.

68 Russell Lewis to author, 22 August 1986.

69 *Ibid.* According to Lewis this lack of debate resulted from trepidation rather than any unwillingness to discuss the voucher issue: 'Knowing Heath's views on the subject Party members were not prepared to risk it'.

70 *Ibid.* William Whitelaw was Chairman of the Conservative Party (1974–75).

71 *Ibid.*
72 In 1973 Sexton (a member of Croydon Education Committee) had joined the PEST (London Group). Here he had met Tony Hutt. Sexton's ambition for an advisory role within the central Party organization had occasioned him to write to Chris Patten to ask for a position on the CRD education desk in the event of a vacancy. Despite Hutt's departure in April 1975 the job had been filled by John Ranelagh. Charles Bellairs, who knew Sexton's name from correspondences received from the Croydon Education Committee, advised Sexton to contact Stevas personally at his office at Old Palace Yard, Westminster. It was this contact that finally led to Sexton's appointment. Charles Bellairs to author, 19 August 1986.
73 'The need for a new Conservative policy on secondary education', address by Professor Cox to the N.W. Area CNACE, 8 November 1975, *The Cox Papers*.
74 The 'Cox scenario' formed the basis of Norman St John-Stevas' *Better Schools For All: A Conservative approach to the problems of the comprehensive school*, CPC. No. 617, December 1977.
75 The timing and manner of Ranelagh's appointment to the CRD education desk was significant. Ranelagh's father was a friend of Sir Keith Joseph and it was on Joseph's personal recommendation to Chris Patten that Ranelagh had been invited to become Education Desk Officer. John Ranelagh to author, 20 February 1986.
76 John Ranelagh to author, 20 February 1986.
77 *Politics Today*, No. 1, 19 January 1976, CRD.
78 As a result of Conservative pressure, the Labour government had announced on 28 August 1974 the creation of the Assessment of Performance Unit (APU).
79 Speech at Swinton, 23 November 1975.
80 *Politics Today*, No. 1, 19 January 1976, CRD.
81 *ibid.*
82 *Times Educational Supplement*, 18 April 1975. Maclure's view may have been influenced by his discussions with Ronald Butt in the All Souls Group.
83 *Times Educational Supplement*, 2 May 1975. Judge was one of the educationalists invited by Stevas to contribute to the second instalment of the Party's educational policy review.
84 *The Right Approach: A Statement of Conservative Aims*, October 1976, CCO.
85 *Ibid*, p. 7.
86 *Ibid*, p. 62.
87 *Politics Today*, No. 20 (Briefing Notes), 8 November 1976, CRD, pp. 366–70.
88 *Ibid.*, p. 367.
89 *Ibid.* All four of these approaches had been outlined in *Labour's Programme 1976*.
90 *Politics Today*, No. 20, p. 369.
91 Open letter to the Prime Minister, from Norman St John-Stevas, CCO Press Release 984/76, 18 October 1976.
92 *Politics Today*, No. 20, p. 370.

Chapter 6

The Crystallization of a Conservative educational policy, 1976–78

Introduction

At a meeting of the NCES in London on 16 May 1976 Dr Boyson announced:

> The forces of the right in education are on the offensive. The blood is flowing from the other side now.[1]

I have pointed out that the CEs had, between 1970 and 1976, established a strong base in the Conservative Party for developing further the notion of *excellence in education*. The Party's difficulties in fashioning a conservative educational policy in line with Conservative philosophy were caused by its problems in defining the aims of education. We saw in the previous chapter how these problems were resolved, and how key CEs had been appointed to influential positions in the Party to help formulate an educational policy founded upon preservationist principles. This chapter seeks to explain how that policy was formulated. From 1976 CEs were playing a central role in the education policy-making process in the Conservative Party. Until November 1976 the position of Deputy Opposition Education Spokesman had been divided between Dr Hampson and Dr Boyson. In Mrs Thatcher's Shadow Cabinet reshuffle in November 1976 Boyson was appointed Junior Opposition Education Spokesman, with Norman St John-Stevas remaining the Chief Opposition Spokesman on Education and the Arts. The main Tory education concerns in opposition were now: continuing the fight against Labour's 1976 Education Bill; Conservative responses to the 'Great Debate'; initiating 'standards' and 'values in education' campaigns (1977/78); promoting the quality of teaching; supporting discipline, parental choice and religious education; and opposing the politicization, as they saw it, of the secondary school curriculum. The latter involved proposals by Stevas and Boyson to abolish the Schools Council (founded in 1963 as a result of the recommendations of the Lockwood Committee). From 1976 both Stevas and Boyson acted in unison over these six broad policy areas but, as will be shown, they were fundamentally to disagree over two other issues — education vouchers and the publication of school examination result league-tables.[2]

It was during the period 1976–78 that the CEs were able to develop so much of what has subsequently become Conservative educational policy in government: the stress on high standards; the extension of parental rights; the sponsoring of the Assisted Places Scheme and the retention of such selective schools as survived. Whilst Sir Keith Joseph and Angus Maude largely determined the direction and coordination of the Party's policy work at this time, the formulation of education policy continued to rest with Stevas, Boyson, Sexton and Ranelagh (succeeded as CRD Education Desk Officer in 1977 by Biddy Passmore). But enthusiasm for *excellence in education* went well beyond these Conservative policy formulators. The Tory press (and its Conservative education correspondents) were now becoming, in the wake of the William Tyndale affair, vigorous sponsors of CE ideas.

The juxtaposition of the *Black Paper* group (now led by Dr Boyson and Professor Cox) and the Conservative Party in the preservationists' *Fight For Education* was shown in the last chapter to have been something more than a lucky coincidence. By late 1976 a number of *Black Paper* ideas had already been adopted as official Conservative Party education policy: that purpose-built comprehensives with an adequate sixth-form and a varied social mix of children would probably prove successful; that a universal system of 11–18 comprehensives should be opposed because many sixth-forms would be too small, and because city neighbourhood schools would drive middle-class parents to buy houses in more favoured areas; and, that selection in some localities should be favoured (preferably at 13+).

The close overlap between the work of the *Black Paper* group and education policy formation in the Conservative Party is illustrated by the way in which each utilized Neville Bennett's study (1976) of classroom teaching styles to popularize the view that formal/traditional teaching methods achieved the best results in training children to be literate and numerate. In the same month that he was appointed Junior Opposition Education Spokesman, Dr Boyson (with Professor Cox) was making preparations for a fifth Black Paper (*Black Paper 1977*). Boyson and Cox were convinced that many children were being deprived of the achievements in basic subjects they could have expected if taught in a more formal manner. The *Black Paper* group now sought to exploit not only the findings of the Bennett study but also the raised public concern over educational standards that had followed upon the events at the William Tyndale Junior School.[3] Their proposition — 'formal classrooms are superior' — now had the support of a number of conservative education correspondents, including Bruce Kemble (*Daily Express*) and John Izbicki (*Daily Telegraph*). Cox informed Boyson:

> I talked to John Izbicki this morning. He was most friendly, and will wait until after Christmas for information about the Black Paper. Bruce Kemble

suggested that Easter Saturday would be a good day for publication. I am not sure about that, but just before the Easter Conferences is obviously a good idea.[4]

Cox also suggested to Boyson:

> Would it not be a good idea to start publishing an annual pamphlet for NCES members? We ought to give them more. If we did this, could there be a link with Churchill Press? It would help if, when I write to tell people their articles are not included in the Black Paper, I could inform them that we were willing to publish them as part of a book. (*ibid.*)

Clearly, the Black Paper editors in their urgency to capitalize on the zeal of their contributors, were seeking every opportunity available to promote their campaign. Given the close relationship between the *Black Paper* group and sections of the Conservative Party, the latter's mission to raise educational standards was now quite obviously influenced by the former's continuing impetus to battle for a complete reassessment of schooling priorities.

The Party's Conversion to 'Excellence in Education'

We saw in the previous chapter how, in the period between 1975/76, the Conservative Party had started to adopt the notion of *excellence in education* and how it had taken the decision to deploy this conservative educational philosophy to oppose Labour's policy for universal comprehensivization. According to Ranelagh,[5] it was the arrival of Shirley Williams as Education Secretary which finally prompted the Conservative Party's wholesale conversion to *excellence in education*. Additionally, her position now became the subject of a new Conservative offensive.[6] In 1975 Ranelagh had helped Stevas to take the political and tactical decision (which Stevas had sold to Mrs Thatcher) to fight Labour's comprehensive policy.[7] Consequently, Ranelagh and Stevas pursued a dual mission in fighting Shirley Williams and concentrated on opposing Labour's 1976 Education Bill on the basis of its costing, arguing that the Labour government should instead create more grammar schools and safeguard educational standards.[8]

According to Ranelagh,[9] the Conservative Party's offensive against Shirley Williams was given intellectual weight by the work of Leon Brittan. Ranelagh has further recalled:

> It was Brittan who largely penned *How To Save Your Schools* in 1975. Stevas wrote very little of that. Brittan was always the number two in education, though officially it was Boyson.[10]

Ranelagh's perception is to some degree supported (though not wholly acknowledged) by Brittan's own recollection of events:

> I was not involved in the formulation of education policy, except in the
> purely defensive role of wanting to protect schools from the Labour legis-
> lation. It was with the intent of doing that that I used my professional legal
> experience, as well as my political knowledge, to help write the 1975
> pamphlet. [11]

As to whether he was, in 1976, the Party's *unofficial* number 2 in education (officially
he was the then Opposition Front Bench Spokesman on Devolution) Brittan has
informed the author 'If I was then I was unaware of it at the time.' [12] And it remains
unclear as to whether Brittan had, in fact, been asked by Mrs Thatcher (in 1975) to
take charge of advising the Party on education issues. What is certain is that he first
acted as the Party's link with the universities. This role sprang from his membership of
the Political Committee of the Carlton Club. According to Brittan, [13] it was the
Carlton Club that decided that the Party should take up the intellectual battle in
education. Thus, it was the Carlton Club — through its spokesman Eric Koops —
which had approached Mrs Thatcher to suggest Brittan's name as the Party's higher
education liaison officer. [14]

The significance of Brittan's appointment (as higher education liaison officer) for
the Party's conversion to *excellence in education*, was that his duties brought him into
direct contact with the educational-right preservationists. Some of these he had already
met when he had addressed the 1973 NCES Conference. But, during 1975/76, he met
Professor Antony Flew at the University of Reading (an NCES member and friend of
Professor Brian Cox) and it was this meeting which appears to have had a profound
effect on Brittan's own educational philosophy:

> I was aware of these preservationists. There was a deliberate Party strategy
> to befriend these groupings. I was drawn to Flew's commitment to defend
> educational standards against an educationally destructive egalitarianism. [15]

It is worth noting here that Professor Flew had been one of those academics canvassed
by Cox and Dyson in 1969 to help in the Black Paper *Fight For Education* campaign.
Flew had then replied from his post at the University of Keele:

> Fine. I have already ordered my copy of the pamphlet, and persuaded our
> bookshop to buy some for sale there. It will be a change from Che' Guevara
> and attacks on all assessment from sociologists. [16]

The Party's conversion to *excellence in education* in 1976 was also assisted by the work of
Stuart Sexton. Bearing in mind Sexton's own commitment to Black Paperite ideology
(he was a contributor to *Black Paper 1977*) it was not unexpected that he should have
liaised so closely between Stevas and Boyson in the promotion of preservationist ideals.

During the period 1976–78 Sexton's role was divided between 'official' Education Adviser to Stevas and 'unofficial' speech-writer to Boyson. Most significantly it was Sexton who drafted and wrote papers on the finance of education specifically for the Tory Opposition Spokesmen on Education. Sexton has commented:

> The CCO press releases on those speeches by Stevas and Boyson were written by myself. My ideas were 'ghosted' as being from their hand.[17]

Sexton's *ideas* included proposals for minimum standards and a minimum curriculum; an effective and independent Inspectorate for all schools to monitor those standards; as well as *schools of excellence* (schools with particular subject specialisms) and greater parental freedom of choice of school (Sexton, 1977, pp. 86–9). All of these, with the exception of the proposal for *schools of excellence* (announced and implemented by Kenneth Baker in 1986/87), would be put into effect by Mark Carlisle and Sir Keith Joseph between 1979 and 1986 (see chapters 7, 8 and 9).

Sexton believed that the Tory Party had lost its way over private freedom in education under the Heath government.[18] Sexton was not alone amongst those CEs who wished to develop policies to guarantee that all children should have the right education. Five other CEs — Chris Tame, Chris Patten, Caroline Cox, Dr John Marks and Fred Naylor — were now to advise the Party to pursue a radical conservative schools programme based on the notion of *excellence in education*.

The libertarian Chris Tame had been appointed as a general assistant at the IEA in September 1975 (a post he held until May 1979).[19] Prior to his appointment at the IEA Tame had rapidly embraced free-market libertarianism.[20] Together with the IEA librarian (Ken Smith) Tame assisted with research for Sir Keith Joseph and others.[21] Tame was one of the principal libertarians whose influence was now beginning to spread inside the Conservative Party.[22] Although Tame was opposed to the views of the ultra-Conservative right he was sympathetic to the Boyson line on education.[23] The Boyson line was, of course, the Sexton line.

It was during the mid-seventies that the role of the CRD had become crucial, being the intellectual repository for the *excellence in education* ideas of the CEs. Both the Chairman (Angus Maude) and Director (Chris Patten) of the CRD were keen to promote CE ideas. For Patten, the CEs were expressing a concern about standards and rigour and a worry that the socialists' obsession with structure, equal access and equality of opportunity (as expressed through comprehensivization) was undermining quality.[24] Patten was conscious that despite increased expenditure on education, the output in terms of results was not as the Party would have liked.[25] His own educational philosophy was shaped, first by the writings of Maude, and later by those of Mary Warnock,[26] both of whom he has acknowledged in his main publication to date.[27] Like Maude, Patten believed in selection, rigour, competitiveness and excellence in education, and that the quality of education should be raised through the provision of a balanced curriculum in well-organized schools.[28] Like Warnock, he believed politicians should set out a more coherent view of what they understood to be the purpose of education and the means of achieving their aims.[29] For Patten, schooling is about preparing young people for 'the good life' and this can only be achieved by the provision of a *good education* that enables the child to learn virtue.[30] Such a view was, of course, shared by other CEs (most notably Stevas, Boyson, Greenway and Maude).

Patten, like other CEs noted in chapter 2, has located the earliest soundings of disquiet amongst Conservatives over modern secondary education to the 1950s:

> A lot of concern was being expressed prior to 1961. It really goes back to Sir David Eccles who, in 1955, felt standards in secondary schools would have to be raised if the evident failure of those schools to educate the technician-class was to be stemmed.[31]

In his five years at the CRD Patten did not find the education policy, as developed at Old Queen Street, to be particularly right-wing.[32] In his view, moderate Conservatism prevailed.[33] He found Stevas to be much more influential than Boyson, simply because Stevas was the Chief Opposition Education Spokesman.[34] Whilst not wishing to downplay the strong views which Stevas himself had on educational matters, Patten has acknowledged that it was Maude's influence that was most important in shaping Stevas' approach to education.[35] Maude has agreed that he influenced Stevas, especially the latter's speeches around the country:

> Stevas was making the same noises as I had been making from the time of the first Black Paper in 1969.[36]

Maude had for a long time been concerned about the failure of the comprehensive schools to educate the lower-ability children. According to Maude[37] his concern was taken up, first by Stevas, and later, by Sir Keith Joseph. That same concern was, between 1976–78, expressed by the new Tory radicals — Caroline Cox, Dr John Marks and Fred Naylor — each of whom established themselves as fierce critics of comprehensives, defenders of selection and proponents of parental choice in education. As CEs they would each make significant contributions to the formation of Conservative education policy (see chapters 7, 8 and 9). All three would join the right of the Conservative Party.

Before she joined the Conservative Party in 1977, Caroline Cox was a Fabian socialist. What changed her political allegiance and caused her to engage in the educational-right debate, was her experiences as an academic and a parent.[38] As a sociology lecturer at the Polytechnic of North London (PNL) from 1969 to 1974 she had witnessed, at first hand, what she believed to be the damaging effects of staff-student militancy on the teaching/learning process. This experience had raised her political consciousness concerning education.[39] The parallel here with Professor Brian Cox's conversion to the educational-right (following his experience of teaching at the University of California during the period of student turbulence in 1964) is quite striking. Caroline Cox's political consciousness concerning education was further developed by her experience as a parent of three children attending comprehensive schools in the early 1970s. In English Literature, the only work which was set for one of her sons for a whole year and half a term was two essays on rock music with no reference whatsoever to English literacy heritage.[40] This was only one example of several similar issues which led her to question the progressive education orthodoxy.[41]

Two years before joining the Conservative Party, Caroline Cox (together with fellow PNL colleagues Dr John Marks and Keith Jacka) had published *Rape of Reason*, the authors' story of how students, staff and governors at the PNL had sought to subvert academic integrity. Dr Boyson, in his review of the book, hailed it as 'the beginning of the fight back'.[42] It had, in fact, been Boyson who had asked Caroline Cox to give the book to Churchill Press for publication following its rejection by Penguin Books.[43] He had learnt of it from Ralph Harris who had invited Caroline Cox to speak on the PNL troubles at an IEA dinner following her mention of the events to Sir Reginald Murley (a friend of Harris).[44] The significance of the book's publication (besides its appearance in the same year as *Black Paper 1975*, Boyson's *The Crisis in Education* and the media coverage of the William Tyndale affair) was its statement of a particular educational philosophy: that education is about the freedom to pursue the truth. For an account of the centrality of this philosophy to Tory education radicals see Wilby and Midgley (1987, p. 11).

Dr John Marks was a Gaitskellite member of the Labour Party until 1974. He joined the Conservative Party in 1977, the year Stevas launched the Party's 'standards' in education campaign (see section below). His changed political outlook was, again, prompted by the events at the PNL (1971–75).[45] Like Caroline Cox, he believed in a respect for traditional structures and academic excellence.[46] Here Marks and Cox found a mutual affinity with Boyson. Indeed, after *Rape of Reason* had been published, they had both been invited by Boyson to address NCES annual conferences and become NCES members.[47] They were then invited by Boyson and Professor Brian Cox to contribute to *Black Paper 1977*.[48] Both Dr Marks and Caroline Cox (in the period 1976–78) were in the *continuity and tradition* grouping of the radical-right in education[49] (later, from 1980, they would join the *free-market* grouping from their positions as, respectively, Secretary and Chair of the CPSESG: see chapters 7 and 8 below). There was now some (albeit limited) overlapping membership between the CPSESG and NCES.[50] One NCES member was Fred Naylor who, significantly, was to join the CPSESG at the personal invitation of Cox.[51] He, like Marks and Cox, would give the Conservative Party close counsel on developing policies based on the notion of *excellence in education* (see chapters 8 and 9).

Naylor had, in the 1960s, taught at Leeds Modern School and become Head of the City of Bath Technical School. Both schools were submerged by the comprehensive tide — and this led him to his role as an intense critic of comprehensives, upholder of selection and defender of parental choice in education.[52] During his time at the Schools

Council (where he worked as sixth-form curriculum examination officer, 1968–73) Naylor had made contact with Dr Boyson through Sir Desmond Lee.[53] In 1973 Naylor and Boyson had met together at Highbury Grove School.[54] They had got on well together as a result of a mutual interest in educational standards.[55] It was also in 1973 that Naylor had joined the NCES and returned to Bath to work as a college of education lecturer. Like Boyson he believed progressive education was responsible for a breakdown of morality.[56]

In the period 1976–78 Naylor was in communication with Boyson, Marks and Cox.[57] All three were pluralists with their attachment to choice and freedom in education.[58] Naylor's particular concern was to counter and expose that notion of the *common school* (which had to have a *common faith* of moral and religious education) which drew its inspiration from John Dewey's book *A Common Faith*.[59] Naylor saw Dewey's formulation of the *common faith* as socialism, and it was this that the Conservative Party had to fight and resist.[60] Naylor wished to demystify, what he saw as, the 'comprehensive mythology' that had developed in Britain in the 1960s. His wish was, of course, shared by Stevas, Boyson, Sexton and Ranelagh.

Naylor felt he and others of the *continuity and tradition* persuasion, were fighting for 'positive freedom' in education.[61] That is, the positive freedom of the child to be taught how to do things (but not given freedom to do as it pleased) and the positive freedom of parents to be allowed diversity of choice in education.[62] In this respect Naylor sees the development of the educational-right in the 1960/70s as more idealistic than Ralph Harris' 'awkward squad'.[63]

Naylor's position was influenced by the work of Torsten Husén at the OECD.[64] Naylor sympathized with Husén's thesis, that in the 1960s education had moved from a traditionalist/conservative to a liberal form, and was moving in the 1970s to a Marxist form (equality of results).[65] It was Naylor's appreciation of this transition that had led him to be strongly critical of the position taken by fellow Schools Council member Maurice Plaskow.[66] Plaskow adhered to the left-of-centre educational tradition of Liberal/Fabian reform of the public education system, based as it was on the rhetoric of hope and optimistic slogans of 'equal value' and 'equal opportunity'. Naylor believed in a differentiated education system and greater choice and freedom — a particular conception of *openness* as opposed to the Conservative orthodoxy which did not believe in upsetting the status quo.[67] As well as Husén's influence, Naylor was also motivated in his traditionalist views by John Dunstan's book *Paths To Excellence and the Soviet School*.[68] It was this study of the Russian secondary education system (a system highly elitist and differentiated, with its emphasis on affecting the general education of young people appropriate to the contemporary requirements of the social, scientific and technical process) which Naylor drew to Boyson's attention.[69] In chapters 8 and 9 we shall see how the Soviet education system, based as it is on intellectual and moral aims (the striving for educational excellence and a belief that education can deliver morality) and technicist objectives (providing citizens with a high level of general education and backing their subsequent training to increase their efficiency and adaptability on the job) was drawn by Naylor to the attention of Mrs Thatcher and Sir Keith Joseph. The important point to note is that henceforth much of the Conservative Party's education policy would be strongly influenced by Dunstan's study.

The 'Standards '77' campaign

Despite the efforts of the Conservative Party to block Labour's Education Bill the Government successfully enacted the Education Act 1976, which required LEAs to 'have regard to the general principle that (secondary) education is to be provided only in schools where the arrangements for admission are not based (wholly or partly) on selection by reference to ability or aptitude'. Whilst Stevas had led Conservative opposition to the Bill in the House of Commons, Conservative opposition to the Bill in the House of Lords had been led by Lord Elton.[70] Elton, unlike Stevas, was a CE with practical experience of teaching in the state education system.[71] He believed he was no backwoods peer and had a very good idea of what was offered by both the direct-grant grammar and the comprehensive school systems.[72] Elton's role in the upper-chamber was supported by Viscount Eccles. It is significant that whilst he was organizing Conservative opposition against Labour's Education Bill in the Lords, Elton was also chairing an *ad hoc* Committee of Governors of London grammar schools threatened with abolition (established by himself and Robert Vigars).[73] This Committee may have had some influence on the paths these schools subsequently followed.[74]

The failure of the Conservative campaign to halt comprehensivization in 1976 did not deter the CEs from their mission to open the education debate to wider public scrutiny. In November 1976 Stevas made preparations for a major public campaign to promote standards in education. He believed in increasing parental choice and influence throughout the education system, and was ready to commit the next Tory government to translating this aim into reality. Labour's position here was more restrictive. Shirley Williams believed in giving maximum choice to parents in education ('voice and choice') but within the maintained system and not on the basis of academic selection. Comprehensivization was, she believed, compatible with a good deal of parental choice.[75] She favoured (and promoted) education maintenance allowances and the experiment to provide nursery centres for the under-5s.[76] It was against this background that CCO announced, somewhat guardedly, the Stevas initiative:

> Mr Norman St John-Stevas, Opposition Spokesman on Education, Science and the Arts, will be discussing standards in education and the implications of the new Education Act at a conference of Conservative education leaders at CCO tomorrow, Friday 26 November. The conference is not open to the Press but Mr St John-Stevas will be available to meet correspondents at 2 Abbey Gardens.[77]

On 27 January 1977 Stevas formally launched 'Standards '77' (the Conservatives' campaign to raise the standard of education in schools) at a press conference also held at CCO.[78] A number of prominent figures in education had agreed to participate in the campaign throughout England and Wales, including Professor Ralph Dahrendorf (Director of the London School of Economics), Lord Vaizey (Brunel University) and Tom Howarth (Senior Tutor, Magdalene College, Cambridge). The latter's inclusion gave some guarantee that a preservationist-line would be maintained.

'Standards '77' may well have drawn inspiration from an essay by the preservationist Vernon Bogdanor (an NCES member and prominent Conservative Oxford City councillor) (see Bogdanor, 1976). Bogdanor had urged the Conservative Party to be less defensive and apologetic about education and to take up three themes as the foundation of Conservative education policy: (i) the maximum degree of local initiative in decision-making compatible with the maintenance of national standards and the rights of parents; (ii) the creation of a new consensus in secondary education; (iii) and the adoption of a programme of recurrent education. These themes paralleled Stevas' education philosophy and belief in a 'socially responsible capitalism'. They also implied a decentralized society restoring choice and opportunity, yet preserving quality.

Significantly, on the day before the launch of 'Standards '77' Stevas had made a statement on educational responsibilities within the Conservative Parliamentary Party[79] in which he announced that during 1977 the Party intended to continue the education team work begun in 1975: Boyson, as Deputy Opposition Spokesman, was to act as spokesman on the schools (as CNACE Honorary Secretary, he was to represent the views of the PEC to the National Union and vice versa); Dr Keith Hampson, Vice-Chairman of the PEC. was to deal with higher education and act as liaison officer between the PEC and Conservative local government leaders; and William Shelton (PEC) was to be concerned with standards in education and the development and implementation of the 'Parents' Charter'.

'Standards '77' was, in fact, the second stage of the Party's campaign to raise standards throughout the education system. The first stage (on parental rights and influence) had been sponsored by the Conservative PEC in 1976. The formation of 'Standards '77' was the result of work carried out by the PEC which had received assistance from local government leaders, the CNACE, the Women's National Advisory Committee, the CPC, the FCS, the YCs, the Bow Group, and by many individuals concerned with education (not all of whom were members of the Conservative Party).[80] Amongst the events planned for the campaign were a series of lectures on the purpose of education. Stevas considered that the ends of education had been neglected in the interests of discussing the means. In May 1977 the Party held four lectures at Westminster before an invited audience. The lectures were given by Professor Dahrendorf, Lord Vaizey, John Izbicki and Tom Howarth. The topics discussed were 'Values in Education', 'The Possible Need for a New Education Act',

'Resources for Education' and 'The Role of the Educational Press'. Stevas also called a series of regional conferences to be addressed by members of the Party's education team for the exchange of views with representatives of local government, teachers, parents and all those concerned with education. These conferences were held in Manchester, Newcastle, Southampton and Canterbury. In connection with these, local educational groups were formed to act as cells concerned with problems of standards and ways of raising them.

As part of 'Standards '77' Stevas also undertook a programme of visits to local government centres to meet Conservative councillors concerned with education. Stevas consulted with the Kent, Oxford and Surrey councils and those in the West Country. At Oxford he consulted Vernon Bogdanor (Vice-Chairman Oxfordshire Education Committee) who, very shortly after, outlined for the Party a strategy for achieving preservationist educational policies (Bogdanor, 1977).[81] Stevas also called a conference on education and industry and a non-party conference (in June 1977) on the role and future of religious education in the county schools, and planned to publish a study on comprehensive schools and how they might be improved. (Stevas, 1977).

Stevas envisaged that this campaign and programme would in no way be dependent on that initiative announced by James Callaghan and Shirley Williams following the former's Ruskin College speech. He asserted:

> We intend to continue to use to the full the freedom conferred by Opposition to develop our ideas on education, and the more these ideas are implemented by the government such as those we have put forward on parental governors, the support for exams, the Schools Council etc, the better we shall be pleased.[82]

That the Conservatives' 'Standards '77' campaign should initially have so closely paralleled Labour's 'Great Debate' is less surprising than the fact that both were avowedly dissimilar in their objective. Whereas 'Standards '77' sought a new consensus on secondary education, the 'Great Debate' made gestures towards the idea of a *core curriculum* (to be developed by the DES), which was just the kind of holistic thinking which Conservatives were being asked to oppose (Bogdanor, 1977, pp. 20–1). Whether Labour's programme for an education debate was ill-planned and cursory in execution (thus allowing the Conservatives to force the terms and context of the public discussion on schooling) still remains a largely unanswered question.[83] However, in his memoirs James Callaghan (1987) has recalled how he was considered by some to have been an 'amateur educationalist', and how it was he who suggested Shirley Williams should hold a series of regional conferences which, because 'the DES was pulling at her coat tails', were not concluded before spring 1977 (pp. 410–11).

If, indeed, Labour's 'Great Debate' was hurriedly organized then one can equally charge the Conservatives' 'Standards '77' campaign with being inconsistent. For example, just when Stevas was welcoming Labour's moderation and seeming conversion to standards and quality in education, Boyson was doing the exact opposite. Speaking to the Midland Area Federation of Conservative Students' Dinner in Nottingham on 12 February 1977 he said:

> The Labour Party's apparent change of front is simply a political tactic without conviction. While Mrs Williams pays lip service to excellence, the measurement of standards and the need for preparation for science and industry, she has agreed for reasons of party doctrine to the closure of two of the most successful schools in London which have opened doors of opportunity to hundreds of working class children — Marylebone Grammar and Mary Datchelor.[84]

The Nottingham address, symbolic of the growing friction between Boyson and Stevas over the direction of Conservative education policy, was important for another reason. According to John Ranelagh, Boyson was now engaged in a campaign amongst backbenchers to popularize his particular ideas inside the Party.[85] Madel has suggested that Boyson's campaign was conducted through the centre-right 92 Group of Conservative MPs.[86] Whatever Boyson's tactic may have been the Boyson-Stevas relationship during 'Standards '77' was not a happy one (see Stevas, 1984, pp. 17–18).

However, 'Standards '77' did allow the Conservatives to capitalize on, what they saw as, Labour's shallow education policy. As one education correspondent who was closely involved in the reporting of the events at the William Tyndale Junior School put it to the author:

> Between 1975–78 the CEs perceived and exploited the intellectual bankruptcy of Labour's education policy on comprehensivization. Labour could not deliver. All Labour offered was a watered-down grammar school education in comprehensive schools that was just not possible for Labour to implement.[87]

During the 'Standards '77' campaign a new CRD education desk officer was appointed. In April 1977 Ranelagh left the education desk for a position in the CRD Foreign Affairs Section and was replaced by Biddy Passmore (CRD Education Desk Officer, April 1977–May 1979). Passmore, though anti-voucher, favoured the consumerist approach to education and took charge of further advancing the *standards and choice* debate within the thinking of the Party's education team.[88] Her contribution was to take up the reins dropped by Ranelagh on his departure and provide information and material in support of the Tory drive on standards and freedom in education.[89]

Stuart Sexton now continued to pen some of Stevas' speeches to Conservative audiences,[90] whilst Passmore was engaged upon the Conservative conferences on education, compiling briefing notes and summarizing the intensive three-month programme of lectures and meetings previously initiated by Stevas in the early spring.[91]. It was at the Ely Conference (12 May 1977) that Stevas outlined the purpose of schools and Conservative policy on schools. And it was here that the essence of the preservationists' platform — the retention of selection — was asserted by Stevas, with his call for variety and flexibility in the education system. Passmore extracted from his speech the following:

> Variety and flexibility implies different kinds of school and a continuing process of assessment which will sometimes lead to selection for schools and sometimes to selection inside schools. You cannot teach all children in the same way and in the same kind of school.[92]

Also highlighted by Passmore was Stevas' prioritization of what should be taught in schools. What should be taught fell into two parts: development of the mind, and training for the outside world. In addition to basic skills, children needed good career guidance and the laying of a solid moral foundation. At the Ely Conference Stevas had claimed that religious education in schools had, in many cases, been transformed into a 'secular travesty' and that this decline had to be halted.[93]

Passmore noted that the Ely Conference had struck a 'new mood of optimism, confidence and even a certain pugnacity on the part of Conservative spokesmen and supporters'.[94] Boyson's role in creating this 'new mood of optimism' was now burgeoning on several fronts. His reaction to his appointment by Mrs Thatcher as the second string education spokesman had been characteristically succinct. He had declared that Party office was not his aim and that he would be happy so long as things went 'the right way'.[95] As well as wanting nationally enforced standards at 7, 11 and 14, he also wished to see the publication of each school's examination results, a stronger HMI, complete parental choice, limited government and the cutting back of the whole education bureaucracy. Why Mrs Thatcher had opted for the right leg of the Boyson/Hampson partnership that had provided such strength in the long campaign against Labour's 1976 Education Bill is unclear. What seems more certain is that Party supporters were gaining confidence from Boyson's public addresses, his media exposure and his speeches to the Conservative Educational Conferences.

Boyson's conception of *equal opportunities for all* (i.e. opportunities to be different) meant that the task of the Conservative Party was not to offer abject, unconditional surrender to Labour dogmatists, but to ensure (on behalf of the nation's children) that the continued debate on the comprehensive and post-comprehensive system was based on properly established facts, variety and local option (Boyson, 1977). Herein lay the seeds of the coming confrontation with Stevas (in 1978) over the publication of school examination results league tables.

In his speech to the Conservative educational conference at Portsmouth on 1 July 1977 Boyson told his audience:

> At the Labour conferences you could discuss any topic, provided it was allowed by Labour Party dogma. The discussion of the educational voucher

was ruled out of order because it was against Labour dogma, people could not query the comprehensive non-selective school and parental choice was suspect since free people are a threat to socialism.[96]

Boyson's reference to the voucher was no mere sop to please the Party faithful. At the end of May 1977 he and Professor Brian Cox had each received from Marjorie Seldon a draft copy of FEVER's 'Voucher Book' (edited by Arthur Seldon) which contained a blueprint for councils wishing to undertake a voucher experiment. Marjorie Seldon hoped the NCES would publish it in time for the Party Conference in early October and that FEVER would promote it at its London Convention on parental involvement on 29 October 1977.[97] Cox was informed:

We have tried to make it a good read for people of modest intellect and yet sufficiently lively and informative so that it doesn't bore the 120 + IQ readers.[98]

According to one co-founder of the FEVER, Boyson was (in 1977) the 'driving force behind the Seldon lobby for the voucher'.[99] Everything FEVER published was vetted by Boyson.[100] Thus, midway through the 'Standards '77' campaign Boyson's unofficial activities (which were probably unknown to Stevas) were being increasingly devoted to promoting a market-solution to the education crisis. Where Stevas and Boyson were agreed, was on the principle that schools should have to defend and explain their policies to parents, and publish a prospectus for parents every year.[101]

The final stage of 'Standards '77' (August–December 1977) saw Stevas making a series of major statements: on Labour's July 1977 circular curtailing LEAs offering free places or partial assistance with the fees for children whose ability indicated suitability for a highly academic independent school; on Labour's consultative document on *Education in Schools*; on the Taylor Report; on restoring direct grant schools; on the restoration of quality and excellence in schools; on political education in schools; on *Better Schools For All*; and on discipline and moral standards in schools.

Of these, Stevas' address to the 1977 Conservative Party Conference on the restoration of quality and excellence in schools and his statement on political education, afford the clearest accounts not only of the direction of Conservative education policy, but also of the influence of the preservationists over that policy.

We saw in chapter 5 how it was at the 1975 Party Conference that Stevas had first declared that the foundation on which Conservative education policy was to be based was the restoration of quality and excellence in schools. At the 1977 conference — where the education debate centred around a motion on 'Standards' — Stevas told delegates that the Party (because of its persistent and indefatigable advocacy of its policy of standards) had changed the education debate in Britain in the Conservatives' favour, moving it on to Tory ground.[102] Stevas' Parliamentary team, who had supported the Party in this battle, included Drs Boyson and Hampson, Nigel

Foreman, Nicholas Winterton and Sir George Sinclair. Stevas referred to his team as an 'ecumenical group' (*ibid.*).

At the Blackpool conference Stevas announced high schooling standards were now the Party's lodestar. The Party would direct the major part of its effort to improving the comprehensive schools and to ensuring that these schools raised their performance. Henceforth, Stevas' Parliamentary team would be rallied around the call 'to put what is wrong, right' (*ibid.*). Stevas prioritized the sphere of moral and religious education as the one sphere in which high standards were more important than anywhere else, and announced the Party's education committees had decided to devote the whole of 1978 to the campaign to promote religious and moral values in schools (see below). Stevas emphasized the Conservative Party did not claim an exclusive mandate here but felt it fitting that for a Party with a history and tradition such as its own, it should take the lead where others were either hostile or indifferent.

The planned campaign for 1978 may well have been influenced by the deliberations of the Conservative Philosophy Group (CPG).[103] The group was, according to one member, anti-permissive.[104] One of its founders has stated, it had been established at a time when the Conservative Party appeared to be 'floundering around' and was concerned to revive and renew Christian morality in Conservative Party thinking.[105] In 1977 Mrs Thatcher, Rhodes Boyson, Peter Utley, Ronald Butt, Enoch Powell, Robert Blake and Julian Amery were all CPG participants.

Though Stevas pledged Conservatives would strive for nothing less than educational excellence for all, he felt the issue of political education in schools to be a major problem which might hinder this overriding objective of Tory education policy.[106] Stevas suggested the Party faced a double danger: either the issue would atrophy and die, leaving the nation faced by a generation of political illiterates, or it would be exploited by those who wished to misuse it for their own totalitarian ends.[107] The way out of this dilemma would be to build up a consensus among the democratic political parties on the approach to the problem. Labour's Green Paper *Education in Schools* had asserted the importance of a greater awareness within schools of the role of the individual participating in a democracy but it had not put forward a scheme for achieving this objective.

Stevas proposed a programme for political education in schools which Sir Keith Joseph would later implement (see chapter 9). Thus, there should be:

> A simple explanation of the problems of social organization, of the alternatives of dictatorship, anarchy or democracy, of the British choice of parliamentary democracy and how it works ... a basic explanation of the relationship between our political system and our economic system — the belief in a mixed economy as a means of combining help for the weak with the safeguarding of freedom. (*ibid.*)

Stuart Sexton's Black Paperite rhetoric was saved for Stevas' view:

> If we allow some of the more lunatic educational and sociological fashions of the past decade to spread unchallenged through our education system, we are storing up for ourselves a violent future. Energy, impatience and half-baked theories are the inspiration of the Baaders and the Meinhofs of the West. (*ibid.*)

Between October and December 1977, the CRD education desk and Sexton continued to supply the kind of education policy agenda which right-wing conservatives had been promulgating since 1970. Despite all this activity, and canvassing for standards and parental choice of school, Stevas' Parliamentary team was, at the end of the year, still awaiting a positive response to its calls from the Labour government. It was Labour's failure to give the Conservative opposition notice it intended to legislate on parental choice of schools which led the Tory Party to increase the momentum of its education campaign.[108]

The 'Values '78' campaign

'Values '78' was the third in a series of campaigns sponsored by the Conservative PEC. The Party regarded this campaign as the most important of the three since it attempted to answer the basic question 'What is education for?'[109] The Party now saw the purpose of education to be:

> to enable all children to develop their talents to the full for their own good and that of society, and to enable them to share and participate in the nation's heritage of cultural and moral values. (*ibid.*)

This development in Conservative educational philosophy was, I have suggested, influenced by the concerns of the CPG. It may also have been influenced by the aims of the Salisbury Group (SG).[110] This group believed that while governments had mainly concentrated on economic problems, such matters as foreign affairs, defence, the constitution, the environment, law and order and education, had been neglected in debates about the meaning of modern conservatism.[111] It believed that important as economic policy was, unless it was seen as part of a general system of ideas (moral as well as intellectual) Conservative policies would seem merely a series of temporary expedients.[112] The difficulties Conservative governments had faced in dealing with such issues as law and order and education, had arisen at least in part from the absence of a firm theoretical basis for their policies.[113]

Discussion on religious, moral and civic values in schools (about which the Conservative Party believed so many parents to be anxious) had, surprisingly, been largley omitted from the government debates on education in 1977. They were all matters of principal concern to Stevas, Boyson, the CPG and SG. Stevas summed up the concern when he announced that effective action was required in the three related spheres if extremist ideologies, of left or right, were to be defeated in the schools.[114]

Though the SG had no formal connection with the Conservative Party it did have a link in Patrick Cosgrave (Special Adviser to Mrs Thatcher, 1975–1979). Cosgrave had attended the inaugural meeting of the SG held at the St. Stephens Tavern, Queen Anne's Gate, Westminster, in 1976.[115] Thus, there is every reason to suspect that Mrs Thatcher was (in 1978) conversant with the activities of the SG, whose members included Dr Roger Scruton,[116] Peter Utley, Professors Norman Gash, Michael Oakeshott and Elie Kedourie, Dr Barry Bracewell-Milnes and Peregrine Worsthorne.

'Values '78' involved a series of regional conferences and a further series of Conservative education lectures at the House of Commons (given by Mary Warnock, Roy Shaw, Stevas and Harry Judge). The CPC, through its branches in over 500 constituencies, conducted a two-way exchange of views on the subject of the purpose and problems of religious and moral education, in order for the Party to obtain a clear picture of the situation at the grass roots. The Party hoped (through 'Values '78') to articulate and crystallize the national mood on a vital topic.[117]

During February 1978 the essence of the Party's new conservative philosophy of education — the opening up of the career to talent achieved by the setting of both basic and high intellectual standards within a disciplined learning environment — was propagated by both the CRD and CCO. A paper by John Ranelagh[118] argued that British schools were failing to guarantee minimum standards in the 3Rs and that a broad curriculum for all pupils up to a high standard was required to stretch pupils of all levels. The paper's publication preceded a speech by Stevas[119] in which he also called for schools to provide for every pupil to develop its talents to the full.

The new conservative philosophy of education was now increasingly focused on the coupling of *Education* and *Industry*. Significantly, the general topic of 'Education and Industry' was the theme of a National Education Conference convened by Stevas on 29 June 1978 at the Post House Hotel, Leicester. To this conference Stevas invited Professor Brian Cox and told him:

> The purpose of the Conference will be to enable those people who are interested to put their views forward so that they may be properly considered when we are formulating detailed proposals to develop our Education Policy.[120]

The contribution of the preservationists to the development of the new conservative philosophy of education had already been considerable and there was every sign in 1978 of their continuing influence. For example, against the background of the opening up of the career to talent, Boyson's brief had been to speak on falling standards of literacy. He had done so and had expressed his increasing desire to see the comparison and publication of school examination results. He had observed that the Labour Party feared any comparison of results achieved over an age-group, between the remaining areas of the country that had selective schools and the comprehensive areas.[121] Boyson's speeches (written by the Roman Catholic Stuart Sexton) had become infected with Christian piety. Thus:

> To destroy the remaining good grammar schools of this country at a time when educational standards are still falling, is as vandalistic as the destruction of stained glass and sculptured treasures at the time of the Reformation. Both are almost irreplaceable (*ibid.*).

Boyson's other preoccupation had been to continue his populist broadsides against teacher incompetency.[122] Boyson now headed a CRD policy group on teacher training but there were signs that his preservationist rhetoric was becoming more extreme. Whilst his official role as an Opposition Spokesman on education was supposedly to assist Stevas in the promotion of Conservative education policy, his unofficial participation in promulgating the traditionalist line of the NCES was beginning to give the impression of a growing impatience with the pace of Conservative educational reform. Not only had Boyson derided the supposed difficulties of settling on a common core curriculum but he had also advocated[123] a school-leaving examination between 15 and 16 (a Certificate of Adult Competency), based on a syllabus drawn up by teachers. Clearly, in these unofficial addresses Boyson was at some variance with Stevas.

Ironically, just when Boyson had been supporting the work of the NCES, the CRD had published a supplement to the 1977 Campaign Guide[124] in which Biddy Passmore castigated the Labour government for failing to offer proposals to increase parental influence, freedom and choice in schools, for rejecting national tests of literacy and numeracy, and for failing to make proposals to strengthen HMI (p. 113).

Boyson's most significant speech in the 'Values '78' campaign was made to the Conservative North-West Advisory Committee on Education (where Professor Brian Cox sat as a member). On 8 April 1978 Boyson had told Party members that Conservatives believed in a society where all could have choice of school for their children according to their ideas of discipline and subject choice.[125] This was an important restatement of radical-right Tory education policy since one area upon which Stevas and Boyson were agreed was the need for improvement in teaching methods and teacher quality in schools.

Underlying Boyson's whole approach to schooling was his particular conception of *equal opportunities for all*. This, in fact, was not dissimilar to Rab Butler's formulation. As Jefferys has shown (1984, p. 311)[126], it had been Butler's desire that secondary schools should provide 'equivalent opportunities to be different'. Similarly Howard (1987, ch. 10) has indicated that whilst Butler's declared objective in formulating the 1944 Act was 'secondary education for all', he intended that his reconstruction of the national system of education would allow for some differentiation. Thus, Boyson was not, at least in his basic educational philosophy, shifting from that Tory belief in inequality as prescribed by the man most responsible for recreating the Conservative Party after 1945.

In April 1978 there were clear signs that the Party's absorption of *Black Paper* thinking had not waned viz.: 'the age of the pupil as guinea-pig must come to an end'.[127] And again:

> the very schools where a sound academic education based on traditional teaching methods had always flourished are being butchered around us . . . we will repeal the main provisions of the 1976 Education Act to stop this slaughter of academic excellence. (*ibid.*)

Henceforth, no Conservative Secretary of State would be empowered to approve re-organization schemes that did away with schools of proven worth. Conservatives and, no doubt many parents, considered schools of proven worth could be judged by their examination performance. However, it is surprising that Stevas and Boyson should have publicly split on an issue less fundamental to Party education policy than some other issues (such as those embraced by the 'Values '78' campaign). Nevertheless, this first major difference of opinion was a precursor of other splits in the preservationist ranks after 1978 (see chapters 7–9).

During the summer and autumn of 1978 the 'Values '78' campaign was be-devilled by the Stevas-Boyson furore over the publication of school examination results league tables. At an NCES conference in London on 17 September 1978 Boyson released the results for Manchester's Schools, angering both Manchester heads and Stevas.[128] According to Boyson the main purpose of the exercise had been:

> . . . to demonstrate conclusively that the government's determination to force reorganization on Tameside and Trafford is precisely tantamount to ordering a forcible lowering of their present rate of educational successes.[129]

Boyson's campaign to highlight the structural disadvantages and academic deficiencies of city comprehensives, may have been prompted by the dangers observed in HMI reports: that in some schools able children were not stretched sufficiently intel-lectually, while the least-able were underachieving and lacking interest.

A split on education policy within the Conservative Party became evident when Stevas publicly rejected any idea of publishing league tables of exam results (see Berliner, 1978). His speech (to constituents at Chelmsford on 22 September 1978) made no reference to Boyson and, though Stevas expected that individual schools would publish exam results, he asserted 'league-tables' were not official Conservative policy. The disagreement within the Party widened the following day when the Monday Club publicly opposed Stevas' view that exam results should be seen in their social context. It felt such a view would lead to a form of social engineering and undeserved egalitarianism which the Party ought to deplore rather than justify.

Boyson was now receiving letters of support from those Conservatives who, like him, wished to reveal the academic decline which, in their view, had followed in the wake of politically-manufactured comprehensive education. One such Conservative wrote advising Boyson to examine the case of Sheffield:

> Sheffield is interesting because it has gone further than most in applying the 1944 principle of tripartism: with a good clutch of grammar schools, technical schools (and secondary mods which would put most modern comprehensives to shame) there was no competition from a direct grant school (unlike Manchester). So a comparison of Sheffield before and after the mid-sixties comprehensive revolution *is* comparing like with like, and gets round all that smokescreen of nonsense being used to rebutt your recent criticisms of the Manchester position.[130]

Despite disagreement over the manner of the publication of school exam results, the Party's enthusiasm for *excellence in education* had not diminished. At the 1978 Party Conference Professor Max Beloff spoke on 'High Standards of Excellence for All'.[131] Stevas welcomed Beloff's speech. His public endorsement of one of the leading preservationists and Black Paperites foreshadowed Beloff's future role in the making of Conservative education policy as a Conservative Peer (from 1981).[132]

At the 1978 Conference the themes of the 'Values '78' campaign were not overlooked. Excellence in education rested upon discipline in the schools.[133] Stevas saw discipline as a means, not an end, and he based his view on Lord Acton's conception of Freedom, which was not the power of doing what one liked but the right of being able to do what one ought. Democracy (a free society) was, above all, a moral and spiritual enterprise, and the importance of schools in transmitting and so preserving that inheritance could not be over-estimated. This was why Stevas was determined to keep religious teaching in schools.

In October 1978 Stevas announced his opposition to the government's plans to move towards a single examination system at 16 + [134]. Pressure for a common examination had been initiated by the Socialist Educational Association and, said Stevas, as Conservatives dedicated in the schools to the pursuit of excellence, the Party believed that a first priority had to be the retention of objective and externally assessed examinations. In chapters 8 and 9 we shall see how Sir Keith Joseph shifted the Party's attitude on a common 16 + examination and, in so doing, angered the preservationist wing. But, in 1978, the Party still wanted evolutionary reform, not the radical revolution proposed by Labour.

Parallel to the Party's concern over school examination reform, grass-root Conservative opinions were being sought on the vexed question of the capacity of the comprehensive school system to meet the needs of able children. Members of the N.W. Area Advisory Committee on Education were informed:

> We have been asked to prepare a report on *The Future of the Brighter Child in the Comprehensive System*. I have, therefore, arranged a meeting on 31

October 1978 at Cheadle and Gatley Conservative Club, and have been fortunate in obtaining the services of Professor Brian Cox as our guest speaker. A report of our meeting will be presented to the Central Advisory Committee. This is a genuine opportunity to make a positive contribution to the policy of our Party.[135]

As in the case of Professor Beloff, Professor Cox's appearance on an official Party platform in 1978 foreshadowed his imminent invitation to play a central role in Conservative education policy-making.[136]

In November 1978 Stevas was promoted from Shadow Education Secretary to Shadow Leader of the House. The decision by Mrs Thatcher to appoint Mark Carlisle (and not Boyson) as Stevas' successor was a surprise Tory choice, bearing in mind Carlisle's lack of knowledge concerning education. But Boyson had become perhaps too outspoken, and his NCES activities and other unofficial speeches had clearly embarrassed the Party on the sensitive issues of vouchers and the publication of school exam results. The split between the national and local levels of the Party over parental choice of schools (some Conservatives believed the national spokesmen had put forward a policy which was impossible to deliver) had caused Mrs Thatcher to act. Although it was believed that Stevas had counselled Mrs Thatcher against appointing Boyson as his successor, Stevas denied this was the case. In a letter to the editor of the *Times Educational Supplement* (1978) he wrote:

> Contrary to some statements in the press the appointment of Mr Mark Carlisle was made entirely on the initiative of Mrs Margaret Thatcher and while she naturally consulted me about it, the choice was her own. I happen to believe it was an excellent one and he has already made it clear that he is going to continue the Conservative education tradition which has been established since the time of R. A. Butler.

In the next chapter we shall see how far the preservationists' vision for Tory education policy was met by Mark Carlisle and his deputy, Lady Young, and to what extent Stevas' hopes for a continuation of the Conservative education tradition of Butler were realized.

Notes

1 Reported in the *Times Educational Supplement*, 21 May 1976.
2 Though Stevas was now engaged in working on restatements of Conservative education policy, the exercise was apparently hindered by Boyson's presence. Stevas and Boyson were disparate personalities. As Stevas has reflected: 'We did not work happily together and, looking back, I regret that I did not make greater efforts if not to bridge the gap, then at least to narrow it'. See Stevas (1984), pp. 17–18.
3 It was significant that Dolly Walker, the disaffected William Tyndale teacher, was recruited as a contributor to *Black Paper 1977*. See her essay 'William Tyndale', pp. 38–41.

4 Letter from Cox to Boyson, 18 November 1976, *The Cox Papers*.

5 John Ranelagh to author, 20 February 1986.

6 *Ibid*.

7 *Ibid*.

8 *Ibid*.

9 *Ibid*.

10 *Ibid*.

11 Letter from Leon Brittan PC, QC, MP to author, 27 February 1986.

12 Leon Brittan MP to author, 1 April 1986.

13 *Ibid*.

14 Leon Brittan MP to author, 1 April 1986. Brittan's role as the Party's Higher Education Liaison Officer was succeeded to by Dr Keith Hampson in 1976.

15 Leon Brittan MP to author, 1 April 1986. For Flew's own preservationist defence of educational standards, see Flew (1976) and (1987).

16 Letter from Professor Flew to the CQS, NDG, *The Cox Papers*. Flew informed the author: 'The New Right is distinguished from the Old Right by the age of its members. Most of its members have been converts in later adult life'. Professor Flew to author, 21 November 1985.

17 Stuart Sexton to author, 3 January 1985.

18 *Ibid*.

19 Tame's responsibilities were officially designated as 'research and editorial'. His work at the IEA was, for a time (June 1977–May 1979), paralleled by responsibilities he undertook as a Research Officer for the National Association for Freedon (The Freedom Association). At the NAFF Tame became an associate of fellow member Russell Lewis, who was now an associate of both Dr Boyson and Ralph Harris in the Mont Pelerin Society.

20 Chris Tame to author, 25 February 1986. In late 1975 Tame had joined the Adam Smith Club (founded in 1973 by Dr Barry Bracewell-Milnes, Peter Clarke and Dr Sudha Shenoy) which met at the same address as the IEA (2 Lord North Street, Westminster) to discuss and exchange libertarian and liberal ideas. Tame's membership of the ASC (where he became Chairman) was made at the personal invitation of Dr Bracewell-Milnes who was employed at the IEA as a Consultant, and who had asked Tame to present a paper to the Club and popularize the group's activities.

21 Chris Tame to author, 25 February 1986.

22 *Ibid*.

23 *Ibid*.

24 Chris Patten MP to author, 19 February 1986.

25 *Ibid*.

26 *Ibid*.

27 See (1983), pp 85–100. In this chapter ('The Ideal of Quality') Patten quotes widely from Maude's *The Common Problem* (1969) and Warnock's *Schools Of Thought* (1977).

28 Chris Patten MP to author, 19 February 1986. See also, Patten (1983), p. 99. Patten had, of course, reasserted the Conservatives' belief in inequality, with the statement that 'Conservatives are not egalitarians. We believe in levelling up, in enhancing opportunities, not in levelling down . . .'

29 Patten (1983), p. 94.

30 *Ibid*.

31 Chris Patten MP to author, 19 February 1986.

32 *Ibid*.

33 *Ibid*.

34 *Ibid*.

35 *Ibid*.

36 Lord Maude to author, 19 February 1986.

37 *Ibid*. Maude recalls that Joseph read his book *The Common Problem* on the first day of its publication. Here it is important to note that the education section of Maude's book contained material also used in his essay 'The egalitarian threat' for the first Black Paper. That essay was, in fact, written originally for *The Common Problem* which was published after *Fight for Education: a Black Paper*.

38 Baroness Cox to author, 5 July 1985.
39 *Ibid.*
40 *Ibid.*
41 *Ibid.* For an account of Professor Brian Cox's experiences as a parent of children attending progressive schools, see Hopkins (1978) pp. 81–2.
42 *The Spectator*, 19 July 1975.
43 Baroness Cox to author, 5 July 1985.
44 *Ibid.*
45 Private Information.
46 Private Information.
47 Private Information.
48 Private Information.
49 Private Information.
50 In the NCES Marks and Cox met Harry Greenway MP, Ralph Harris, Professor Bantock, Ruth Garwood-Scott (FEVER) and Max Beloff. All were committed to observing, investigating and reporting what was happening in education, in order to alert public opinion and to stimulate corrective action when and where necessary. The NCES is an independent body and non-political, aiming to influence all the major Parties by presenting arguments based on careful study of facts and by evaluating educational and cultural trends.
51 Fred Naylor to author, 6 November 1985.
52 *Ibid.*
53 *Ibid.*
54 *Ibid.*
55 *Ibid.*
56 *Ibid.* See also, Fred Naylor, 'Comprehensive mythology', in *Black Paper 1975*.
57 Fred Naylor to author, 6 November 1985.
58 *Ibid.*
59 *Ibid.* See Dewey (1934).
60 Fred Naylor to author, 6 November 1985.
61 *Ibid.*
62 *Ibid.*
63 *Ibid.*
64 *Ibid.* In particular *Source Influences on Educational Attainment*, OECD, 1975.
65 *Ibid.* Husén's thesis was developed in his *The School In Question: A Comparative Study of the School and its Future in Western Societies*, 1979.
66 Fred Naylor to author, 6 November 1985.
67 *Ibid.*
68 *Ibid.* see Dunstan (1978).
69 Fred Naylor to author, 6 November 1985.
70 Front bench spokesman on Education for the Conservative Opposition in the House of Lords (1976–79); Conservative Whip, House of Lords (1974–76).
71 Assistant Master, Loughborough Grammar School (1962–67); Assistant Master, Fairham Comprehensive School for Boys, Nottingham (1967–69); Lecturer, Bishop Lonsdale College of Education (1969–72).
72 Letter from Lord Elton to author, 10 September 1986.
73 *Ibid.* Vigars was the Committee's most active member and a contributor to *Black Paper 1977*. See Vigars, 'How comprehensive?', *Black Paper 1977*, pp. 68–71. In this essay Vigars questioned the capacity of comprehensive schools to offer and staff that range of scientific and technical subjects formerly available at the grammar, the secondary modern and the technical school. Vigars argued that the tide against the large comprehensive was turning and that it was, thus, all the more urgent to encourage the schools to develop specialist interests (the creation of 'technical comprehensive' schools).
74 Letter from Lord Elton to author, 10 September 1986.

75 Shirley Williams to author, 27 September 1985. The requirements on parental appeals and school information, as embodied in the 1980 Education Act, were originally formulated by Mrs Williams.
76 *Ibid.*
77 'Standards in education', CCO Press Release 1170/76, 25 November 1976.
78 'Standards '77', CCO Press Release 51/77, 20 January 1977.
79 'Educational responsibilities within the Conservative Parliamentary Party', CCO Press Release 82/77, 26 January 1977.
80 Statement by Stevas, CCO Press Release 85/77, 27 January 1977.
81 In this essay Bogdanor again argued the case for decentralization in education and warned the Conservative Party not to be tempted to agree with the centrist solutions to the crisis in education offered by James Callaghan and the DES. He suggested that the defence of educational standards could only be achieved by the retention and strengthening of a decentralized system of education which had not failed because it had not been really tried. A greater degree of 'parent power', the right as Rhodes Boyson had put it 'to secure a passport out of the school', would, according to Bogdanor, help ensure that schools responded better to national priorities.
82 Statement by Stevas, 27 January 1977, CCO Press Release 85/77.
83 For one assessment, which is critical of the eight regional conferences organized by Labour in the wake of Ruskin, see CCCS (1981), pp. 219–20.
84 'Labour knock down the educational ladder', speech by Boyson to the Midland Area FCS Dinner, Nottingham, 12 February 1977, CCO Press Release 168/77.
85 John Ranelagh to author, 20 February 1986.
86 David Madel MP to author, 15 April 1986. Madel was elected MP for South Bedfordshire in June 1970. He was Vice-Chairman: Conservative Backbench Employment Committee (1974–81); and Conservative Backbench Education Committee (1981–83); and Chairman, Conservative Backbench Education Committee (1983–85). Member of the Carlton Club. The 92 Group was founded in 1966 by Patrick Wall and Ronald Bell 'to keep the Conservative Party conservative'.
87 Mark Jackson to author, 20 February 1986.
88 Biddy Passmore to author, 5 December 1985.
89 *Ibid.*
90 On 'The Conservative Party as the party of local option and individual effort' (to a CNACE meeting, 18 June 1977); and on 'Mixed-ability teaching and the decline in educational standards' (to Welwyn and Hatfield Conservative Association, 4 July 1977).
91 *Politics Today* No. 12, Briefing Notes, CRD, 25 July 1977.
92 *Ibid.* pp. 223.
93 Stevas' prescription for the content of the secondary school curriculum was given support by Devlin and Warnock (1977) published just after the Labour Government's eight regional 'Great Debate' conferences had been held.
94 *Politics Today* No. 12, p. 223.
95 'Right leg forward', *Times Educational Supplement*, 26 November 1976.
96 Speech by Boyson to the Conservative Educational Conference, Portsmouth, 1 July 1977, CCO Press Release 697/77. In this speech Boyson called for a 'core curriculum' which, he asserted, should grow naturally from the grassroots, rather than a centrally imposed curriculum, which would only be necessary if teachers and LEAs failed to develop their own agreed core. Boyson believed genuine educational progress normally arose from spontaneous evolution and not from government direction.
97 Marjorie Seldon to author, 6 June 1985.
98 Letter from Marjorie Seldon to Professor Cox, 31 May 1977, *The Seldon Papers*.
99 Linda Whetstone to author, 19 August 1985. Linda Whetstone is the daughter of Antony Fisher (founder of the IEA) and first met the Seldons at a Mont Pelerin Conference in Oxford in 1956 and, in the late 1950s, helped at the IEA's original office in Hobart Place, Westminster. She was formally introduced to Marjorie Seldon by Ralph Harris in 1970, when the IEA had moved to 2 Lord North Street, Westminster.
100 *Ibid.*

101 Both requirements had been canvassed as Party policy by Boyson at a meeting of the CNACE at Nottingham on 23 April 1977, and at the Portsmouth Conservative Educational Conference on 1 July 1977.

102 Address by Stevas to the Conservative Party Conference, Blackpool, 11 October, 1977, CCO Press Release.

103 The CPG was founded in 1975 by Dr Roger Scruton, Hugh Fraser, John Casey and Jonathan Aitken and first met at the home of Jonathan Aitken's mother, later moving to Jonathan Aitken's home at 8 Lord North Street, Westminster. Peregrine Worsthorne to author, 4 February 1986.

104 Peregrine Worsthorne to author, 4 February 1986.

105 Dr Roger Scruton to author, 10 January 1986. One of the objectives of the CPG has been the re-moralization of national life, an objective which has been carried forward by the Conservative Family Campaign (formed in April 1986) which has sought the restoration of the traditional patriarchal family. Both the CPG and CFC have viewed permissiveness as the main cause of contemporary social problems and have treated teachers, social workers and other education and welfare workers as responsible, not for Britain's economic decline, but for its moral decline.

106 Stevas to the Conservative Party Conference, Blackpool, 11 October 1977.

107 Stevas to the Birmingham Bow Group at Birmingham, 18 November 1977, CCO Press Release 1194/77.

108 The Queen's Speech opening the Parliamentary session 1977/78 had been widely expected to contain the promise of an Education (Miscellaneous Provisions) Bill incorporating, amongst others, proposals on parental choice of school. Shirley Williams was known to favour amendments to the 1944 Act to give parents new legal safeguards clarifying their rights to send their children to a school of their choice. She had set out her proposals in a confidential consultative document. These included proposals (such as the right of parents to express preference for particular schools and be informed by their LEA of admission arrangements) which Conservatives had been advocating for several years and the Opposition was ready to welcome the Bill. However, there was no mention of such a Bill in the Queen's speech.

109 'Values '78'. Statement by Stevas, 24 January 1978, CCO Press Release 63/78.

110 Formed in 1977 by Diana Spearman, Lord Coleraine (Richard Law) and Robert Hamilton Wills for the purpose of 'promoting discussion of current issues on the basis of the traditional Conservative principles associated with the third Marquis of Salisbury (Leader of the Conservative Party 1881–1902), and exemplified in the thought of those who have developed these principles, and adapted them to modern conditions'. The Group has sought to enlist support from Conservatives in the Universities, professions and serious journalism, in order to foster a climate of opinion favourable to the reception of Conservative ideas. Conservative MPs and other officials of the Tory Party are not allowed membership of the Group. The Group met at the home of Diana Spearman (7 Lord North Street) next door to the CPG's base at 8 Lord North Street.

111 Diana Spearman to author, 5 July 1985. From 1946–61 Diana Spearman worked at the CRD.

112 *Ibid.*

113 *Ibid.*

114 'Values '78'. Statement by Stevas, 24 January 1978.

115 Diana Spearman to author, 5 July 1985. This meeting took the form of a luncheon party given by Lord Coleraine and was also attended by Diana Spearman, Robert Hamilton Wills, Maurice Cowling, Lord Salisbury and Professor Auty. The luncheon party was given as a result of an article written by Spearman ('Tell immigrants what to expect', *Daily Telegraph*, June 1976) which had attracted the interest of Wills, and who had suggested a group be formed to defend English national culture. As Lord Coleraine had invited Lord Salisbury to the luncheon it was decided to call the group the SG in honour of the third Marquis of Salisbury.

116 Editor, *The Salisbury Review* (1982–); member, Executive Committee of SG (1978–).

117 'Values '78'. Statement by Stevas, 24 January 1978.

118 John Ranelagh, *Science, Education and Industry*, Old Queen Street Paper No. 2, CRD, 6 February 1978. Ranelagh's focus upon the wastage of talent amongst the bottom 40 per cent of the secondary

school population may have been the precursor to Sir Keith Joseph's own interest in the 'under-achieving pupil' which he announced at the 1982 North of England Education Conference at Leeds.

119 Speech by Stevas to the YCs' National Conference, Harrogate, 11 February 1978, CCO Press Release 190/78.

120 Letter from Stevas to Professor Cox, NDG, *The Cox Papers*.

121 In a speech to the SE Area YCs' Annual Meeting, 18 March 1978, CCO Press Release 403/78.

122 For example, in his address to a meeting of the NCES in London on 12 March 1978 he had called for competency tests as the prerequisite for teacher promotion. See, 'No jobs and no promotion without tests — Dr Boyson', *Times Educational Supplement*, 17 March 1978. Boyson's advocacy of a more active force of HMIs to provide a critical assessment of what was happening in schools was pursued by Sir Keith Joseph at the DES (1981–86).

123 Speech by Boyson to meeting of the NCES, London, 12 March 1978.

124 *The Campaign Guide Supplement 1978*, CRD, March 1978.

125 Speech by Boyson to the Conservative N.W. Advisory Committee on Education, Withington Conservative Club, 8 April 1978, CCO Press Release 470/78.

126 Jefferys makes the point that Butler had been convinced that the power of the state should be increased after the war, though still used to enhance individual enterprise, and had urged that the Beveridge idea of universal provision in social policy be adopted but never turned into uniformity. Jefferys argues that this points to the paradox of Butler's reform: the 1944 Act, by removing many of the iniquities of the inter-war education service, was presented and accepted as a progressive measure, but it was simultaneously designed to accommodate Conservative Party interests. Jefferys suggests that by reinterpreting these interests in the light of wartime circumstances, Butler foreshadowed the new style of Conservatism which was to emerge after 1945: accepting a more active role for the state and encouraging the creation of a more flexible, meritocratic social order.

127 Speech by Stevas at the Conservative Central Council Meeting, Centre Hotel, Leicester, 7 April 1978, CCO Press Release 489/78.

128 Professor Cox informed the author 'I spoke to Rhodes at the NCES meeting in London on 12 March 1978 and told him to put together a league-table on Manchester's schools exam results. Myself and Raymond Baldwin compared the Manchester and London Areas'. Professor Cox to author, 21 February 1986. In fact the London results were provided by Robert Vigars at Baldwin's request. Raymond Baldwin was an NCES member, a former co-opted Member of Manchester Education Committee (1967–71) and contributor of an essay in *Black Paper 1977* ('The dissolution of the grammar school'). In 1978 Baldwin was Chairman of the Governors of Manchester Grammar School.

129 Letter from Boyson to Councillor K. Eastham, November 1978, *The Cox Papers*. Boyson told Eastham 'It is not our Party's policy to make further radical changes in established schemes of secondary school reorganization, but to seek to improve their results'.

130 Letter from Christopher Meakin to Dr Boyson, 30 September 1978, *The Cox Papers*. Meakins' letter was passed by Dr Boyson to Professor Cox for the attention of the NCES.

131 During 1976 both Joseph and Thatcher had publicly demonstrated their support for excellence in education by their patronage of the University College at Buckingham. Both (with Professor Max Beloff) had been closely involved with the college since its inception. At the official opening of the college in 1976 Mrs Thatcher welcomed its 'pursuit of excellence'.

132 Professor Max Beloff was a member of the Liberal Party until 1971. From 1972 he was an NCES sponsor. In 1982 he was appointed Chairman of the CRD's Quality of Education manifesto policy committee.

133 Speech by Stevas at the 1978 Conservative Party Conference, 13 October 1978, CCO Press Release 1305/78.

134 Stevas in a speech at Canon Park School, Coventry, 26 October 1978, CCO Press Release 1355/78.

135 Circular letter from Ted Radcliffe (Acting Chairman, N.W. Area Advisory Committee on Education, Sub-Committee for Greater Manchester), NDG, *The Cox Papers*.

136 In 1981 Professor Cox would pen for the CPC his *Education: The Next Decade* (CPC No. 511-521-684, December 1981) and, in 1982, he would be invited to join Lord Beloff's Quality of Education policy group.

Chapter 7

The 'Conservative Educationalists' and the social-market economy: The emergence of disunity and resistance, 1979–81

Introduction

Until 1979 the role of the CEs in promoting quality in education and parental choice of school had been largely restricted to populist exhortations concerning the need for diversity in types of schooling and appeals to self-interest where parents, not the state, should have the power to determine a child's education. Demands for educational excellence (as the goal of Conservative education policy) had been pressed since 1975 but as these were made by a party in Opposition they may perhaps be interpreted as more a defence of the citadels of academia rather than a serious contribution to improving the public schooling system.

From its election to office in May 1979 the Conservative Party set about developing and implementing the policies of the *social-market economy* (Holmes, 1985, chapter 2). The *social-market economy* is the hallmark of contemporary Conservatism, implying as it does a particular approach by Conservatives to the financing of public services such as health and education. This approach involves taking steps towards rationalizing the existing nationalized and state sector. In a series of speeches Sir Keith Joseph had, since 1974, spelt out the case for a *social-market economy* (Kavanagh, 1987, p.115) and a central and important tenet of Mrs Thatcher's Conservatism was the emphasis put on the use of markets and free enterprise to produce and distribute goods and services wanted by consumers (Holmes, 1985, p. 40). However, the very notion of the *social-market economy* would be seen by some CEs (notably the preservationists) as posing a threat to their particular view of excellence in education and the centrality of a public, state provided, schooling system. The lines of disunity amongst the CEs, created by the Prime Minister's pursuance of a radical approach to public policy, would centre on the issues of the voucher and the financial restraints on education.

This chapter shows how the CEs responded to the idea of the *social-market economy* and how some CEs offered resistance to its application to Conservative education policy. It is argued that disunity amongst the CEs became more pronounced in the period 1979–1981 and severely jeopardized the implementation of preservationist educational policies.

Bringing Conservative common-sense back to education

Between November 1978 and May 1979 the main Opposition Party spokesmen on education had sought to bring 'Conservative common-sense back to education'.[1] The rhetoric of *common-sense*, bearing in mind the 1978–79 'winter of discontent', was aptly chosen by Stuart Sexton. His formulation of the restoration of Conservative common-sense to education had included an offensive against Labour's Education Bill (which was seen by Conservatives as limiting parental choice of school by enabling LEAs to alter the intake to all their schools every year irrespective of the wishes of parents); a pledge to bring back an assisted places scheme for the ex-direct grant schools and so promote the ladder of talent and social mobility for all pupils (such schools, Sexton maintained, would be 'centres of excellence' to which all could aspire); a commitment that the next Tory government would review the whole relationship between schools, further education and training; opposition to Labour's proposals for a common exam system at 16 + ; a promise to introduce a Bill embodying the Party's 'Parents' Charter'; the promotion of *selection by ability* and the discouragement of mixed-ability teaching; and a challenge to Labour's manifesto for its failure to consider the issues of educational standards and discipline.

Sexton's role as Education Adviser to Mark Carlisle had brought him into close contact with Professor Brian Cox. As the Runcorn MP, Carlisle had encouraged Sexton to join the regional CNACE — the NW Area Committee[2] — the group to which Professor Cox was already affiliated. However, unlike Sexton and Boyson, Professor Cox was not an advocate of the social-market.[3] Although as editor of the Black Papers he had given some support to the idea of education vouchers, he did not see the voucher principle as the best vehicle for achieving excellence in education.[4] Believing as he did that creativity came from discipline, he instead favoured *selection* as the best promoter and measure of individual excellence.[5] Mark Carlisle, too, was unhappy about vouchers[6] and in this respect he was following the line taken by Stevas. Carlisle's predecessor, speaking on the publication of the Kent Council's Feasibility Study on Vouchers, had endorsed the report's conclusion that vouchers would not necessarily be the only or the most satisfactory means of achieving parental choice of school.[7]

Carlisle has suggested[8] that most of the educational ideas of the Conservative Party between 1979 and 1981 were devised in Stevas' period as Education Opposition Spokesman; but his own speeches (albeit written by Sexton) give evidence of the pervasive influence of Sir Gilbert Longden. For example, in an election address he said:

> Only a Party dedicated to excellence in every sphere can stop the decline to
> mediocrity. Only a Party which fights for freedom and diversity can halt the
> movement towards compulsion and uniformity. Only by teaching different
> abilities separately can each child reach the top of his personal tree.[9]

Carlisle's resurrection of One Nation philosophy, part of which was a belief in
maximizing the performance of all children (the pursuit of excellence), was not
unexpected given Chris Patten's continuing incumbency as Director of the CRD.
Indeed, in April 1979, raising education standards was the central feature of Conservative education policy.[10] However, it did put Carlisle in some disagreement with the
economic evangelicals, particularly Sir Keith Joseph, who had achieved ascendancy in
the Tory Party in the late 1970s.[11] For example, in recollecting his term at the DES,
Carlisle has said:[12]

> The main issue, as I saw it, was the financial restraints on education. I was a
> liberal on the right of the Party. Keith Joseph was one of the opponents of
> further educational expenditure.

Holmes has suggested (1985, p. 32) that soon after the Conservatives' General
Election victory of 3 May 1979, departmental ministers were resisting cuts relating to
their departments, and that Carlisle privately warned his colleagues that educational
standards would be badly affected if cuts as high as 7 per cent were implemented. It is
probably a measure of the politician's dexterity in handling his brief when in office that
in his public statements Carlisle gave no indication of his misgivings about the implications for education of Mrs Thatcher's economic experiment.[13] The view that public
expenditure must be controlled and inflation eliminated meant education would, like
other public services, have to take its share of the planned capital reductions.

The location of the key personnel overseeing Conservative education policy

The election of a new Conservative government in May 1979 had necessitated a
number of ministerial appointments and changes in Party organization personnel to see
through the pledges contained in the Party's manifesto — a manifesto which had
promoted the virtues of free enterprise and a philosophy of freedom.[14] Riddell (1983)
has argued that for all her promises to form a Cabinet of like-minded people, Mrs
Thatcher's choices in May 1979 were cautious and traditional (p.42). It was a Cabinet
with a mixture of the old paternalist wing (Carrington, Soames, Whitelaw, Pym,
Gilmour and Carlisle) plus the economic Thatcherites (Howe, Joseph, Nott and
Howell) (*ibid.*). We saw in the previous section how this mix presented Carlisle with

difficulties over the financing of education. His position may well have been restricted by another feature of Mrs Thatcher's first administration. According to Wapshott and Brock (1983) after Mrs Thatcher became Prime Minister there was little Cabinet discussion of general educational policy (p. 104). This would suggest either that the Prime Minister was happy to leave her ministers (Mark Carlisle and Lady Young) in charge of implementing agreed education policy or that she no longer felt education to be of sufficient significance to her overall government strategy to warrant Cabinet debate.

The main change in Party organization personnel that was to influence the further shaping and delivery of Conservative education policy between 1979 and 1981 was the appointment of Alan Howarth[15] as the new Director of the CRD. The son of the preservationist Tom Howarth, he succeeded Chris Patten, following the latter's election as MP for Bath.[16] His appointment by Mrs Thatcher was made with the agreement of Lord Thorneycroft, the Conservative Party Chairman to whom he had been Private Secretary.[17] Howarth's arrival at the CRD and the appointment of Christine Chapman[18] as the new Education Desk Officer were particularly significant. Both were committed to a more vigorous statement of the educational radical right's case for excellence in education.[19] Howarth believed that the views of the 'right' on education had not on the whole prevailed on the process of Party policy formation, in which the CRD had played its part before 1979.[20]

New ministers and the interruption of the market right's plan for education

Stephenson (1980) has suggested that the appointment of Mark Carlisle as Education Secretary was a clear indication of Mrs Thatcher's unwillingness to make radical experiments and that Carlisle worked quietly to dilute the impact of the Radical Right on the Party's education policy, which his predecessor Stevas had encouraged (pp. 14–15). That Carlisle was distinctly out of sympathy with the views of right-wing Conservatives on education is confirmed by the former Secretary of State's recollection of the events concerning Dr Boyson's position at the DES:

> It was my preference to put Lady Young in charge of schools and not Boyson. I thought Boyson was too over-zealous on schools. When I took over in 1979 the education system was still in a fair amount of disarray and I did not want Boyson to upset the teachers. I wanted a conciliatory rather than provocative approach.[21]

Lady Young's appointment as Minister of State in the DES gave her responsibility for all matters relating to schools and teacher employment.[22] Dr Boyson was given charge of higher education. His promotion meant he had to relinquish the Chairmanship of the NCES to Professor Cox.[23] The marginalization of Dr Boyson had begun.

The liberal right domination of the DES by Carlisle and Lady Young was paralleled by a centre left hold on the PEC by William van Straubenzee (Chairman, 1979–82) and CNACE by Demitri Argyropulo (Chairman, 1979–82). Between 1976 and 1979 Argyropulo had served as a Parliamentary Research Assistant to Straubenzee. Like Straubenzee and Carlisle he was both anti-voucher and paternalist in his approach to education.[24] Argyropulo had joined the CNACE in 1974 and was elected Chairman in April 1979. His determined and calculated strategy was to defeat the advocates of the market-economy approach to schooling: on the CNACE the market-right was kept at a distance whilst the paternalists, mostly the Tories from the shire counties, ruled. It should be remembered, however, that the CNACE had limited power in Party policy-making: it constitutional position was, as its title indicates, advisory only.[25]

The CNACE now comprised eighty-nine members. The paternalists included Straubenzee, Harry Greenway (the newly-elected MP for Ealing), Les Lawrence (CNACE Vice-Chairman), Philip Merridale (Wessex Area) (the Conservatives' LEA Leader) and Maurice Venn (Greater London Area), whilst the market right was represented in John Barnes, Angela Rumbold[26] and Peter Bruinvels.

Evidence of Argyropulo's disdain for the ideas of the education market right can be found in his Young Conservatives Policy Statement *Comprehensives and the Conservative Party* (1976).[27] In this report he argued:

> Some Conservatives do not like the comprehensive idea at all, and would like to see the Party oppose it in principle. However, whether they like it or not, comprehensives are here to stay. It is therefore essential that comprehensives should work...The way in which the vast majority of the nation's young are educated is far more important than the minority interests with which the Party is already far too closely identified. A constructive Conservative policy towards comprehensives must include the rejection of any Party commitment to a voucher system and support for a common examination system at 16 + .

Such a position meant that Argyropulo was a natural ally for Mark Carlisle.[28] His power base in the CNACE seems to have been unaffected by a move within the Party to obstruct his plan to expand the Committee's activities. It appears that CCO (because of a shortage of funds) wished to persuade the CNACE to amalgamate with the National Local Government Advisory Committee and to cease functioning as a separate organization, where its role was considered fairly marginal.[29]

Carlisle's resistance to the pro-voucher arguments of his junior colleague Dr Boyson, was a major set-back for the free-marketeers on the far right of the Conservative Party, of which a section was hostile to the very idea of public education (because for them it embodied the heresy that the public interest is more than just the sum of private desires). We shall see in chapters 8 and 9 how Sir Keith Joseph, Carlisle's successor, may have been predisposed towards vouchers but could not accept the logic behind them.

Between them Mark Carlisle and Lady Young concentrated their time at the DES on developing a core curriculum and pupil profiles of assessment. They were united by their wish to retain and advance school sixth-forms (perhaps the only point on which they were in agreement with Boyson) and sixth-form colleges for non-academic pupils. Their efforts to reform 16 + /17 + examinations were crucial to the realization of this objective. Both felt that it was the growth of comprehensive education which had logically led to the call for a single 16 + exam.[30] Significantly, it was Carlisle and not Sir Keith Joseph who was the first Conservative minister to push for reform towards the GCSE.

Carlisle believes that his two major achievements at the DES were the introduction of the Assisted Places Scheme (APS) in 1980 and his recognition of the Professional Association of Teachers (PAT) on the Burnham Committee.[31] His dismissal by Mrs Thatcher from the Department in September 1981 was, he maintains, the result of her determination to strengthen the balance towards the Right in the Cabinet but may also have been prompted by his decisions to allow Tameside to go comprehensive and not to allow Erith School (Bexley) to revert from a comprehensive school to two separate grammar schools.[32]

Lady Young's principal concerns as Schools Minister were to propagandize against those teachers who appeared to accept pupil under-achievement (for example, girls in maths and science in ILEA schools) and to oversee the 1981 DES paper *The School Curriculum* and the merging of the GCE/CSE examinations.[33]

Much of the policy which Mark Carlisle and Lady Young furthered during their period at the DES had actually originated at the NCES. A pamphlet by Vernon Bogdanor (1979) had recommended a number of reforms to reverse the downward drift in British education — reforms that could be adopted without any large-scale legislative upheaval and which would not involve any significant increase in public expenditure (*ibid*, p.20. Significantly the reforms did not include a voucher system.) These included securing a consensus between teachers, industrialists and government about the skills with which the schools should equip young people; encouraging comprehensive schools to develop their own specialisms, and encourage cooperation between the maintained sectors; placing parental rights upon a statutory basis, and ensuring that admission limits were sufficiently flexible to allow for genuine parental choice; and encouraging the formation of a General Teaching Council to regulate professional standards (*ibid*, pp.20–21). The correspondence between Bogdanor's proposals and the Carlisle-Young Line at the DES is so close that some cross-fertilization of ideas here seems more than likely.

The precise role of Stuart Sexton as Carlisle's Special Adviser during the temporary eclipse of the market right's plan for education is not easily determined though it would appear that, with the exception of the voucher, he had a virtually free rein. Significantly, between 1979 and 1982, Mrs Thatcher's Policy Unit at Downing Street had no remit to formulate education policy.[34] Thus, with the two central organs of government policy-making (the Cabinet and PM's Policy Unit) quiescent on education, Sexton was able to establish himself as the *eminence grise* of Tory education policy.[35]

As an exponent of both market right and preservationist policies, Sexton believed a free-market could solve most educational problems (all schools should be independent and all parents should have vouchers to pay for places); parents were the best guardians of educational standards and grammar schools should be restored.[36] In Sexton's view, Carlisle did not go as far, or as fast, as the educational radical right wished.[37] Unlike Carlisle, Sexton was not a paternalist in the traditional High Tory sense.[38] For Sexton the market right and peservationist/paternalist right were only compatible in as much as the former wished parents to have the choice of preserving the best in education.[39]

As well as from Mark Carlisle, Lady Young and Demitri Argyropulo resistance to features of the market right's plan for education also came from Robert Rhodes James.[40] Like Carlisle and Young, he was a paternalist on the liberal right wing of the Party and favoured a pragmatic approach to educational issues.[41] As the Party's liaison officer for higher education he was in direct contact with both Carlisle and Boyson. His was a Prime Ministerial appointment and not a political position. While his work as PPS to Peter Carrington might partially explain his appointment, his selection seems incongruous when set against the general philosophy of Thatcherism (i.e. individualism) with its determination to replace those state collectivist institutions spawned by socialism, by a myriad of new institutions fostered by the market.

Like other CEs, Rhodes James had believed that more things were going wrong than right in education.[42] Despite this he opposed Boyson over student loans and vouchers.[43] Though he was pro-voucher at the ideological level he considered they would be administratively impractical.[44] He believed the principle of the voucher was only attractive because it implied parent power, and good schools would not be able to cope with parental demand.[45] Such pragmatism gave Carlisle yet another ally in the move to block the more extreme ambitions of the educational radical-right.

A 'shopping list' of items for discussion

A possible explanation for Carlisle's success in deflecting particular policies of the educational radical right may be found in Mrs Thatcher's style of government between 1979 and 1981. Dale (1983) has quite rightly commented that Thatcherism by no means had things all its own way as far as education strategy and programmes were concerned (p.250). Less critically, Salter and Tapper have claimed (1981) that Mrs Thatcher merely oversaw more concrete proposals (notably in the field of curriculum development and in the restructuring of higher education) for a readjustment of educational goals (p.39). Sexton's view is that the Prime Minister did not initiate policies but preferred to allow her ministers to give her a 'shopping list' of items for discussion.[46] Carlisle's 'shopping-list' did not include vouchers or any of the other proposals favoured by the educational radical right for privatizing parental choice of school. Indeed, the only item which Carlisle brought to Mrs Thatcher was the Micro-Electronics Project (MEP) for schools, implemented via the Department of Industry in 1980/81.[47]

The MEP may be seen as epitomizing the Conservative Party's growing enthusiasm for linking schooling more closely to the needs of economic regeneration. The change had been signified in Carlisle's address to the 1979 Party Conference:

> What we mean when we talk about raising standards in education is raising the standards of achievement for all, raising the standards of literacy and numeracy, raising the quantity and quality of mathematicians, scientists and linguists, raising the standards of behaviour and discipline in our schools. If we are to achieve those improved standards we shall do it only by the pursuit of excellence. The Conservative Party is still the party of one-nation and its education policy has to be the policy of one-nation.[48]

Sexton's composition of Carlisle's address — an amalgam of the new Thatcherite economic strategy and the old *One Nation* philosophy — had placed the notion of *excellence in education* in a new (technicist) context which differed from its earlier humanist one. Sexton's usage of the phrase 'the pursuit of excellence' would become the bedrock of the Party's education policy as contained in the 1983 General Election manifesto and as carried forward by the second Thatcher government (see chapters 8 and 9).

Carlisle's critics take the offensive

Following the passage of the government's new Education Bill, the educational radical right's impatience with Carlisle's approach to schooling appears to have become more acute. At the CRD Alan Howarth took the view that the 1980 Education Act was only one step along the road down which he wanted the Government to travel to further strengthen parental rights.[49] Whilst Carlisle had envisaged that the measures in the new Education Bill would form 'a complete package' and would have 'a considerable effect on parental participation and on improving opportunities and standards'[50], Howarth doubted whether the legislation would guarantee the delivery of real parental choice although he regarded it as a useful advance.[51] For him, the exclusion of vouchers meant that only a token, cosmetic form of parental choice would be realized by the new Act.[52]

Carlisle's critics had some cause for irritation. The 1980 package was, in effect, a *soft* mixture of Stevas' original 'Parents' Charter' and calls from Boyson to safeguard popular schools and publish school examination results. It did not satisfy all CEs.

The educational radical right's influence within the CRD was now strong. When Angus Maude had entered the Cabinet as Paymaster-General, in May 1979, the post of CRD Chairman had been abolished. The executive direction of the CRD (between May 1979 and December 1981) was held solely by Alan Howarth. During this time Howarth was listening with increasing interest to the ideas of Alfred Sherman, a former adviser to Mrs Thatcher.[53] Sherman had much in common with the Prime Minister, Howarth and Boyson. All were fervent believers in the free-market and the minimal State. From 1980 Howarth and Chapman (both members of the CPSESG) were meeting Sherman at the CPS whilst Howarth met Arthur Seldon from time to time at the IEA.[54] The pro-voucher CEs at the CRD and CPS were now more than just a source of intellectual stimulus to the Conservative Party. One of the tasks of the contemporary Right was to extend the limits of the thinkable and sayable. Between 1980 and 1981 the CPSESG sought to influence a change in Conservative education policy regarding the voucher though this was not in any sense a subversive strategy launched from the CRD.[55]

The changed relation between the CRD and CPS in 1980 meant that the task facing the educational radical right appeared, though daunting, to be at least surmountable.[56] Until 1979 the CRD had seen the CPS as a rival in influencing Conservative policy, and the period 1974–79 had been marked by Chris Patten's antipathy towards the pro-voucher Alfred Sherman.[57] Howarth's agreement with Sherman over vouchers suggested a possible healing of ideological divides within the Tory hierarchy that might lead to a more rapid implementation of free-market policies.

However, the prospect for the application of such policies to education hinged upon the replacement of Mark Carlisle and Lady Young by Conservatives (Sir Keith Joseph, Dr Boyson and Robert Dunn) more attuned to the philosophy of the *social-market economy* (see chapters 8 and 9). Among those who favoured Carlisle and Young's replacement was Teresa Gorman.[58] Herself a former teacher, member of the Adam Smith Club, FEVER, CPS and Westminster City Council, she was, more significantly, an associate of Sir Keith Joseph.[59] According to Gorman, the 'new ideas people' of the Tory Party (i.e. the free-marketeers) came, in 1980/81, to the view that Carlisle and Young — as representatives of the old Tory paternalist education establishment — had to go.[60] Her view of events fits well with Edwards, Fulbrook and Whitty's suggestion (1986) that there was in this period of crisis (displayed by the tension between the requirements of state expenditure and the demands of capital for a real return on its investment) considerable pressure to find a new way forward (p.128).

Evidence of this pressure may be found in both the activity, and the private correspondence of, particular free-market groupings who were now intent upon directing a new way forward in Conservative education policy. Principal amongst these were the Selsdon Group and IEA, both of which supported education vouchers and major cuts in public spending. The Selsdon Group now included Nicholas Ridley MP, Professor Middleton (Cranfield), Stephen Eyres and Philip Van Der Elst (Eyres and Van Der Elst were also members of the Freedom Association). It was one of the well-established groups within the Conservative Party promoting right-wing views (privatization of nationalized industries, private provision in health and welfare and major cuts in taxation) akin to those of the Prime Minister. Crucially, Ian Gow (PPS to Mrs Thatcher, 1979–83) was a Selsdon member.

As well as the Selsdon Group, Mrs Thatcher now had an affinity to the IEA. In February 1980 she wrote to the IEA's founder:

> On the day I am due to lunch at the IEA, I am delighted to underline my admiration for all the IEA has done over the years for better understanding of the requirements for a free society. The Institute's publications have not only enabled us to make a start in developing sound economic policies. They have also helped create the intellectual climate within which these policies have commanded increasingly wide acceptance in the universities and the media. I wish you every success in your efforts to advance the principles in which we all believe. I am one of your strongest supporters.[61]

Mrs Thatcher clearly felt that the IEA's sustained research and education relating to the correct role of government had aided the formation of her own political thinking.[62] Her letter to the IEA was preceded by a similar plaudit from Friedrich von Hayek who had told Antony Fisher:

> What I argued thirty years ago, that we can beat the Socialist trend only if we can persuade the intellectuals, the makers of opinion, seems to me more than amply confirmed. Whether we can still win the race against the expanding Socialist tide depends on whether we can spread the insights fast and wide enough.[63]

These correspondences occurred at a time when Carlisle was engaged with announcing a positive look ahead to education in the new decade. His proposals for a core curriculum (*A Framework for the School Curriculum*, DES, January 1980 which identified the central importance of English, mathematics, science, modern languages, RE and studies for the preparation for adult and working life) were based on one of the key precepts of the CEs: that 'an agreed view must reflect the best of current practice, and it must also help to bring about the improvements that are required'.[64] *A Framework for the School Curriculum* contained what Carlisle called the 'essential education', and it was his firm intention to contain the reductions in education expenditure to what was necessary (but no more), to make sure what was spent was better spent than it was before, and see savings were made as far as possible outside the classroom and not within it.[65]

To the educational radical-right, Carlisle's *making savings and improving the efficiency* approach (though government inspired) lacked conviction and appeared as a sop to the demands for a *social-market economy*.[66]

What Carlisle had achieved, in bringing the interests of education and industry closer together, was an understanding that standards of excellence applied as much to vocational training as to other academic standards in the education system. But his failure (in the eyes of the educational radical right) was his preference for making minimum changes to existing arrangements, and his insistence upon following the Longden view that there could be no merit in change for the sake of change.[67] The Longden view was no longer tenable in a period requiring radical initiatives, and Carlisle's too frequent resort to the resolution of matters in what he often referred to as 'true-lawyer's fashion', perhaps illustrated his reluctance to be a part of the new way forward.

The CEs were united by their desire to see academic excellence in the schools preserved but the *new attitude to the school curriculum* (as advanced by Mark Carlisle and Lady Young) embodied little more than a reemphasis on the primacy of basic subjects and skills which traditionalists had canvassed throughout the 1960s and 1970s.

The publication of the DES paper *The School Curriculum* (March 1981), intended by the Secretary of State to give all pupils equality of educational opportunity via the curriculum[68], did nothing to pacify Carlisle's critics. It even incensed some on the educational centre right (represented on the Conservative Education Committee by Harry Greenway, David Madel and Patrick Cormack) by its failure to ensure the position of moral education in schools.[69] Like Carlisle, they opposed the manner and momentum of the influence of the New Rights' laissez-faire economists over the Conservative Party.[70] Their anti-voucher position had given Carlisle considerable support. But their participation in the 1981/82 session of the House of Commons Education, Science and Arts Committee suggests even they had grown tired of Carlisle's encouragement of limited educational reform.

The 1981/82 session of this Committee specifically addressed the question of the secondary school curriculum. When, on 13 July 1981, Greenway questioned Lady Young on the issue of religious education and the apparent lack of religious or moral education in many schools beyond the third year, she replied:

> I hope schools, governors and LEAs will look at this area of the curriculum
> as being something which they would regard as of importance.[71]

This was not enough to placate the educational centre right.[72] After nearly two years Mark Carlisle and Lady Young had not only failed to meet the demands of the educational radical-right they had now alienated some of their own keenest supporters.

Signs that the nature and pace of Conservative education policy would imminently change, with the succession of Sir Keith Joseph as Education Secretary and Dr Rhodes Boyson as Junior Education Minister (Schools), were evident in the latter's address to Hereford Conservative Association on 24 July 1981. Boyson informed Party members:

> The basis of all good education is high quality teaching. As a Conservative Government we are still not satisfied with the standard of education. The main aim of our Conservative Government is to bring pride, enterprise and integrity back to Britain.[73]

In September 1981 Mrs Thatcher decided that Carlisle's commitment to a *One Nation* conservatism and his Cabinet opposition to monetarism did not fit him to take part in the new way forward.

We shall now see how Joseph and Boyson pursued the belief that there was no direct link between how much was spent on education and what could be achieved in the schools. It would be a pairing of like-minded intellectuals with no inborn aversion to radical educational reform.

Notes

1 In a statement issued two days before the 1979 General Election Dr Boyson claimed Tory education policy: 'was striking a welcome chord in the hearts of anxious parents, employers and teachers' and that the people of Britain were not interested in 'bogus theories of social engineering'; he predicted: 'on Thursday they'll be voting to bring Conservative common-sense back to education'. CCO Press Release, 1 May 1979, GE 791/79.

2 Mark Carlisle MP to author, 18 April 1985.

3 Professor Cox to author, 15 August 1986.

4 Professor Cox to author, 21 February 1986.

5 *Ibid.* Cox added: 'My position on educational excellence and my opposition to the excesses of progressive education were both influenced by Jacques Barzun's book *The House of Intellect*'. Barzun's book, published in America and England in 1959, argued that the notion of helping a child (in the USA) had displaced that of teaching him, and that even apart from its hostility to Intellect, systematic coddling was as dangerous as it was impertinent.

6 Mark Carlisle MP to author, 18 April 1985.

7 Statement by Stevas, 5 June 1978, CCO Press Release 742/78.

8 Mark Carlisle MP to author, 18 April 1985.

9 Speech, by Mark Carlisle, Opposition Spokesman on Education and Conservative Parliamentary Candidate for Runcorn, at the Town Hall, Bolton, 25 April 1979, CCO Press Release, GE 704/79.

10 *The Conservative Manifesto 1979*, CCO, pp. 24–6. The education section of the manifesto (divided into two sections: 'Standards in Education' and 'Parents' Rights and Responsibilities'), was not penned by any one individual but was the result of the deliberations of a CRD education policy group meeting under the secretaryship of Biddy Passmore and consisting of a number of invited academics and MPs (including Sir Keith Joseph, Angus Maude and William Shelton). Chris Patten's role was to draft the final agreed position.

11 For an account of the rise of the 'economic evangelicals' in the Tory Party, see Keegan (1984) chapter 2.

12 Mark Carlisle MP to author, 18 April 1985.

13 For example, Carlisle's speech delivered at the opening of the National Association of Headteachers' Conference in Oxford on 28 September 1979 was on the theme 'Education standards can be maintained despite cut in planned expenditure'. It had been announced on 31 July that local authorities should plan on the basis of a reduction of 5 per cent on the plans for current expenditure in 1980/81.

14 As well as education, the virtues of free enterprise and the philosophy of freedom underpinned the Conservatives' policy proposals for reviving the private rented sector, protecting the environment, council housing, health and welfare.

15 Assistant Master, Westminster School (1968–74); Private Secretary to the Chairman of the Conservative Party (1975–79); Director, CRD (1979–81); Vice-Chairman, Conservative Party (1980–81); CBE 1982; MP. Stratford-on-Avon, since 1983; Member, CPSESG (1980–87); Founder Member, No Turning Back Group of Conservative MPs (1983–86); Party's Higher Education Liaison Officer (1986–87).

16 Patten became PPS to Norman St John-Stevas, Chancellor of Duchy of Lancaster and Leader of House of Commons (1979–81).

17 Alan Howarth MP to author, 24 April 1986.

18 Christine Chapman was appointed to the CRD by Howarth's predecessor, Chris Patten, as a result of her graduate research at the University of London Institute of Education on the education voucher. Alan Howarth MP, to author, 24 April 1986.

19 Alan Howarth MP to author, 24 April 1986.

20 *Ibid.* According to Howarth, both Patten's and Stevas' influence over Conservative education policy can be seen in the omission of the voucher from the Party's 1979 Election manifesto.

21 Mark Carlisle MP to author, 18 April 1985.

22 Lady Young was a Vice-Chairman of the Conservative Party Organization (1975–77) and Deputy Chairman (1977–79). Between 1957–72, she was a member of the Oxford City Council, and served as Chairman of the Planning and Education Committee (1957–67). In 1972 she joined the University Women's Club in Audley Square — a Conservative club for academic and professional women and the female counterpart to the Carlton Club in St. James' Street.

23 Cox had now joined the St James Society. The brainchild of Dr Madsen Pirie, the SJS was founded for all those who wished to create an Open Society. As a forum for all academics and educationalists who cared passionately about high culture and who were prepared to fight for their beliefs in the market-place and in the schools, it was the first real attempt to unite Conservatives behind the idea of 'education for a free society' and a campaign to maintain and improve professional standards in law, architecture, the sciences, teaching, medicine and nursing. The SJS arranged a number of meetings in London during 1979, including one addressed by Sir Geoffrey Howe, but then it faded, largely as a result of Dr Pirie devoting his time to the Adam Smith Institute (ASI). Letter from Professor Cox to author, 26 November 1986.

24 Private Information. In March 1987 Argyropulo co-founded the moderate Conservative Education Association (CEA), a body formed to preserve the state maintained sector as built upon the ideals of R. A. Butler and Sir Edward Boyle.

25 Private Information.

26 Chairman, Kingston upon Thames Education Committee (1978–79); Chairman, Education Committee, AMA (1979–80); Chairman, CLEA (1979–80); Minister of State, DES (1986–); Member, No Turning Back Group of Conservative MPs (1985–86).

27 Argyropulo served as S.E. Area YC Chairman (1975–77) and National YC Vice-Chairman (1977–79). He had been elected to Surrey C.C. Education Committee in 1973 and was CNACE Vice-Chairman (1976–79). In 1981 he became a member of the British Atlantic Committee, a body which also counted the anti-voucher and paternalist Harry Greenway among its membership.

28 The Carlisle-Argyropulo line may have been supported by Walter Ulrich (Deputy Secretary, DES, 1977–87).

29 On 13 April 1979 a meeting was held at Central Office to clarify the future position of the CNACE. It was agreed there should be no increase in the existing CNACE budget and that the CNACE would be encouraged by the Local Government Department to join in with their activities (for example, joint conferences and policy groups), but if they were not prepared to do so, then Local Government would include education in its own conferences since councillors were now demanding that it be discussed by them. Private information.

30 Mark Carlisle MP to author, 18 April 1985; Lady Young to author, 16 April 1985.

31 Mark Carlisle MP to author, 18 April 1985. In 1979 the APS was opposed by most Conservatives

involved in education and was not popular at the DES. Despite such reservations the scheme passed on to the Statute Book because it was based on a manifesto commitment.

32 *Ibid.*

33 Lady Young to author, 16 April 1985.

34 Sir John Hoskyns' letter to author, 31 July 1986. Hoskyns was Head of the PM's Policy Unit (1979–82). He informed the author: 'When I was in the Policy Unit we did not deal with education policy at all. I think therefore you would get the information you require from Stuart Sexton'.

35 The first public sign of Sexton's importance as Special Adviser to Conservative education ministers was his attendance at a CNACE meeting on 15 September 1979 at the Central Hall, Westminster. It was at this meeting that Sexton presented his formulation of the Assisted Places Scheme. Besides formulating the APS, Sexton had been responsible for coordinating delaying tactics among councils faced with Labour laws requiring abolition of selection and drafting the 'Parents' Charter' that went into the 1979 Election manifesto.

36 Stuart Sexton to author, 18 December 1986.

37 *Ibid.*

38 *Ibid.*

39 *Ibid.*

40 MP Cambridge (1976–); PPS, FCO (1979–82); Party Liaison Officer, Higher Education (1979–85).

41 Robert Rhodes James MP to author, 4 March 1986.

42 *Ibid.*

43 *Ibid.* James, like Boyson, was a member of the CPG. Between 1980–83 James sat on a CRD advisory group on vouchers and student loans set up by Peter Thorneycroft. This group included Lord Beloff and Hugh Thomas. No report was submitted by the group.

44 *Ibid.*

45 *Ibid.*

46 Stuart Sexton to author, 3 January 1985.

47 Mark Carlisle MP to author, 18 April 1985. The MEP was supported by Sir Keith Joseph (Secretary of State, DoI, 1979–81), David Young (Special Adviser, DoI, 1980–82), and Kenneth Baker (Minister for Information Technology, DoI, 1981–84).

48 Speech by Carlisle to 1979 Conservative Party Conference, 9 October 1979.

49 Alan Howarth MP to author, 24 April 1986.

50 Speech by Carlisle to 1979 Conservative Party Conference, 9 October 1979.

51 Alan Howarth MP to author, 24 April 1986.

52 *Ibid.*

53 Howarth had been in touch with Sherman since the days when he was Private Secretary to the Party Chairman, Lord Thorneycroft. It was part of his job to be in touch with all strands of Conservative opinion.

54 Howarth's membership of a number of CPS Study Groups was sought by Alfred Sherman. They both saw value in bridging what had been a gulf between the CRD and CPS. Howarth was also personally sympathetic to much of the tenor of CPS thinking. It was, however, his responsibility as Director of the CRD to uphold and support official Government policy, and this he did scrupulously.

55 *Ibid.*

56 *Ibid.*

57 *Ibid.*

58 Teresa Gorman to author, 16 August 1985.

59 *Ibid.*

60 *Ibid.*

61 Letter from Mrs Thatcher to Antony Fisher, 20 February 1980, *The Fisher Papers*. The IEA is credited by Mrs Thatcher and the press for creating the climate of opinion which made her election possible.

62 For an assessment of the considerable advance made by the New Right within the Conservative party and the increasing pressure it was able to exert on the leadership, by the linking of the principles of a free-market with more congenial Conservative emphases on a stronger state, see Gamble (1981), p. 147.

63 Letter from Hayek to Fisher, 1 January 1980, *The Fisher Papers*.
64 Lady Young to Education Conference of the NUT, London, 11 January 1980.
65 Speech by Carlisle during a tour of Staffordshire, 1 February 1980, CCO Press Release 53/80.
66 Teresa Gorman to author, 16 August 1985.
67 Following his decision not to approve Bexley's proposals to restructure Frith School as a separate grammar and secondary modern school, Carlisle told Conservatives in Chislehurst: 'I take great account of local wishes. Overall we must all aim for high standards and academic excellence. There can be no merit in change for the sake of change'. Speech by Carlisle to the Chislehurst Conservative Association, 7 March 1980, CCO Press Release 195/80.
68 Mark Carlisle MP to author, 18 April 1985.
69 David Madel MP to author, 15 April 1986.
70 Private Information. Before becoming an MP Patrick Cormack, like Greenway, had been a teacher (Assistant Housemaster, Wrekin College, Shropshire, 1967–69); Head of History, Brewood Grammar School, Stafford, 1969–70).
71 *Second Report From The House of Commons Education, Science and Arts Committee 1979–83, Session 1981–82, Vol II, Minutes of Evidence*, (HC.116-II), p. 504, para. 1345. In the light of the inner-city disturbances and breakdown in law and order during the summer 1981 there was considerable pressure on the government to concern itself with the issue of moral education in the school curriculum.
72 David Madel MP to author, 15 April 1986.
73 Speech by Boyson to Hereford Conservative Association, 24 July 1981, CCO Press Release 585/81.

Chapter 8

In pursuit of excellence, 1981–83

Introduction

The last chapter showed how the increasing divisions amongst the CEs had appeared and how these divisions were, in part, the result of reactions to Mrs Thatcher's new style (monetarist) and new substance (radical reforms) of government. A number of commentators, notably Dale (1983) have noted these divisions and have attempted to construct a typology which might help explain the range of influences underpinning Thatcherite education policy between 1979 and 1983.

Dale's typology (of the *Industrial Trainers*, the *Old Tories*, the *Populists*, the *Moral Entrepreneurs*, and the *Privatisers*) whilst suggestive does not fully indicate the extent to which a number of influential CEs, including Sir Keith Joseph and Dr Rhodes Boyson (seen by Dale as respectively the chief ideologue and the chief propagandist of Thatcherism (*ibid.*, p.233)) fall into more than one category. Nevertheless, the typology is useful in highlighting the tensions over education policy which continued to emerge and develop within the Conservative Party during the first Thatcher government. For example, prior to the appointment of the new Education Secretary, two of the principal CE groups — the NCES and the CPSESG — had been the object of considerable inner discord. Press coverage of the views of some members of the CPSESG (who also happened to be members of the NCES) had caused both groups to be seen by the public as 'right-wing'. As a result the Black Paperite Stephen Woodley (NCES Executive Committee) had advised Professor Brian Cox:

> It is one thing for *The Guardian* to describe us as 'right-wing' when they can't prove it, quite another when the names on our NCES notepaper are also identified with one of Keith Joseph's groups.[1]

The unsettled alliance of the *Populists* and the *Privatisers* in the NCES and the CPSESG was not quickly resolved. The eventual outcome of the deepening conflict would be the decision (taken in the spring of 1986) by Dr John Marks (NCES

Chairman (1985/86) and CPSESG Secretary) and Baroness Caroline Cox (Chair, CPSESG) to split from the NCES to work at their own Education Research Centre (established by Dr Marks in 1985).[2]

The case of the NCES/CPSESG rift is important because, as we shall now see, its development paralleled not only Sir Keith Joseph's ascendancy and Mrs Thatcher's preference for market-forces, but also the CRD's increasing acceptance of CPSESG ideas for the formation of Conservative education policy.

Carrying forward 'excellence in education'

It was during Sir Keith Joseph's tenure as Secretary of State for Education and Science (1981–86) that the pursuit of *excellence in education* was promoted as something more than a Conservative ideal. Under Joseph a clearer vision of what education should be was formulated and policies to deliver that vision (of educational excellence) implemented. The policies themselves are discussed in chapter 9.

Joseph's vision of what education should be was formulated against the background of a fundamental rethink of the role to be played by the education system in a general strategy for social and cultural change. It is in this context that Judge's statement, 'The mood and pace of educational policy were changed', should be read (Judge, 1984, p. 192).

Joseph's reappraisal of Conservative educational policy — the first since Stevas' exercise of 1974/78 — was based on a technical/vocational conception of education. In chapter 5 it was shown how Joseph (as a defender of educational excellence) had once argued the importance of young people having access to *good education* in order that they might be given the mental resources to enjoy their freedom. This view of education, postulated by Joseph in 1959, now formed the basis of the Secretary of State's 'Good Schools for All' address to the 1981 Conservative Party Conference. Joseph's speech drew attention not only to the concern about academic standards but also to pupil behaviour, discipline and work habits. Joseph suggested that policy had to be orientated to meet the needs of the non-academic pupil, for whom the key basic subjects would mean more if they were associated with a greater prevocational content in parts of the curriculum. This, Joseph believed, might be a more effective education for many pupils.

Though earlier CEs (principally David Eccles and Angus Maude — see chapters 2 and 3) had identified the needs of the non-academic pupil as a focus for Conservative education policy, it was Joseph who was the first to articulate *excellence in education* as a meaningful aim. His transposition of educational excellence to *effective education* would bring with it a conviction that the attainment of good schools for all rested upon the teaching of *sound knowledge*.[3]

In order to understand how Joseph came to make such a radical formulation of *excellence in education*, it is necessary to trace the development of his own educational philosophy. It was, by Joseph's own account, firmly-rooted in the thinking of the original One Nation Group:

> Like Angus Maude, I was a One Nation group member in 1956. We believed levelling in schools had to stop and that excellence (discrimination) had to return. Our key perception was *differentiation*. We equated the stretching of children, at all levels of ability, with caring. Our aim was to achieve rigour in the school curriculum. Later, I was much influenced by Maude's views in *The Common Problem*, and the Black Papers. The Black Papers responded to a strong national perception, that there was a vast gap between what people received and what people needed in education. Because of the fall in the birth-rate and school rolls I decided, when I took office in 1981, to go for *quality* not *quantity*. For too long popular high expectations of education had led to popular disappointments. Large sections of the nation were eager for improvements. We wanted to satisfy the thirst for good education.[4]

In 1981 Joseph was fully aware of the group of CEs that thought there could be a market-solution to the crisis in state education and personally associated himself with their cause.[5] In September 1981 Stuart Sexton became his Special Adviser. The reasoning behind Sexton's appointment says much about Joseph's approach to the education brief:

> I took Sexton on because I felt he had *parallel forms of thought* to myself. But the ideas I brought to education were mine, not Sexton's.[6]

Whilst it is true that Joseph did bring to education some original ideas — for example, the notion that a market solution could only proceed (and succeed) in conjunction with a paternalistic Inspectorate[7] — it is not the case that his ideas were wholly his own. A number of his 'ideas' closely matched those of other CEs, who were either commissioned by the Conservative Party to provide scenarios for the future of education (for example, Professor Brian Cox's *Education: The Next Decade*, CPC, 1981) or whose proposals were put to the CRD for active consideration (for example, CPSESG, 1981, *The Right to Learn: A Conservative Approach to Education*).

Within Professor Cox's pamphlet can be found the genesis of Joseph's ideas for the *new selection* (see below). Cox's personal view of the crisis in state education was that:

> Any realistic solution must include some element of selection . . . . The aim of all schools should be to keep alive the best values, to transmit to young people high ideals of excellence. Through the humanities, through literature and history, we keep alive all that is best in our traditions; we help

the voices of the past to live again in the experience of the student. Through maths and sciences we train the informed, rational mind . . . . All these values involve discrimination between good and bad, true and false; such discrimination involves selection, the choice of high standards, the rejection of the third-rate. Unless our school system reflects such hierarchies of value it will inevitably degenerate into relativism and impotence (Cox, 1981, pp. 22–3).

The similarity between Cox's call for *hierarchies of value* and Joseph's push (from 1982) for *relevance* and *fitness for purpose* in the school curriculum suggests that Black Paperite discourse was far from redundant. Indeed, the CPSESG's policy-study (completed in June 1981) was prepared under the general editorship of the then Chairman and Secretary of the Group (Caroline Cox and Dr John Marks respectively) who had both been contributors to the Black Papers. It had been submitted to the CRD on 1 August 1981 and was a 'document designed to serve as the basis for discussion of Conservative Party education policy for the mid-eighties' (CPSESG, 1981, p. 1). For the present author the significance of the CPSESG's document was its observation that there was no identifiable Conservative Party philosophy of education in the way that there were recognizable Conservative approaches to economic policy, labour law, constitutional questions, defence, law and order and Europe (*ibid.*). In matters of education (from primary to higher) Conservatives had, according to historical record, been content to tag along behind the Liberals, and subsequently behind Labour (*ibid.*). In matters educational, the Conservatives had appeared primarily as the party of the transient 'status quo', and as the party of the public schools and older universities — in a word — privilege (*ibid.*). In post-war British society — as Sir Keith Joseph among others, had cogently explained — clinging to the 'status quo' had invariably meant letting the socialists make the running, whether with a greater or lesser degree of reluctance, tempered by resignation or even the appearance of enthusiasm and one-sided bi-partisanship (Joseph, 1976). In the CPSESG's view, hanging on to the 'status quo' out of the combined (if self-contradictory) convictions that the 'clock cannot be turned back', that all change is likely to be for the worse, but that to oppose change too determinedly would court misunderstanding and unpopularity, did not provide propitious ground from which new initiatives might be launched (CPSESG, 1981, p. 1).

As well as Caroline Cox and Dr John Marks, the contributors to the CPSESG's policy study included Professor Antony Flew, Fred Naylor, Lawrence Norcross (Headmaster, Highbury Grove School) and Professor Arthur Pollard (University of Hull). Like Caroline Cox and Dr John Marks, they had each been contributors to the Black Papers. The Group's policy proposals for secondary education were based on a conviction that there was a need to halt and reverse those post-war educational policies which, in the view of the CPSESG, had been increasingly dominated by the socialist principle of compulsory equality — one type of school for all, no selection either within or between schools, the abolition of examinations which pupils could fail (*ibid.*, p. 14). Above all, the Group asserted:

> We need to make our education system proof against the irreversible structural changes now intended by the Labour Party which is now committed to the abolition of independent schools (Labour Party Discussion Document *Private Schools*, Socialism for the Eighties Series), with compulsory enforcement of mixed-ability teaching and the destruction of religious and single-sex schools, (*London Labour Party Manifesto*, GLC Elections, 1981) (*ibid.*).

The CPSESG's document which was aimed at 'the pursuit of excellence' suggested a range of policies for schools, based on Conservative principles, to achieve the major purpose of education — to provide all future citizens with reasonable access to worthwhile skills and bodies of knowledge, including knowledge of the culture and traditions of Britain's free and democratic society (*ibid.*). It suggested: (a) that a range of examinations was needed in order to cater for the diverse needs of children with differing aptitudes and interests, and that the proposed merger of GCE 'O' level and CSE should be carefully monitored; (b) increasing at successive educational stages the amount of grouping by ability; (c) that measures should be taken to increase parental choice of schools and to facilitate children and young people changing schools if they and their parents wished (the choice and appeals provision of the 1980 Act should be widely publicised); (d) that flexible transfer arrangements should be encouraged to enable pupils to change schools; (e) that more information about individual schools (including details of public examination results) should be freely available to parents; (f) that a greater variety of types of school should be encouraged (including specialist schools/centres of excellence within the state system; (g) that educational allowances should be given to parents to spend in schools of their choice, either in the state or the independent sector; (h) that schools which had good sixth-forms working well should be retained; and (i) the introduction of a national system of educational vouchers (*ibid.*, pp. 12–19).

Although Sir Keith Joseph would not pursue all of the CPSESG's package of suggested policies (for example educational allowances, educational vouchers and specialist schools/centres of excellence) his initiatives would be based on one of the CPSESG's main recommendations — that to achieve 'the major purpose of education' Conservatives had to stimulate a greater awareness of costs and of the need for better value for money in the national investment in education (*ibid.*, p. 15). Additionally, the broad thrust of the CPSESG's proposals — that the Conservative Party should implement policies to foster excellence and elites rather than equality of condition — was already in keeping with Joseph's political philosophy.[8] Finally, we should note that between 1981 and 1983 Joseph gave responsibility for the pursuit of excellence in education to a number of CEs — Dr Rhodes Boyson (Parliamentary Under-Secretary of State (Schools) 1981–83),[9] William Shelton (Parliamentary Under-Secretary of State (Further Education), 1981–83), William Waldegrave (Parliamentary Under-Secretary of State (Higher Education), 1981–83) and Oliver Letwin (Education Desk Officer, CRD, 1982–83 and Political Adviser to Sir Keith Joseph, 1982–83) — each of whom would show themselves strongly committed to the search for quality and value for money.

The 'new selection'

When Sir Keith Joseph introduced his Parliamentary education team at the 1981 Conservative Party Conference, he declared:

> I am glad that there is a connecting link between the new team and the former team. The unique Dr Boyson remains, I am glad to say.[10]

Joseph's choice of rhetoric could not have been more apt. The history of the CEs is, as we have seen, rooted in connecting links or, as Joseph has preferred, 'reactions'.[11]

In his reply to the education debate at the 1981 Party Conference, Joseph indicated his intent to effect a return to traditional classroom teaching styles:

> I welcome the fact that the mixed-ability tide seems to have ebbed. Mixed-ability teaching calls for very rare teaching skills if it is to benefit every child in a non-selected class.[12]

For nearly a decade (see chapters 4–6) Dr Boyson, in association with the NCES, had opposed the spread of mixed-ability teaching. Now, as Joseph's deputy, it appeared that he was to oversee the restoration of selection for which he had so long campaigned. Within just three years, however, the advent of the GCSE examination reform would thwart Boyson's ambition.

Although Joseph was pledged to make the comprehensive system work, he lamented the pressure towards comprehensivization of the 1960s and early 1970s, and (like Angus Maude before him) wished the Party had proceeded more slowly. In 1981 he believed the educational practice of the 1960s and 1970s had prevented differences of talent and aptitude being developed and evaluated.[13] He believed the attitude and motives which had nourished egalitarian politics (pursuit of power and envy of those who are different) meant a dislike of diversity.[14] Here Joseph shared a view common to all CEs: that education had seen an unholy alliance of socialists, bureaucrats, planners and directors of education acting against the true interests and wishes of the nation's children and parents by their imposition on the schools of an ideology (equality of condition) based on utopian dreams of universal cooperation and brotherhood.

Throughout Joseph's period of office the CEs were divided between those who desired the maximization of parental choice (the educational radical right), and those who preferred the maximization of pupil performance (the One Nation Tories) as the principal objective of Conservative education policy. However, it was because the *pursuit of excellence* was inherent in the *One Nation* philosophy that maximizing the performance of all children (whatever their ability) became the Secretary of State's overriding concern.

Between September 1981 and June 1983 Sir Keith Joseph launched a series of initiatives designed to raise the educational standards of children of all abilities: (i) the systematic initiation of a programme to make initial teacher training much more rigorous; (ii) the pursuit of agreement on a national curriculum; (iii) the transformation of the public examination system; and (iv) the preparations to introduce pupil records of achievement.

Of these, the second initiative (the pursuit of agreement on a national curriculum) appeared to promise the best hope of promoting a traditional style of schooling which many CEs had advocated. The search for a consensus concerning the content of a national curriculum was, in September 1981, already proving difficult. An illustration of this contention was the conflict between the government and the representatives of teachers' associations about the introduction of courses in technology. In September 1981 a conference at Lancaster House, presided over by Mrs Thatcher, stressed the need to restore technology teaching to the curriculum. More girls were to be induced to take higher education courses in science and technology. Sir Keith stated that children should understand how business and the economy worked. Sir Clive Sinclair talked about the need for commercial values to replace academic values. No teachers' representative was invited to speak. The teachers' exercise of control over the curriculum was already being reduced by the work of the Manpower Services Commission.

Sir Keith Joseph's address to the 1982 North of England Education Conference in Leeds (on 6 January) was significant for its focus on the needs of low-attaining pupils. In his speech Joseph returned to conceptions of education he had earlier formulated and advanced at the 1981 Party Conference. The key phrase he set before the North of England delegates as an aim of Conservative education policy was, a 'more effective education for all children'. In its 1981 presentation, it had been limited to a 'more effective education for many pupils'. Although the needs of the less academic pupils deserved greater emphasis than they had been receiving, Joseph believed they could not be tackled in isolation. What was required was a stronger awareness of how policies which applied to all pupils could best serve the interests of the less academic.

For Joseph, what constituted *effective education* would depend on the need of each child. For those who were deemed unsuited to an academic curriculum, education would be 'effective only if it directly prepared for life and for the world as the pupils themselves could be enabled to see it'.[15] Such children were, in Joseph's view, a 'very large minority' (*ibid.*).

Joseph envisaged that the most promising basis for future developments lay in a curriculum which would provide a broad programme of general education (but with a practical slant), which would develop young peoples' personal attributes (such as a sense of responsibility and the capacity for independent work) and help them to discover what kind of job they might expect to tackle with success.

Despite its leanings towards a *back-to-basics* curriculum, Joseph's *curriculum* did not satisfy some CEs — not even all Black Paperites. For example, Raymond Baldwin responded by arguing that secondary schooling was 'no place for dogmatic absolutes of any colour' (Baldwin, 1982, pp. 150–3). Baldwin was strongly opposed to any standardized diet of teaching throughout all schools. He believed such a scheme would cause any potential academic stream to be the victim, not the leaven, of the school environment. For Baldwin, the way forward to secure the best education for all children was not through an attempt to reform the comprehensive system. Rather, the true glory of a successful national secondary school system would lay in the richness and variety of the provision it made for the full development of all types of ability and aptitude in all kinds of social environment (*ibid.*, p. 153). Baldwin appealed to Conservatives to make a patient effort to discover the facts, admit the shortcomings of the schooling system, recognize the strong features and preserve what was excellent and efficient and amend what was not (*ibid.*).[16]

Both in his 1981 Party Conference and 1982 North of England Education Conference speeches Joseph signalled a retreat from the *curriculum common to all pupils* advocated for secondary schools by the government in *The School Curriculum* (DES, 1981). What the government now seemed to be saying was not that the curriculum should be of 'a broadly common character' with 'substantial common elements' but rather a greater degree of differentiation was required in what was taught to various categories of pupils. In effect, there should be a return (either by the reorganization of schools or within the existing comprehensives) to a version of the old tripartite system which the *common school* was supposed to have replaced. Joseph's formula (the *new selection*) may have been contrary to orthodox curriculum theory but it was an appropriate assumption on his part that the mixed-ability tide appeared spent.

Both speeches may be seen as marking 1981/82 as the period where Joseph embarked upon a more utilitarian approach to education. Conservative education policy was now displayed as valuing education only for the things it enabled persons (or collectively, a state) to do or make. This approach would be repeated and reinforced in Joseph's 1984 and 1985 North of England Education Conference speeches (see chapter 9).

Centralizers versus decentralizers

Sir Keith Joseph's education team comprised CEs representative of the two major schools of right-wing educational thought — the *centralizers* (paternalist-right) and, the *decentralizers* (market-right). It is important to note this division because, as we shall now see, although Joseph's team was united in its broad support for raising educational standards, it displayed less agreement over precise schemes to improve the mechanics of *parental choice*. Significantly, each grouping was distinguished by its varying degrees of support for, and opposition to, the education voucher.

The *centralizers*, opposed to the voucher, included Joseph (initially sympathetic to vouchers but, from 1981, sceptical of their administrative practicality) and Robert Rhodes James (liaison officer for higher and further education). It is worth noting that in May 1982 Rhodes James joined the anti-voucher advocate Lord Belloff[17] as a member of a newly-constitued CRD Advisory-Board, meeting under the chairmanship of the then Party Chairman (Cecil Parkinson). This Board had as its remit to 'advise on the conduct of policy work and propose new lines of investigation and research'.[18] The appointment of the Black Paperite Lord Beloff to the CRD was shortly to have a much deeper significance (see below). The *decentralizers*, proponents of the voucher, now included William Shelton and Dr Rhodes Boyson (the latter supported by Robert Dunn and James Pawsey) and Stuart Sexton. William Waldegrave's political position at the time did not permit him to be categorized by the author as either a *centralizer* or *decentralizer*. Though a One Nation Tory he saw a more centralized education system as anathema to him and whilst he acknowledged the case for vouchers on social justice grounds, he advised Joseph against them on practical grounds.[19]

The divisions between the *centralizers* and *decentralizers* appear to have deepened markedly between 1982 and 1983. On the relationship between ministers, advisers and civil servants in this period, Waldegrave has said:

> The most important figure on schools was Walter Ulrich. Sexton's influence was negative, he had very little influence over Sir Keith.[20]

Waldegrave, like William Shelton, casts the name of Ulrich as the key determining influence over Conservative schools policy. However, one can be less sure of Waldegrave's assessment of Sexton. Admittedly, Sexton was not acting as Joseph's DES Special Adviser at the time of the Department's paper on education vouchers (December 1981) (see below). He had, nevertheless, returned to the DES by the beginning of 1982 and did pen Joseph's 1982 North of England Education Conference speech.[21] Furthermore, he appears to have set about the reinforcement of Joseph's *new selection* by the initiation of a *new direction* in Conservative education policy-making. Sexton has said of his return to the DES:

> Policy formulation at the Department was very informal. There was no set procedure. I certainly did not get my marching orders from Sir Keith. Once a month, I invited other Special Advisers from other Departments to dinner, to discuss education policies. Employment and Industry were represented. Discussion around tables at the DES and All Souls were important channels of influence.[22]

Three months after Sexton's return to the DES, the voucher issue was still before the Secretary of State for consideration though, by March 1982, it had been effectively 'killed'. At the 1981 Party Conference Joseph had told delegates:

> I have been intellectually attracted to the idea of seeing whether eventually a voucher might be a way of increasing parental choice even further . . . .There are very great difficulties in making a voucher deliver, in a way that would commend itself to us, more choice than the 1980 Act will deliver. It is now up to the advocates of such a possibility to study the difficulties, and they are real, and see whether they can develop proposals which can cope with them.[23]

Following Joseph's declaration on the voucher, the NCES and the FEVER had requested from the Minister an account of the problems that would need to be resolved before an education voucher scheme could be defined, and its implications assessed, for the purposes of educational policy. The Minister's response,[24] detailing some fifteen problems, had made it very clear that unless the proponents of the voucher (who now included John Barnes and Professors Mark Blaug, Antony Flew, Alan Peacock and Jack Wiseman) could convincingly describe its operation and suggest how the practical difficulties of its implementation might be tackled, its general introduction was far down the list on the government's immediate agenda.

In March 1982 the FEVER replied to Joseph by stating that the essential task in public policy on education in Britain was to find a means of universalizing parental choice as far as practicable.[25] Its fifteen-page paper to the Secretary of State stressed the role vouchers might play in assisting lower-income parents to escape from undesirable school environments such as the William Tyndale School, and questioned whether it was fundamentally within the power of government to command the pace of adaptation to a voucher system. The FEVER document noted:

> The dislocation anticipated by officials indicates a pre-occupation with the state sector as well as understandable predilection to continue with education systems unchanged (*ibid.*, p. 8).

And:

> It is implausible to suppose that parental influence or control would have allowed standards of teaching the elementary skills to have fallen so far that the political parties have had to propose centrally-designed or centrally-imposed *core curricula*. The boot is here very much on the other foot (*ibid.*, pp. 14–15).

The FEVER response was signed by its Chairman, Marjorie Seldon, who had sought for several years to impress the voucher principle on Joseph. It is, therefore, surprising that the tenor of the FEVER response should have so blatantly attacked Joseph's centralist approach at a moment when he might well have reconsidered his position on the voucher.

The *centralizers* versus *decentralizers* battle over the voucher did not end in March 1982. During the autumn, the arena of conflict was to switch from the DES to the CRD. But before this happened, there were two developments. In June 1982 Oliver Letwin was appointed as Sir Keith Joseph's political adviser and CRD Education Desk Officer and, in July 1982, Sir Geoffrey Howe (Chancellor of the Exchequer) delivered his speech on *Conservatism in the Eighties*. Letwin and Howe were to prove to be key-actors in the voucher-battle (see below).

Howe's speech suggested a voucher system as part of a future Conservative Party policy agenda:

> Widening choice, encouraging private provision, ensuring more flexibility, while improving value for money: those are our proper goals. The 1980 Education Act was a significant step towards ensuring parental freedom of choice and encouraging parental involvement. A voucher system, whereby parents would have an even greater choice of schools for their children, and whereby standards might be raised through more competition is one possibility.[26]

The viability for a voucher system was discussed by the Conservative Group on Education, established by Sir Geoffrey Howe as part of the preparation for the 1983 election manifesto and chaired by Lord Beloff.[27]

The 'Quality of Education' policy group

The remit of the Conservative Education Policy Group was less to suggest items for the manifesto than policy for the longer term (i.e. five years ahead) (Butler and Kavanagh, 1984, p. 39). It is significant that the group's report was submitted not only to Sir Geoffrey Howe and Cecil Parkinson but also to Ferdinand Mount (the Head of the Prime Minister's Policy Unit and the person responsible for writing the 1983 Party manifesto) (*ibid.*).

Lord Beloff's appointment as Chairman of the Conservative Education Policy Group was not unexpected. The Secretary of State had told delegates to the 1982 Party Conference that, in seeking ways to improve choice and standards in education, he would 'strongly bear in mind the views of Lord Beloff'.[28]

The views of Lord Beloff were now very close to those of the Education Secretary. Like Joseph, he felt it was essential for central government to accept more responsibility than previously because many local authorities defied demands by parents for higher educational standards and greater choice.[29] Recalling his time as

Chairman of the Conservative Education Policy Group, Lord Beloff informed the author:

> I adhered to the philosophy *more means worse*. There had been a considerable ebb to and fro as to what constituted a *teacher* in schools. The development of education as a profession had concentrated on things like psychology and sociology, which helped the teacher as a *communicator* but did little to help teachers as *educators*. I believed teachers should be *skilled scholars*. I had long felt that educational standards had been falling, particularly in modern language teaching and in standards of teacher training.[30]

Lord Beloff's views were reflected in his group's report. Members of Lord Beloff's group included fellow Black Paper writers such as Professor Brian Cox and Raymond Baldwin (Chairman of the Governors of Manchester Grammar School), as well as moderates like Lady Platt (the newly-appointed Chairman of the Equal Opportunities Commission). The other members were David Smith (Headmaster of Bradford Grammar School) and the MPs Malcolm Thornton (Garston), James Pawsey (Rugby) and Harry Greenway (Ealing North). Oliver Letwin and Stuart Sexton, political advisers at the DES, attended the Group's meetings as assessors. The Group's report made a recommendation (on whose advice it is not clear) for a General Teaching Council, and considered proposals to strengthen moral and religious education in schools, as well as a more vocational slant to the curriculum.[31] It rejected the idea of education vouchers as the great majority of the Group were not convinced that the voucher scheme was the best method of increasing parental choice and thereby improving standards, and because its cost would be hard to justify to a highly sceptical public at a time of stretched resources.

Here may be found both the reason for the exclusion of vouchers from the Party's 1983 manifesto (see below) and Sir Keith Joseph's subsequent rejection of the voucher idea at the 1983 Conservative Party Conference (see chapter 9). Lord Beloff did not publicly disclose his opposition to the introduction of education vouchers until February 1983.[32] His Group's report advised that more thought and public discussion were essential, and only when outstanding questions had been settled and when there was evidence of a public demand should a pilot voucher scheme by attempted, particularly since it would have to be preceded by legislation.[33] All this would seem to confirm the view of one of the principal advocates of the voucher that its 1983 abandonment was ultimately political (see Seldon, 1986, chapter 4) though even he fails to examine in any detail the impact of the deliberations of the Beloff policy group.

In addition to its voucher recommendation, the Beloff policy group also made two other significant proposals: that personal school records of achievement for pupils be developed, and that the GCE 'O' level examination be retained.

'Schools: the pursuit of excellence'

One point of common agreement between Sir Keith Joseph, Dr Boyson and Lord Beloff was their wish to see the industrial and technical revival of Britain. Each were agreed on the fundamental aims of education — the preservation and extension of learning and culture, and the fitting of the individual for adult life. At the 1982 Conservative Party Conference Joseph had announced that the diluted academic curriculum offered to the 40 per cent or so of children whose potential was not academic, was not an ideal vehicle to equip them for life.[34] Boyson welcomed the proposed joint enterprise of the MSC and LEAs to set up ten technical and vocational pilot projects for the 14–18-year-olds which, he suggested 'will help fit our young people for the competitive world in which we live'.[35] Beloff's position had similarly undergone some modification. He now believed that the work of the MSC was essential and he was strongly in favour of more technical and vocational studies in schools.[36]

The framing of Conservative education policy upon a particular principle — 'specialist enrichment on a broad educational base'[37] — now seemed to have a wide consensus within the Party. It was a consensus which viewed education as part of society having a responsibility to recognize that the nation required a new emphasis on technical efficiency and innovation at every level, from the research scientist to the technician or craftsman at the workbench. Technical and vocational education would be vital in re-establishing a technical elite in Britain:

> Between what happens in the schools, the colleges, the polytechnics and the universities there is a close link, and a link with the quality of life for the whole population. It is our task to pass on to future generations that excellence that exists.[38]

In the 1983 Conservative manifesto *The Challenge of Our Times*, the Party's proposed education policy was described as 'Schools: The pursuit of excellence'. In education, as in economics, the manifesto sought both to create and reflect a change in public attitudes and expectations. For two years Joseph's education team had engaged itself in what it saw as the rebuilding and development of education with an emphasis on excellence and order in schools (i.e. selection, structure, curriculum control and firm standards). Joseph's notion of *ability teaching* and the Boyson/Sexton vision of *specialist schools*, were indications of a traditionalist rather than a fundamentalist view of schooling which had gained some currency within the Party.

The proposals for education described in the 1983 Conservative manifesto suggest the educational radical-right's '*dream ticket*' of Joseph and Boyson had not offered any ideas or innovations significantly different from Carlisle's period at the DES. Lord Beloff's views were prominent in the list of education proposals:

> We are not satisfied with the selection or the training of our teachers. Our

White Paper (*Teaching Quality*) sets out an important programme for improving teacher training colleges.[39]

And, again:

We shall encourage schools to keep proper records of their pupils' achievements (*ibid.*, p. 30).

Both proposals had been pressed in the Beloff policy groups's report. However, one Beloff proposal – the retention of the GCE 'O' level examination – was not included in the manifesto. The document noted:

The public examination system will be improved, and 'O' level standards will be maintained (*ibid.*).

The exclusion of the voucher idea from the manifesto was a major triumph for the *centralizers* over the *decentralizers*. In addition to Lord Beloff, both Harry Greenway and Professor Brian Cox had, as members of the policy group, voted against the voucher.[40] According to Robert Rhodes James,[41] vouchers had effectively been killed by Sir Geoffrey Howe prior to the launch of the 1983 Election manifesto purely on costing and that were was no ideological barrier to their implementation.

The triumph of the *centralizers* went beyond the issue of the voucher. The *centralizers* case which had been argued between 1982 and 1983 for stable schools (with maximum choice of school subject), strong discipline and clear moral standards,[42] had largely been adopted in the manifesto.[43] More noteworthy than this, the manifesto had not taken up the proposals of the *decentralizers* on the Beloff policy group (James Pawsey, Oliver Letwin and Stuart Sexton) to expand the APS and to introduce excellence awards for schools (something akin to the Queen's Award for Industry) whereby schools would be encouraged to compete amongst themselves for an improvement in standards.[44]

Though the Party's manifesto proposals for the raising of educational standards were placed under the banner 'Schools: The pursuit of excellence', they contained no clear policy on school examinations. This was surprising in the light of the Government's desire to improve the quality of education and its commitment to a 'resolute approach'.[45] Equally noteworthy in the manifesto was the continued support on the part of Joseph and Boyson for their long-term aim of radically reforming education and taking further steps in the government's chosen direction — towards a *better education for all*. They had acquiesced to the major platform of the CEs' approach — that educational evolution not revolution, was the national need. Educational evolution meant progress and change in response to pupils' real needs and altered circumstances. The Beloff policy group recommendation for the retention of the GCE 'O' level examination did not fit into the dynamic of *educational evolution* as envisaged by Joseph and Boyson. The failure to implement the Beloff recommendation was balanced by the government's publication of its White Paper *Teaching Quality* (DES,

1983), which went some considerable way towards satisfying the demands of Lord Beloff and other traditionalists who now looked for controls by which the DES might exercise greater regulation over initial teacher training and the means whereby LEAs managed the teaching force.[46] The White Paper placed particular emphasis on both academic and professional content of initial training courses, and thus met Lord Beloff's view that teachers should be skilled scholars as well as effective communicators. Improvements in the content and structure of initial teacher training courses now meant newly-trained teachers would be expected to have greater knowledge and expertise in the subjects they were to teach, as well as more practical experience, and would have to provide satisfactory evidence of classroom competence.

In the next chapter we shall see how a tide of *new realism* in education, inspired by the CEs, was directed towards a fundamental rethink of secondary education.

Notes

1 Letter from Stephen Woodley to Professor Cox, 7 January 1981, *The Cox Papers*. In 1981 Woodley was playing an important role in the NCES, organizing speakers for conferences and contributors to the NCES Bulletin. He obtained the services of Kenneth Minogue, David and Bernice Martin and Arthur Hearnden for the NCES Conference (8 March 1981) and Peter Dawson (PAT) and Donald Naismith (CEO, Croydon) for the NCES Bulletin.

2 Professor Cox to author, 15 August 1986.

3 Sir Keith Joseph to author, 5 June 1986. For Joseph 'sound knowledge' incorporated the traditional basic subjects plus business studies and technology. It did not incorporate the teaching of ideology or subjects like peace studies, urban studies, sociology and politics.

4 *Ibid.*

5 *Ibid.*

6 Sir Keith Joseph to author, 5 June 1986. With regard to Sexton's position, it should be noted that just after he became Education Secretary Joseph temporarily dismissed his Special Adviser (though why is not known) and brought in to the DES David Young (Joseph's Special Adviser at the Department of Industry). As a result Sexton briefly became a political adviser to Dr Boyson, until the latter successfully counselled his return (in 1982) upon the appointment of David Young to the Chairmanship of the MSC.

7 Sir Keith Joseph to author, 5 June 1986.

8 Joseph believed that at no point in their lives were men equal in ability and capacity to exploit the opportunities which all equally enjoyed, nor at any point in their lives could they be made so. See Joseph and Sumption (1979), p. 35.

9 Boyson's PPS (1981–82) was Robert Dunn, who had been Joint Secretary of the Conservative Backbench Education Committee (1980–81). Boyson's PPS (1982–83) was James Pawsey, who had been Secretary of the Conservative Backbench Education Committee (1979–80) and Joint Secretary (1980–81). Both, like Boyson, held views akin to the educational radical-right.

10 Conservative Party Conference 1981, CCO Press Release, 755/81.

11 Sir Keith Joseph to author, 5 June 1986.

12 Conservative Party Conference 1981, CCO Press Release, 755/81.

13 Sir Keith Joseph to author, 5 June 1986.

14 *Ibid.*

15   Speech by Sir Keith Joseph to the 1982 North of England Education Conference, CCO Press Release 7/82.

16   Here it should be noted that Baldwin's own analysis (*Secondary Schools 1965–1979*, NCES Occasional Pamphlet No. 2, 1981), which sought to demonstate a decline in GCE 'O' and 'A' level achievement following a steady rise through the 1950s and 1960s (when the schools were selective and many new grammar schools were built), may in actual fact have influenced Joseph's decision to reform both the secondary school curriculum and the system of examinations at 16+.

17   Lord Beloff to author, 17 April 1985: 'I am an unashamed centralist. I favoured the French national education system model'.

18   CRD Advisory Board, CCO Press Release 409/82, 27 May 1982.

19   William Waldegrave MP to author, 7 April 1986. Waldegrave's assessment of the practical problems of vouchers are to be found in *Education Vouchers: A DES Paper*, December 1981. For Waldegrave's proposals to limit the destuctive power of an ever-expanding state, see his *The Binding of Leviathan* (1978).

20   William Waldegrave MP to author, 7 April 1986.

21   Stuart Sexton to author, 3 January 1985.

22   *Ibid*. Both Joseph and Waldegrave are Fellows of All Souls, Oxford.

23   Conservative Party Conference 1981, CCO Press Release 755/81.

24   *Education Vouchers: A DES Paper*, December 1981.

25   *Vouchers to Universalise Parental Choice in Education: Response to Secretary of State for Education on administrative questions*. FEVER, March 1982, *The Seldon Papers*.

26   Sir Geoffrey Howe, 'Conservatism in the eighties', speech given at the CPC Summer School, St. John's College, Cambridge, 3 July 1982.

27   The Conservative education policy group was one of nine small policy committees established by Sir Geoffrey Howe in early autumn 1982. The remit of these committees was to identify measures which a second term Conservative administration might implement. The other groups established looked at issues concerning the inner cities, family life, tax and social security, trades unions, unemployment and Europe. Altogether Sir Geoffrey Howe invited approximately seventy Conservatives, mainly MPs, but also including some peers, some MEPs, some local government activists and some people from the Bow Group and from academic life, to serve on these policy committees. They were invited to report by 31 March 1983. For a full account of the background to these committees, see Butler and Kavanagh (1984), pp. 38–9.

28   Sir Keith Joseph, replying to the education debate, Conservative Party Conference, 5 October 1982.

29   Lord Beloff, speaking in the 1982 Conservative Party Conference education debate. Reported in *The Times*, 6 October 1982.

30   Lord Beloff to author, 17 April 1985.

31   Private information.

32   See, 'Beloff strongly opposes the voucher system', *Times Educational Supplement*, 25 February 1983.

33   Private information.

34   Speech by Sir Keith Joseph to the Conservative Party Conference, 5 October 1982.

35   Speech by Boyson to the Kings' College Conservative Association at the Waldorf Hotel, London, 19 November 1982, CCO Press Release 754/82. Boyson had seen such technical and vocational courses in other countries in Europe where they had played a great part in those nations' economic advance.

36   Lord Beloff to author, 17 April 1985.

37   The phrase, though used by Boyson in his speech delivered at the Waldorf Hotel, London, on 19 November 1982, would appear to bear the hand of Stuart Sexton.

38   Speech by Sir Keith Joseph to the Conservative Party Conference, 5 October 1982.

39   *The Conservative Manifesto 1983*, CCO, p. 29.

40   Professor Cox to author, 21 February 1986.

41   Robert Rhodes James MP to author, 4 March 1986.

42   Harry Greenway MP to author, 23 January 1986.

43   Significantly, the proposals for education were outlined in the 1983 manifesto under the section 'Responsibility and the family'.

44 Private information.
45 *The Conservative Manifesto 1983*, CCO, p. 47. The manifesto stated: 'This Government's approach is straight-forward and resolute. We mean what we say. We face the truth, even when it is painful. And we stick to our purpose.'
46 One of the levers available to the Secretary of State concerned the recognition of courses offered by universities and colleges, as conferring on a successful participant, 'qualified teacher status' (QTS). It was decided, therefore, to use this legal power to establish criteria which courses would have to satisfy to be accredited for this purpose.

Chapter 9

Rethinking secondary education, 1983–86

Introduction

The previous chapter noted how CEs coming from both the traditionalist-paternalist and market-right wings of the Party viewed *quality of education* as being of central importance to Conservative education policy. In this chapter I shall argue that the Conservatives' election victory of June 1983 and the allocation of new ministerial responsibilities within the DES led the government to see improving the *quality of education* as synonymous with restoring *relevance* to the secondary school curriculum. The government believed that such a restoration could best be effected by responding more quickly to changing needs and national priorities.[1] (see below).

The reallocation of minsterial responsibilities within the DES was announced on 22 June 1983. Besides having overall responsibility for the work of the Department, Sir Keith Joseph's specific responsibilities were to include the education of 16–19-year-olds, vocational education, relations with the MSC (including the technical and vocational education initiative TVEI), education research and information technology. Dr Boyson transferred to the DHSS as Minister for Social Security. The new Schools Minister was Robert Dunn.[2] Dunn's earlier role as PPS to Boyson at the DES[3] was not his only link with the *voucher-men* of the educational radical-right. His membership of the Carlton Club had brought further contact with Boyson and other pro-voucher members, including William Shelton and Russell Lewis.[4] Like Boyson, Letwin, Pawsey and Sexton (the latter stood unsuccessfully as the Conservative candidate in Warrington North in the June 1983 General Election), Dunn would be especially committed to the creation of 'centres of excellence' (for example, crown schools and technical schools).[5]

As Parliamentary Under-Secretary of State for Education Dunn's responsibilities were to include educational aspects of local government finance, teacher employment, training and qualifications, schools and business, educational technology (including the MEP) and educational broadcasting. Like his predecessor Dr Boyson, his speeches would be written by Stuart Sexton.

On his appointment as the new Schools Minister Dunn was conscious of a clear Conservative educational policy slowly emerging from behind the years of rhetoric.[6] His analysis of that policy's evolution is reminiscent of that presented by several other CEs interviewed by the author:

> For nearly forty years from the time of Butler the Party had had no real education policy. The Party has always been nervous about its lack of a conservative educational philosophy. Up until about 1974 the Conservative Party in Parliament did not have in it men with any real experience of the state education system. Boyson's arrival changed all that. From 1975 the Party was at last able to begin to devise a positive educational policy of its own.[7]

Dunn's links with Boyson were at a personal as well as a political level. Both were Lancastrians, both were educated in the state school system and Boyson was godfather to Dunn's two sons.[8] As Dunn put it to the author, 'my links with Rhodes placed me firmly in the Boysonian tradition'.[9] Clearly Boyson and Sexton's dedication to liberating the state school sector had found an ally in Dunn.

Changing needs and national priorities

The Conservative Party's planned direction for state education was along the lines of what has been termed the *new vocationalism* (see Finn, 1987, chapter 7)[10] making schools more responsive to employers' and parental needs by the introduction of curricula concerned with new technologies and relevance to the world of work. The guiding philosophy behind Conservative educational policy — *excellence in education* — was now being interpreted by the government in terms of the creation of appropriate curricula for different groups of pupils to be derived mainly from their assumed destination in the division of labour (*ibid.*, p. 168).

The failure of the government to alter the structure of local authority control over education via a market-oriented voucher system (at the Conservative Party Conference in October 1983 Joseph had declared the voucher to be dead) may well have been the reason for its renewed concentration (from November 1983) on the issue of pupil achievement in public examinations. This issue was important because the government, as we have seen, believed the educational system should be responsive to the collective choice of parents. It was also a matter on which CEs had long united in their defence of the selective schools. Dunn voiced the Sexton view that children were most likely to achieve the best examination results in the selective schools,[11] but Joseph was decidedly cautious in offering his opinion on the respective attainments of the different types of secondary school and the use of published data on school examination results as a mechanism for improving public understanding of the quality of education offered.[12] Joseph's reluctance to accede to the position of the NCES lobby[13], namely, that the large variations in GCE/CSE examination achievements among LEAs highlighted the poor performance of comprehensive schools, suggested a wish on the part of the Secretary of State to move the education debate away from issues of academic excellence and towards curricula review.[14] These events were an indication of a growing divergence of thinking between Joseph and Dunn over not only the variety of schools to be provided but also the whole vexed question of how best to balance parents' wishes (choice and standards) and pupils' needs (a broad, relevant curriculum). The Dunn-Sexton fusion later came to emphasize that achievement in public examinations did matter to parents and schools should be specialist/work-orientated.

The theme of the 1984 North of England Education Conference (held in Sheffield on 6 January) — 'Catastrophe or Watershed?' — marked a new epoch in the history of Conservative education policy. Joseph believed that the English maintained education system was poised for reform. His speech to the Conference was specifically and purposely directed to the schools sector. The bold and ambitious objective to raise school standards and pupils' achievements required a new approach to the primary and secondary curriculum, and to examinations at 16 +. Joseph argued that in both phases the curriculum needed to be more in accord with four principles — *breadth, relevance, differentiation and balance*. However, the notion of a *coherent curriculum* owed much to the thinking of Lord David Young. Lord Young was closely attuned to the Thatcherite stress on relevance in education. As well as wanting a more relevant education, he wanted subjects to be broader. Like Joseph he believed that secondary schools had been guilty of force-feeding an academic menu to the less-able child. Both sought more clearly defined learning objectives.

From 1984 Lord Young's influence over the formation of Conservative education policy became increasingly pronounced. His influence is evident not only in Joseph's plans to define the objectives of the main parts of the 5–16 curriculum (1984 North of England Education Conference) but also in various White Papers (for example, Cmnd 9135, 1984 and Cmnd 9482, 1985), circulars and statements[15] dealing with the need for schooling to be more closely linked to the requirements of industry. Young's own philosophy — that employers' views should be more fully represented in any reconstruction of the secondary school curriculum — was shaped not only by his own considerable industrial background[16] but also by his previous work at the CPS and Department of Industry. Young's close association with Joseph between 1979 and 1982 had meant they had been able to exchange ideas which, in 1984, emerged as a mutually-agreed view for a strategic framework for state secondary education. They agreed that employers were looking for broader learning in young people and both believed in a more efficient learning process whereby pupils would be encouraged to work to targets under pressure.

It was significant therefore that in his speech to the 1984 North of England Education Conference, Joseph called for a broad consensus regarding the definition of objectives for the curriculum of pupils aged 5–16. In principle such a definition was to encompass four strands: the objectives of learning at school; the contribution of each main subject area or element; the content of the 5–16 curriculum as a whole; and objectives for attainment at the end of the primary phase and for the secondary phase. The pursuit of *excellence in education* now meant the pursuit of *clear objectives*. Here, Joseph was responding to the definition of schooling which traditionalist CEs had popularized during the 1970s — namely, *good education* meant effective well-ordered schools in which pupils developed, learnt and achieved. The curriculum was to be relevant to the real world and to the pupils' experience of it.

The government was now not only setting out proposed national guidelines on the school curriculum, it was also establishing priority areas for curriculum development, as announced by the Secretary of State on 3 February 1984. Joseph's 1984 North of England Education address had already contained three major shifts in Conservative education policy. First, it would no longer be acceptable for only 50 percent of all pupils to achieve the minimum standard. In future, between 80 and 90 percent of all pupils would have to aim at better than the existing average. *Excellence in education* now meant a new, much higher target for pupil performance. Put in another way, there might still be a bottom 10 percent, but no longer a bottom 40 percent. Second, the examination system would be gradually shifted from an emphasis on relative values to stressing absolute values (from *norm-referencing* to *criterion-referencing*).[17] This was a direct response to the perceived requirement of employers who, Joseph believed, wanted to know what skills, levels of understanding and competence, young people possessed. Third, for the attainment of these higher absolute standards, teachers would need to have clearly defined curricular objectives agreed by all (not least by parents and employers). In other words, to define more clearly what children should expect to be taught, to what level of attainment, in accordance with each child's stage of development and ability. These three shifts in education policy were radical in design. The weakness of Joseph's national curriculum proposals however, was how to deliver them in a period of limited resources.

Some CEs were in favour of a more centrally-directed *national timetable* of learning. Like Joseph, they argued that *clutter* subjects were dominating the curriculum and obstructing pupil attainment in literacy and numeracy (see, for example, the contributors to O'Keefe, 1986). And yet even such an enthusiastic advocate of the preservationist position as Dr Roger Scruton was not happy with the government's notion of *relevance* in education as espoused by Joseph. To Scruton, *relevance* was 'educational fantasy' (Scruton, 1984, p. 6).[18] He believed the more you aimed at it, the less you achieved it (*ibid.*). A truly educational subject forced pupils to understand something which had no immediate bearing on their experience — it taught them intellectual discipline, to make considered judgments in matters which were interesting in themselves, whether or not they could see their *relevance (ibid.)*. Scruton believed it was often the *irrelevant* subjects — the great dead languages, higher mathematics and literary criticism — that provided the most useful and most repeatedly applicable discipline *(ibid.)*.[19] Scruton's approach was shaped by a belief that the origin of the individual's moral sense was that human understanding derived from a humanistic education (see Scruton, 1980b).[20]

Joseph (in 1984) did not apparently share Scruton's priority. It is possible that he viewed it vague for the generation of policies which could be implemented. Significantly, this period witnessed the gradual demise of the CPG.[21] By now the CPG was hardly ever meeting.[22] Scruton's disillusionment with Joseph's consumerist/technicist approach to the curriculum emanated from his belief that Joseph was wrongly attempting to turn the ideology of the market into a universal political principle.[23]

'We now have a vision of what education is about'

Between May and October 1984 a number of CE groupings pressed for changes in both the school curriculum and school government.[24] The 1984 Conservative Party Conference showed clear signs of a tide of *new realism* in education about state schools. Joseph announced: 'We now have a vision of what education is about'.[25] Young people when they left school were to be equipped with *relevance* (attitudes, skills and work habits) to live fulfilling lives as adults, citizens, as members of families and at work. This model of education had been commended to Joseph by (amongst others) George Walden.[26] Walden's work as an overseas diplomat (1967-78) and civil servant at the Foreign Office (1978-83) had allowed him to view Britain's problems in an international context.[27] Himself a product of the state education system, he had witnessed with disappointment what he saw as the gradual decline of the English grammar school.[28] He believed Britain was suffering both from an economic lethargy and cultural decline.[29] Walden's association with Joseph between 1984 and 1985 brought together two like-minded Conservatives, each committed to reviving English secondary education:

> When I was PPS to Sir Keith we both believed Britain had a national economic problem. The cost of state public education and its institutionalized educational mediocrity, were, in my view, related in the issue of teachers' pay.[30]

Walden's view of Britain's educational malaise was shaped by his work in France where he was impressed by the French educational system with its emphasis upon rigour, and where his own children were attending school.[31] His admiration for the French Technical Baccalauréat — whereby 11–15-year-olds go to a 'collège' to study for *le brevet secondaire examination* and 15–18-year-olds attend a 'lyceé' to study for *le baccalauréat* (with the less academic entering the 'techniques' to train in practical skills for employment) — was characteristic of a number of CEs (most notably Lord Beloff).

> From my experiences abroad I told Joseph that British schools were self-indulgent, that they were anti-business and anti-industrialist. Getting Britain into the twentieth-century could only be done if schools stressed the practical as well, and not instead of, the abstract. I therefore urged a short-term emphasis upon science and technology. There was so much to be done to restore an ethos of quality to the schools. We had to revive science, technology and business education but also the humanities.[32]

Walden's belief that too much of the nation's educational culture was not just anti-business but also anti-intellectual led him to counsel Joseph to place more emphasis on intellectual achievement in the humanities both as a good in itself and for sound vocational reasons.[33] Both believed the arts as a whole trained the mind in rigour and adaptability. For them there was no 'either/or' about arts and sciences, no conflict between thinking and doing. More science and more training could (and had to) go together with greater expectations in the humanities. Both Joseph and Walden were convinced that higher cultural aspirations did not conflict with prosperity — they underpinned and transcended it. An intellectual culture was not a luxury, but a practical economic and political necessity.

Besides Walden, other CEs were also putting forward trenchant ideas for radical changes to the educational system. Lord Vaizey, a Thatcher adviser, proposed (Vaizey, 1984, pp. 50–1) that the £15.4bn education bill in 1984–85 be halved by reducing the scope of education. He argued for a reduction in the total number of teachers and linking teachers' pay to performance (*ibid.*). Vaizey's ideas for cost-cutting in the classroom may have developed from his earlier view (Vaizey and Clarke, 1976) that the benefits of new educational ideas had not always shown themselves and that the feelings of hope that accompanied educational reform had long since given way to disillusion. Thus, during late 1984, CEs who were close associates of the Prime Minister and Education Secretary were questioning education's relation to society and the economy — in particular why, in spite of the substantial amounts of public money that were being invested in the education system, attempts to raise schooling performance were still proving strangely ineffective. Their resolve — also endorsed by Professor Bantock (1984, p. 328) — was to preserve the traditional curriculum from adulteration by providing alternative and more suitable provision for the lower achiever to manifest his/her own excellence.

The adulteration of the traditional curriculum was now of particular concern to Sir Keith Joseph. His speech to the 1984 Party Conference had addressed the question 'what is happening in the classroom?' He acknowledged there had been complaints of indiscipline, illiteracy, innumeracy and of bias. Here he was referring not only to the findings and views of HMI but also to the expressed concerns of Lady Olga Maitland's Women and Families for Defence (WFD). Indeed, there was a marked similarity between Joseph's question 'what is happening in the classroom?' and WFD's campaign slogan 'what is happening in schools?' In his speech Joseph referred to the WFD's Chairman as 'that formidable woman Olga Maitland', and praised her work in alerting the public to possible bias in the classroom *vis-à-vis* 'peace-studies'.

Lady Olga believed the education service had to work with the family.[34] Though not affiliated to the Conservative Party, the campaign waged by the WFD (to promote balanced teaching and a respect for well-ordered schools free from politically motivated governing bodies) paralleled not only Joseph's own position on these issues but also the work of the Party organization in formulating strategies to monitor the politicization of the school curriculum.[35]

The reception given by the Conservative Party to the work of the WFD lobby was a direct result of personal Parliamentary and extra Parliamentary contact. Lady Olga and Sir Keith Joseph were acquaintances.[36] As a member of the Conservative Party (she had joined the Bow Group in 1967) Lady Olga had close links with the CPS. In 1983 she had been introduced to Dr John Marks (CPSESG) by Alfred Sherman.[37] At this time she was a serving member of the CPS Defence Study Group, and had already begun to pursue her campaign against 'peace studies' teaching in schools.[38] Her opposition to 'peace studies' teaching arose from her belief that it was 'anti-self-reliance, anti-initiative and anti-nation'.[39]

Joseph's position on the teaching of peace-studies' may have been influenced by a WFD report written by Dr Marks (1984).[40] This report recommended that: lessons or courses labelled 'peace studies' should find no place in schools; the government should issue guidelines to LEAs, school governors and teachers which would define how, and to what extent, contentious political topics should be discussed in the classroom; politically contentious subjects should normally form no part of the curriculum for pupils below the age of 16, and should be rigorously excluded from primary schools; and the Education Act be amended so that there should be a duty under it to prevent the political indoctrination of minors at schools (*ibid.*, pp. 1–2). These recommendations did, in the long term, influence Conservative education policy on the depoliticization of school curricula.[41] If the government's vision of what education should be embraced policies to encourage young people to have an understanding attitude towards the imperatives of work, then it also embraced policies to prevent the erosion of traditional morals and values in state schools.

Changing the curriculum experience of youth

At the 1984 Conservative Party Conference, Sir Keith Joseph announced:

> David Young and the education service together are making sure that a
> technical ingredient is returned to more and more curricula in more and
> more of the country; they are only just beginning.[42]

According to one officer working at the TVEI Unit (then in High Holborn),
what was being attempted was 'a radical change to the curriculum experience of
youth'.[43] Joseph now intended to see that the curriculum dominated school
examinations.[44] Meanwhile the *industrial trainers* were arguing that industry's needs
and educationalists' aims were to a very large extent identical.[45] A civil servant has
suggested that Lord Young's Enterprise Unit was engaged in gathering ideas from
education and industry to formulate proposals for government action.[46] Ideas were
certainly in proliferation. For example, the Enterprise Unit did see and consider the
National Institute for Economic and Social Research report *Competence and
Competition*.[47]

By 1985 there was growing support amongst CEs for the general thrust of
Conservative education policy. Even such diverse journals as *The Salisbury Review*
(edited by Dr Roger Scruton) and *Crossbow* were carrying articles pointing
Conservative thinking on education towards an acceptance of the only type of
schooling system which might enable Britain to foster the talent to compete in the
international market place: a system geared to the needs of employers and industry, and
not one which turned out a society of consumers quite unprepared for the world and
disciplines of work (see, for example, Morgan, 1984 and Jones, 1984). Between them
Sir Keith Joseph and Lord Young had begun to identify *the pursuit of excellence* with *the
pursuit of the Realschule ethos*.[48] It should be noted that their extrapolations from the
German model of education followed closely upon James Prior's own study of the
German training system, which itself had acted as a prelude to his plans in 1981 to
replace the old Youth Opportunities Programme with a new Youth Training Scheme
(Prior, 1986, p.141).[49]

Dissension amongst CEs from the general thrust of Conservative education
policy still centred on the issue of just how far the state should use its power to favour
and promote one kind of learning (science and technology) to the disadvantage of the
other (arts and humanities). Enoch Powell, declared that Thatcher's state was:

> ... an inhuman and barbarous state which would, in the end, bring down
> upon its subjects the penalties which attend upon all inhumanity and
> barbarism when the greedy expectations attached to the advancement of
> science turn to bitterness and disillusionment.[50]

In similar vein, Professor Ronald Fletcher made a defence of education as a creative force in society (Fletcher, 1984), and stressed the role of professional educators and their specialist studies in preserving 'excellence' and 'standards', in expressing and transmitting the achievements of the past, in defending and protecting the child from ignorance and exploitation, in warding off a collapse into barbarism.

The Party's debt to Black Paperite ideology

The government's newly-found vision of education was outlined in its White Paper *Better Schools* (Cmnd 9469, March 1985). This proposed a full basic curriculum in all primary schools and a balanced curriculum in all secondary schools. In the latter, all pupils up to the age of 16 were to study English, mathematics, a broad science course, RE, the humanities and the arts. Most pupils were to study a foreign language. Additionally, all pupils were to be given an understanding and knowledge of the values and traditions of British society.

By serving to focus the world of education upon those basic facts of the need to learn (and to learn well), to learn the 3Rs and to know and understand British culture and history, *Better Schools* was a kind of modern Black Paper. This was clearly the view of the CRD's Education Desk Officer, Andrew Turner, who subsequently briefed Tory MPs:

> The present government is determined to undo the damage caused by the misconceptions of the 1960s. A series of policies is being painstakingly developed and gradually implemented — policies necessarily using many different instruments, but unusually coherent in their approach and with the potential to bring about a restoration of a common-sense approach to education in place of Labour's dogma.[51]

Andrew Turner's rhetoric was based on a summary of Black Paperite ideology. In chapter 7 it was shown how Dr Boyson had urged a return to a 'common-sense approach to education'. Sir Keith Joseph had sought to introduce initiatives formulated in accord with such an approach. In its attempt to offer the prospect of an education policy largely based on a view of education in its traditional sense the government had been placing emphasis on output rather than input, on the efficient use of resources rather than fruitless spending, on the skills manifested by teachers and acquired by pupils rather than on grandiose social aspirations. Such objectives were in keeping with some of the key demands made by Black Paper writers in the 1970s.

For the government the task of restoring common-sense, clarity, variety, choice and respect for excellence had not proved easy.[52] But the CRD's education desk officer had been prepared to openly acknowledge the government's indebtedness to those CEs who had so painstakingly battled to alter the climate for educational change. Thus:

Ten years ago those Conservatives and other deeply concerned groups who wished to reverse the socialist tide in education often found it difficult to gain a hearing: their campaign for proper standards, high quality teaching and clear tests of ability was frequently derided as a grossly unfair attempt to undermine a broadly successful system. Today, the case for fundamental reform is widely accepted.[53]

At the 1985 Conservative Party Conference in Blackpool, Sir Keith Joseph's speech (written by Stuart Sexton) was also the product of a summary of Black Paperite ideology. Joseph observed, what he considered to be, a major advance:

I think that the pendulum has swung from teaching that tended to wait upon the child to teaching that leads the child.[54]

This, of course, was what the Black Paperites had campaigned for since 1969. Joseph gave further endorsement to their efforts with his affirmation that 'stretching is part of caring' (*ibid.*), whilst Mrs Thatcher (already advised by the CNACE and others that some LEAs were introducing politics into the classroom) reminded delegates:

the schools of this country are for teaching and learning and not for political indoctrination.[55]

The Party's debt to Black Paperite ideology was also evident in Norman Tebbit's First Disraeli Lecture.[56] Attacking the politics of the permissive society, the Party Chairman argued:

Who would have expected that our whole education system would have been turned upside down, discouraging competitive achievement, despite the accepted fact that even the lowest achievers in school or job wish to be stretched? (*ibid.*, p. 6)

Tebbit's endorsement of *Black Paper* thinking was significant for two reasons. This was an instance of the power and influence of the CEs over a Conservative administration committed to a return to traditional values and standards. It also marked the zenith of the Party's moral crusade (Conservative policies were now reflecting the voice of the so-called *Moral Majority*). The fight for education was now redefined as a fight for the moral health of the nation.

Mrs Thatcher, Sir Keith Joseph, Chris Patten, Norman Tebbit and Robert Dunn (whose wife was a religious education teacher) were not the only moralist CEs at the vanguard of the government's fight for morality. Within the CRD, Lord Beloff tended to represent the viewpoint of the *Moral Majority*. He believed most parents expected schools to give children the skills to enable them to earn a living and the ability to live a moral life, accepting and contributing to the social order (Beloff, 1985, p. 18).

It was largely Lord Beloff's ideas which now informed the Party's education spokesmen in their conduct of the teachers' pay dispute. For Beloff, the teachers' pay dispute was only a symptom of a growing incompatibility between the needs of the community and the educational instruments it had inherited (*ibid.*). He considered the example set by teachers to children during the dispute as nothing other than 'deplorable' (*ibid.*). Their actions over the issue of remuneration were, according to Beloff, indicative of attitudes which were incompatible with an educational system properly doing its assigned job (*ibid.*).

Chris Patten's approach to resolving the teachers' pay dispute followed closely upon Lord Beloff's counsel that the teachers' action was 'threatening social chaos' (*ibid.*). Thus, he told the CNACE:

> The teachers' unions will meet again next week. They have one vital decision. Will they drop disruption and get back to negotiation? We all know which is the responsible course to take. What is the real logic of the teachers' argument that it is either Houghton for them or bust for the schools of this country?[57]

Joseph and Patten's conduct of the teachers' pay dispute (as advised by Beloff) was fundamentalist in character and clearly sought to mobilize the *Moral Majority* in support of the government's case that order had to be restored to the teaching profession. It would appear that Joseph and Patten not only listened to Beloff's advice about teachers but also to his proposals for a national core curriculum. Beloff saw local authorities as responsible for educational provision and teacher employment, but the bulk of education monies were coming from central government whose powers were legally limited. In Beloff's opinion the situation had to change (Beloff, 1985). Beloff advocated a national system, such as had enabled the French to reverse the trend towards scholastic anarchy in favour of a return to tradition (*ibid.*). There was as yet no national blueprint for education, but national guidelines were being formulated for the 16+ examination and broadly agreed national objectives for the 5–16 curriculum were under discussion; additionally, Joseph had canvassed the idea of a national framework within which local teacher appraisal schemes might operate.[58] Despite these movements, the Joseph-Beloff line ran counter to the Dunn-Sexton position which favoured a much greater degree of decentralization with facilities for the establishment of new types of school outside the maintained sector under independent management. In December 1985 Chris Patten announced:

> The triple aim for all pupils is to develop their full personal potential, to prepare them for citizenship and to equip them for employment.[59]

This apparent assimilation of Beloff's idea for schools to equip pupils with the ability to live a moral life into 'preparation for citizenship' may have been occasioned by the government's desire to restore Christian values, both to the schools and to the family. As Patten put it 'Good schools should work in partnership with good parents' (*ibid.*).

In chapter 8 it was noted how Beloff's thinking had begun to be absorbed into Conservative education policy. One of Beloff's principal concerns — improving teacher quality — was now high on Patten's agenda. Thus, at Trowbridge, Patten spoke of the need for teachers to be 'experts in one or more curriculum areas' (Beloff's *teachers as scholars*) and the need for teachers to 'take note of the honour and organization of their profession' (Beloff's warning that the teachers' unions were bringing teaching into disrepute). Teacher expertise coupled with the need to create a higher public confidence in teachers were now major objectives in the government's programme to restore order and esteem to the education system.

In March 1986 there was further evidence of the government's adoption of Beloff's thinking. The Greater London Conservatives published their manifesto for the ILEA elections to be held in May. Its very title *Pupils Before Politics* indicated the Conservatives' determination to progress with their agenda for a moral cleansing of the school curriculum.[60]

Joseph's inclination towards the Beloff line was not arrested by his announcement (in February 1986) that he would leave Parliament at the next election. Despite sources close to the Prime Minister criticizing his failure to afford parents the opportunities provided by the old grammar school ethos (see, for example, Butt, 1986b, p. 16)[61] he had continued to reprieve grammar schools from the threat of closure.[62]

The fight for Joseph's succession

CEs have recognized the need for the education system to be redefined as circumstances change. News of Joseph's planned departure from government office caused, somewhat paradoxically, a number of CEs to seriously question much of that Conservative education policy which they had hitherto supported. Thus, Chris Patten declared:

> We are not going to measure the success of schools by the canons of a narrow utilitarianism. To do so would not only deny some of the most important values of education. It would not help us to prosper economically. Nor are we more concerned that all should reach the same minimum standard rather than that everyone should reach the highest standard of which they are capable. That would be falsely and debilitatingly egalitarian. What is now necessary is to tackle pupils' under-achievement, which is not the same as low achievement.[63]

Patten's abandonment of some of Joseph's most cherished objectives was ironic considering he was judged by many in the Conservative Party to be the Secretary of

State's natural heir apparent. But he was not alone amongst moderate-liberal CEs in voicing concern about the impact of Joseph's education policies on the schools and teachers. Mark Carlisle, conscious of the damaging effects on teacher morale by Joseph's continuous reference to the poor quality of what was taught at some schools without apparent recognition of the success and high standards of many others, cautioned:

> Let us repair the house that exists rather than attempt to replace it with another. (Carlisle, 1986, p. 386)

Another CE on the liberal-wing of the Party, possibly fearing the Government might adopt Oliver Letwin's proposal (Letwin, 1986a and 1986b) to make schools more 'consumerist', was moved to write:

> The trouble with the so-called new radical approach to education is that it is so old hat, espoused by the Party in the 1970s and rejected by Sir Keith as impracticable. (Hampson, 1986, p. 6)

If Sir Keith Joseph's resignation as Secretary of State for Education and Science on 20 May 1986 was a boon to liberal CEs, it was also a fillip to the educational radical-right. Such had been his pragmatism that Joseph the great individualist had, for them, become Joseph the centralizer (see below).

The act of resignation was itself poorly timed. Joseph informed the Prime Minister:

> As you have known for some months, I have thought that a fresh voice is needed at DES to carry forward and develop our policies for better education at all levels of ability in schools . . .

But what the government and DES needed was not a 'fresh voice' but 'one voice' on education. In the event the appointment of Kenneth Baker[64] as the new Education Secretary on 21 May 1986 suggested tactical skill and administrative ability in the presentation of Conservative educational reform were considered greater attributes for securing electoral success than the talent to initiate policy itself.

Joseph's record: an assessment

Any verdict on the *Joseph years* must be provisional. However, it is helpful to situate Sir Keith Joseph's approach and assess how its development was influenced.

In chapter 2 a central tenet of One Nation Conservatism — *selection* as a guarantor of educational excellence — was identified. Chapter 8 noted that Joseph had, since 1956, been a member of the One Nation Group. Significantly, chapters 2–7 showed that between 1956 and 1981 public discussion about education had taken the form of an often crude debate over selective versus comprehensive schools and that for many in the education world (for example, teachers and LEAs) the argument had gone against selection. Arriving at the DES in September 1982 Joseph found himself in the chronic position of someone unsympathetic towards egalitarianism and nationalization (he believed the state had a role but that it should be in providing a framework, rather than in providing all the services itself) (see Joseph, 1987, p. 26) and yet compelled to try and make better the nationalized school system.

Although selection between schools had almost abated in 1981, Joseph did try to move the issue of schooling to make more certain that there was selection within schools. One result of the contraction of the grammar school was Joseph's eventual focus on *differentiation* (his belief that if one wished to do justice to the needs of all levels of ability this could only be achieved if teachers discriminated)[65] which, in effect, has forced the 'grammar school' curriculum on comprehensive schools. Here, at least, Joseph cannot be viewed as a truly radical Education Secretary.

Joseph's thinking on education was not always original. For example, the four curricular philosophies which informed his plans for school change after 1984 — school education should include the development of personal qualities; skills were best learnt by reference to facts; order in the process of learning was conveniently achieved by arranging most of the curriculum by subject; teachers had to hold specialist qualifications — were hardly *new* ideas.

Joseph's observations of low pupil motivation and attainment were in line with mainstream educational orthodoxy. However, the remedies to cure the shortcoming were peculiarly his own. Instead of letting children find their own interests and aptitudes he decided to set them goals to strive towards. However, the '*Joseph years*' marked a period of deep unease within the Party over the best strategy to deliver a *better education for all*. Significantly, both the economic evangelical, Sir Keith Joseph, and the preservationist, Lord Beloff, had questioned whether a combination of parent power and the market was the right way forward.

Notes

1 Significantly, Oliver Letwin was now transferred to the Prime Minister's Policy Unit to become Mrs Thatcher's personal adviser on education. Letwin retained this post until January 1986. The Policy Unit was now charged with formulating economic and social policy plans for the future, and was intended to provide a kind of advice that would not be obtained from 'experts' in the government hierarchy. For an account of the history and work of the Policy Unit, see Willetts (1987), pp. 443–54.

2 Vice-President Eccles Conservative Association (1974–); Councillor, London Borough of Southwark (1974–78); MP Dartford (1979–); Joint-Secretary, Conservative backbench Education Committee (1980–81); PPS to Parliamentary Under-Secretaries of State, DES (1981–82); PPS to Paymaster General and Chancellor of the Duchy of Lancaster (1982–83); Parliamentary Under-Secretary of State, DES (1983–88).

3 Dunn had first met Boyson in 1968 when, as Chairman of Eccles YC's and Deputy Chairman of the Eccles constituency, he helped approve the latter's nomination and selection as the prospective Conservative Parliamentary Candidate. Robert Dunn MP to author, 13 October 1986.

4 Robert Dunn MP to author, 13 October 1986. For an account of the Carlton Club as the social centre of Conservatism, see Phelps (1983).

5 Robert Dunn MP to author, 13 October 1986.

6 *Ibid.* Significantly, it had been the Black Paperite Kingsley Amis who had made one of the strongest appeals for the Tory Party to rid itself of its timidity over education and formulate a clear education policy regardless of notions of political possibility or impossibility. See Amis (1978), pp. 51–9.

7 Robert Dunn MP to author, 13 October 1986.

8 *Ibid.*

9 *Ibid.*

10 According to Oliver Letwin the Prime Minister's Policy Unit was, in 1983–84, 'seriously considering IEA and CPS publications'. Oliver Letwin to author, 19 February 1985. According to Dr Elizabeth Cottrell (Director of Research, CPS, 1980–85) Oliver Letwin was, in 1983–84, a 'frequent visitor to the CPS'. Dr Elizabeth Cottrell to author, 26 October 1984.

11 In a speech to the Annual Conference of the Kent Young Conservatives at the Athelstan Hotel, Margate, 19 November 1983, CCO Press Release 784/83.

12 On 28 November 1983 Joseph gave a written reply to a Question from Harry Greenway MP about the report by the NCES, *Standards In English Schools.* He told the House of Commons: 'The report has illustrated the importance and difficulty of research in this area. I have asked the Department to assess various possibilities for further research as a preliminary to deciding whether further public funds should be committed'. DES Press Notice 411/83.

13 Represented in the House of Commons by Harrry Greenway and, in the House of Lords, by Baroness Caroline Cox, Lord Max Beloff and Lord Ralph Harris of High Cross.

14 Joseph had already demonstrated this objective by his issue on 4 October 1983 of a draft circular, 'Progress report on curriculum review', to LEAs asking them what steps they had taken to draw up policies for the curriculum in their primary and secondary schools and what action they had taken to put those policies into effect. The circular was issued for consultation with a request that all LEAs responded by 16 April 1984.

15 For example, 'Schools and the world of work', 19 March 1984, DES Press Notice 41/84, and 'Economic awareness in the school curriculum', 22 March 1985, DES Press Notice 69/85. In 1982 David Young had been a member of the National Economic Development Council. The NEDC document *Education and Industry* (1982) had argued the benefits of a more practical form of secondary education and warned against the continued predominance of the academic curriculum.

16 Executive, Great Universal Stores Ltd (1956–61); Chairman, Eldonwall Ltd (1961–75); Chairman, Manufacturers Hanover Property Services Ltd (1974–84); Director, Town and City Properties Ltd (1972–75); Chairman, British ORT (1975–80).

17 The introduction of the new GCSE examination was announced by Sir Keith Joseph in June 1984. The aim of the exam was to set down, for the first time in Britain, 'national-criteria' (i.e. agreed statements as to the objectives, content and assessment methods for all future public examinations and syllabuses for 16-year-olds).

18 Significantly, this article was published on the same day that Joseph announced his prioritization of areas for curriculum development. The article asserted that changes in the school curriculum had to have an educational (rather than a political) purpose.

19 For a full description of Scruton's view of high culture, see Scruton, 'The politics of culture', in Cowling (1978); Scruton's view of relevance in education is found in his *The Meaning of Conservatism* (1980) pp. 149–50.

20 Here Scruton argued that the humanities were what remained when science was removed. He suggested that they were nearer to our apprehension of ourselves than any science.

21 Roger Scruton to author, 10 January 1986.

22 *Ibid.*

23 *Ibid.*

24 For example, the CPSESG in its response to the government's consultative paper *Parental Influence at School* (Cmnd 9242, May 1984) had urged greater boldness and clarity in enhancing the position of governing bodies and for increasing parental involvement with them, but advised that trying to fit in all three parties (teachers, parents and LEAs) into a major role in running schools was an 'unsatisfactory troika' (CPSESG, *Comments on the Green Paper Parental Influence at School*, July 1984). The ASI's education group (comprising Digby Anderson, Baroness Cox, Professor Antony Flew, Professor David Marsland, Lawrence Norcross and James Pawsey MP) called for greater de-centralization of education, especially parental control through school boards, as well as more technical and specialist education — 'centres of excellence for different types of aptitudes' (ASI Omega Report: *Education Policy*, September 1984).

25 Sir Keith Joseph, in reply to the education debate, Conservative Party Conference 1984, CCO Press Release 661/84.

26 George Walden MP to author, 8 September 1986. Walden was MP Buckingham (1983–); PPS to Secretary of State for Education and Science (1984–85); Parliamentary Under Secretary of State (Higher Education), DES (1985–87).

27 George Walden MP to author, 8 September 1986.

28 *Ibid.*

29 *Ibid.*

30 *Ibid.*

31 *Ibid.*

32 *Ibid.* For an assessment of how the new educational philosophies of the 1960s/70s had carried on many of the traditional biases against economic enterprise and technical innovation, see Wiener (1985) pp. 132–4.

33 George Walden MP to author, 8 September 1986.

34 Lady Olga Maitland to author, 15 April 1985.

35 The CNACE had, in 1983, established a working party (Chairman, Marina Oliver CNACE Greater London Area) to monitor 'Politics in Schools'(political indoctrination in the teaching of subjects like peace studies, world studies and politics). Other members of the group included David Liddington (Voluntary Honorary Secretary CNACE) and Graham Leon-Smith (Headteacher). Its draft report was sent to the DES in September 1984 as well as to the various arms of the voluntary wing of the Conservative Party – the YC's, FCS, CTU and Women's National Committee (Lady Olga Maitland). Private information.

36 The Secretary of State had on 3 March 1984 addressed a conference on Peace Education in Schools organized by the National Council of Women, of which Lady Maitland was a member.

37 Lady Olga Maitland to author, 15 April 1985.

38 *Ibid.*

39 *Ibid.*

40 This report was prepared with the assistance of Lady Olga Maitland. It was, in fact, Lady Olga's collected information on 'peace-studies' teaching, derived from her contacts with Dr Marks and Baroness Cox (both of whom had had children in ILEA schools) and fellow WFD member Angela Browning (Devon), which formed the basis of the report.

41 For example, Sir Keith Joseph's issue on 4 February 1986 of a draft statement of principles (The Treatment of Politically Controversial Issues in Schools And Colleges') and draft circular ('How To Approach Politically Controversial Issues When Teaching'). These draft papers were sent for comment to local authority associations, teachers' organizations, Churches, voluntary bodies and others. Measures to prevent the political indoctrination of minors at school were debated in the House of Lords on 5 February 1986 on the motion 'Education — Avoidance of Politicization' (moved by Baroness Cox) and incorporated in the 1986 Education Bill.

42 Conservative Party Conference 1984, CCO Press Release 661/84.

43 Private information. Though Sir Keith Joseph and Peter Morrison (Department of Employment) had originally intended that the TVEI would cater for non-achievers, the TVEI Unit was now ongoing for its extension to all young people aged 14–18.

44 Conservative Party Conference 1984, CCO Press Release 661/84.

45 See, for example, *Action on Education — Education Policy Panel Report: The New Initiative*, British Institute of Management, October 1984. This report's recommendation, that young people needed to understand the social and economic functions within society of the various forms of work and that a broad appreciation of technology should be introduced at 16 + , were already part of the Education Secretary's long-term strategy for curriculum change.

46 Private Information. Lord Young, in 1984–85, served as Minister-without-Portfolio, coordinating the work of the Enterprise Unit based at the Cabinet Office. The government had established the Enterprise Unit in September 1984. Here Lord Young, together with two advisers (Richard Knight, CEO, Bradford, and David Wilson, a small business consultant) began to formulate further 14–18 education and training initiatives. The Enterprise Unit consisted of ten members (all full-time civil servants) all on secondment from six government departments (Trade and Industry, Employment, Transport, Environment, Health and Social Security and the Treasury). There was no representation of the DES. The Enterprise Unit was not a think-tank but rather a coordinating department. At the Unit Lord Young headed discussions concerning the education/employment relation and advised other Government departments. The Unit had a formal link with the MSC training division/TVEI Unit based at High Holborn.

47 Private Information. The NIESR study (1984) revealed that whilst West Germany spent 15 per cent of its education budget on vocational training, Britain spent only 8 per cent, and in jobs requiring intermediate vocational qualifications of a commercial or technical nature West Germany had 60 per cent of the workforce qualified, compared to Britain's 30 per cent.

48 An important aspect of Germany's education system was that it was selective. At the age of 11, on the advice of its teachers and at the choice of its parents, the child transferred to the Gymnasium (the counterpart of the grammar school) or to the Realshule (a school geared to producing technically qualified pupils). The ethos which each school possesses is different. The Realschule does not become concerned with inappropriate academic values, nor the Gymnasium with any value other than the pursuit of excellence.

49 Prior was Secretary of State for Employment (1979–81) and, unlike Howe and Joseph, then the only economic Minister who was not of the monetarist Right.

50 Enoch Powell, 'Education — a good thing', speech to the Merchant Taylors' Company, London, 12 December, 1984. Powell's speech attacked the government's bias in spending money towards branches of education which it regarded as signally useful and economically advantageous.

51 Education, *Politics Today*, No. 14, CRD, 9 September 1985, p. 282.

52 For example, the government had encountered long-ingrained prejudices and well-entrenched vested interests, a single instance being the attitude of the teacher union leaders who, in September 1985, had been unhappy to discuss proposals that would enable teachers to achieve promotion and higher pay in return for regular appraisal of performance.

53 *Politics Today*, No. 14, op. cit., p. 286.

54 Conservative Party Conference 1985, CCO Press Release, 540/85.

55 *Politics Today*, No. 18, CRD, 4 November 1985, p. 344.

56 Norman Tebbit, 'Britain's future: a Conservative vision', speech delivered at St. Stephen's Constitutional Club, Queen Anne's Gate, 13 November 1985. Published as CPC pamphlet No. 0510/750 December 1985. During 1985 quarterly 'policy-dinners' of the Party's centre-right 92 Group of MPs (which was committed to 'keeping the Party conservative' and to following a rightward path in economic, social and domestic policy) were taking place. In 1985 the Group's chairman, George Gardiner, arranged a series of policy group meetings, held monthly at the House of Commons Committee Rooms. Two meetings on education were called, both attended by Dr Rhodes Boyson and Robert Dunn. According to Gardiner the Group was now making 'a positive response to the debate on education policy within the Party and was uniting both paternalist-right and market-right views, with the common aim of fixing items for a future manifesto. The balance and direction of the Group was Thatcherite and there was a strong overlap between members of the 92 and the No Turning Back Group of Conservative MPs'. George Gardiner MP, to author, 3 September 1986.

57 Speech by Chris Patten, to the CNACE Conference, Conservative Central Office, 30 November 1985, CCO Press Release 646/85.

58 In an address to a DES National Conference on 'Better Schools: Evaluation and Appraisal', Birmingham, 15 November 1985, DES Press Release 289/85.

59 Address by Chris Patten to the National Association of Headteachers Conference, Trowbridge, 12 December 1985, DES Press Release 313/85.

60 It was during its Second Reading, on 10 June 1986, that Kenneth Baker (the new Secretary of State for Education and Science) amended the 1986 Education Bill forbidding political indoctrination in schools. The amendment was successfully pressed by, among others, Baroness Cox and Lord Beloff.

61 Butt had remained a close confidant of Mrs Thatcher, having formerly served her as a speech-writer. Butt's counsel may have influenced the Prime Minister's decision to replace Joseph earlier, rather than later, in 1986.

62 In March 1986 Joseph reprieved the grammar schools at Sherborne, Stroud and Gloucester. Their closure had been proposed at the behest of the local authorities but against the wishes of local parents.

63 Speech by Chris Patten, to the Secondary Heads Association Annual Conference, Christ Church, Oxford, 20 April 1986, DES Press Release 90/86. Patten was now supporting plans for a nationwide network of 'Crown Schools', run directly by the government, with the aim of restoring standards and discipline in the inner city-areas. These plans had gained increasing support from Cabinet ministers as part of a proposed review and restructuring of state education. It had already been decided that education would occupy a prime place in the next Conservative manifesto, and it seemed that the concept of 'Crown Schools' (initially to be set up in fifty–sixty places) could form the core of a new education policy. The first proposal for 'Crown Schools' in Conservative literature is to be found in C. B. Cox, *Education: The Next Decade*, p. 22.

64 A liberal-moderate Tory, Kenneth Baker had been PPS to Edward Heath (1974–75); Heath's campaign manager during the 1974–75 Party leadership context; Minister for Information Technology (1981–84); and Environment Secretary (1985–86). His first act on arriving at the DES was to dismiss Stuart Sexton. In October 1986 Sexton was appointed Director of the IEA Education Unit by Lord Harris of High Cross.

65 Sir Keith Joseph to author, 5 June 1986.

Appendix 1: Conservative Party Organization

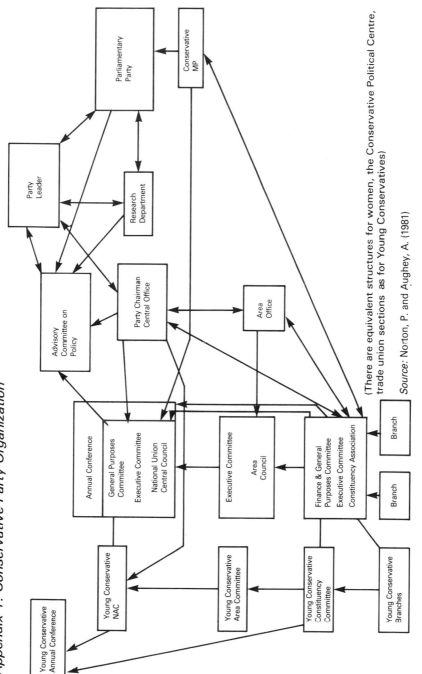

(There are equivalent structures for women, the Conservative Political Centre, trade union sections as for Young Conservatives)

Source: Norton, P. and Aughey, A. (1981)

Appendix 2

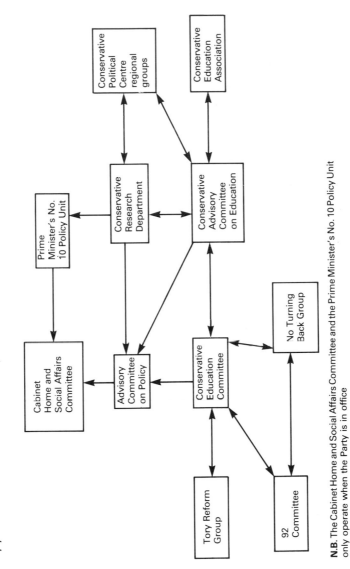

Appendix 2: Educational Policy Formation in the Conservative Party

N.B. The Cabinet Home and Social Affairs Committee and the Prime Minister's No. 10 Policy Unit only operate when the Party is in office

Bibliography

Primary sources

Official Publications
    Cmnd. Papers
    Parliamentary Debates and Papers
    DES Papers and Circulars

Publications of Political Parties
    Conservative Party
    Labour Party

Newspapers and Periodicals
    Dailies
    Weeklies
    Monthlies
    Others

Unofficial Annuals, Almanacs and Guides

Private Papers

Other Unpublished Sources
    Theses

Memoirs

Official Publications

Command Papers

Education: A Framework for Expansion (Cmnd 5174) (1972)

Teaching Quality (Cmnd 8836) (1983)
Training for Jobs (Cmnd 9135) (1984)
Parental Influence At School (Cmnd 9242) (1984)
Education and Training for Young People (Cmnd 9482) (1985)

Parliamentary debates and papers

Minutes of Evidence taken before The Select Committee on Education and Science,
    3 March 1970
Hansard, Oral Answers to Questions, House of Commons, 6 May 1975
Second Report from The House of Commons Education, Science and Arts Committee
    1979–83, Session 1981–82, Vol II, Minutes of Evidence (HC. 116–II)

DES papers and circulars

A Framework for the School Curriculum (January 1980)
Education Vouchers: A DES Paper (December 1981)
Progress Report on Curriculum Review (4 October 1983)
Schools and the World of Work (19 March 1984)
Economic Awareness in the School Curriculum (22 March 1985)
How To Approach Politically Controversial Issues when Teaching (4 February 1986)
DES press releases

Publications of political parties

Conservative Party: Published material

CPC pamphlets *The New Conservatism: An Anthology of Post-war Thought* (CPC.
No. 150, October 1955)
Educating the Individual Child, Keith Hampson and Simon
Jenkins, PEST Education Series 1 (CPC. No. 337, February
1966)
Education: Quality and Equality, Angus Maude (CPC. No. 391,
February 1968)
Re-Think on Education, Kathleen Ollerenshaw (CPC. No. 432,
March 1969)
Battle Lines for Education, Rhodes Boyson (CPC. No. 538,
December 1973)
Standards and Freedom, Norman St John-Stevas (CPC. No. 557,
September 1974)
How To Save Your Schools, Leon Brittan and Norman St John-
Stevas (CPC. No. 573, July 1975)

	Parental Choice, Rhodes Boyson (CPC. No. 561, January 1975)

Parental Choice, Rhodes Boyson (CPC. No. 561, January 1975)
Better Schools for All: A Conservative Approach to the Problems of the Comprehensive School, Norman St John-Stevas (CPC. No. 617, December 1977)
Education: The Next Decade, C. B. Cox (CPC. No. 511–521–684, December 1981)
Britain's Future: A Conservative Vision, Norman Tebbit (CPC. No. 0510/750, December 1985)

Other pamphlets *Make Life Better* (1968)
The Right Approach: A Statement of Conservative Aims (1976)
Science, Education and Industry, John Ranelagh (Old Queen St Paper, No. 2, CRD, 6 February 1978)
Manifesto of the Conservative Party, 1955
Manifesto of the Conservative Party, February 1974
Manifesto of the Conservative Party, 1979
Manifesto of the Conservative Party, 1983
Official Reports of 88th–105th Annual Conferences, 1968–85

Bound volumes *The Campaign Guide 1974*
The Campaign Guide 1977
The Campaign Guide Supplement 1978
The Campaign Guide 1979
The Campaign Guide 1983
Centre Forward, 7 volumes, 1971–77
Notes on Current Politics, 13 volumes, 1974–86
Politics Today, 11 volumes, 1976–86

CCO press releases

Conservative Party: Unpublished material
(Conservative Party Archive, Bodleian Library, Oxford)

Conservative Policy on Comprehensive Education, AGLB/CRD/519/08, Letter No. 37, May 1967
Education — Conservative Policy, AGLB/CRD/519/08, May 1967
PEC Comments on Cmnd 5174 'Education: A Framework for Expansion', AGLB/CCO 4/10/95
Two Aspects of the Current Comprehensive Battle, CRD memoranda, author not assigned (NDG), AGLB/CRD/519/08
CUTA/Focus on Education correspondences CCO/4/10/88/95–96
Letter and draft article from Rhodes Boyson to Peter Baguley, 14 November 1968, CCO/4/10/88/95—96
Text of Motion as adopted by the CEA at its AGM, 5 March 1973, AGLB/CCO 4/10/95

NACE Minute Book Vol. 2, 1965–77
NACE Minute Book, 1970–74
Letter from Mrs Thatcher to Secretary of the CEA, 2 April 1973, AGLB/CCO4/10/95
Speech by Mrs Thatcher to the AMA, Manchester, 29 December 1972
    Parental Choice, CNACE draft report, April 1973
    Opportunity and Choice in Education, CNACE draft manifesto, January 1974

CCO 4/9	1961–66
/119–120	Conservative Teachers' Association
/1137–138	Education

CCO 4/10	1966–78
/88	Conservative Teachers' Association
/95–96	Education

CRD 511/06	Schoolbuilding 1956–65
510/02	AGM Greenland's Letter Book 1963–64
516/02	AGM Greenland's Letter Book 1965–68
519/08	AGM Greenland's Letter Book 1967
519/03	Education Committee 1955–64

Papers of the Conservative and Unionist Teachers' Association (subsequently the National Advisory Committee on Education), 1965–74.

Labour Party

Labour's Programme 1976
Private Schools, Labour Party Discussion Document
London Labour Party Manifesto, GLC Elections, 1981

Newspapers and periodicals

Dailies

Daily Mail
Daily Telegraph
The Independent

The Observer
The Times

Weeklies

Education
New Society

Times Educational Supplement (TES)
Times Higher Education Supplement (THES)

The Spectator
The Teacher

Sunday Telegraph
Sunday Times

Monthlies

The American Scholar
The Cambridge Review

Director
Marxism Today

Others

The Colston Papers

Contemporary Record
Critical Quarterly
Crossbow
Doughty Street Papers
Focus on Education
History of Education
Journal of Education Policy
Journal of Social, Political and Economic Studies

Kay-Shuttleworth Papers on Education (NCES)
NCES Bulletin
NCES Occasional Pamphlets
Political Quarterly
Political Studies
Public Administration
Research Papers in Education
The Salisbury Review
Swinton Journal

Unofficial annuals, almanacs and guides

Parliamentary Profiles
The Times House of Commons, 1983, 1984, 1985, 1986
Who's Who annually

Private papers The following were consulted:

BOYLE — Brotherton Library, University of Leeds
COX — private possession, University of Manchester
FISHER — private possession
LONGDEN –– private possession
SELDON — private possession

The Boyle Papers

Letter from Sir Edward Boyle to Sir Michael Fraser, 26 February 1964, MS. 660/22684
Speech by Sir Edward Boyle to meeting of the National Union of the Conservative and Unionist Associations Central Council, 6 March 1965, MS. 660/22929

Speech by Sir Edward Boyle to the Conservative Party Conference, 14 October 1965, MS. 660/22930/2

Speech by Sir Edward Boyle to the Conservative Party Conference, 12 October 1966, MS. 660/22937/1

Speech by Angus Maude to the Mechanics' Institute, Bradford, 9 May 1967, MS: 660/22632

Speech by Sir Edward Boyle to the 1967 Conservative Party Conference, MS. 660/22938

Speech by John Vaizey to the Annual Conference of the NACE, 22 June 1968, MS. 660/22640/1

Speech by Sir Edward Boyle to the 1968 Conservative Party Conference, MS. 660/22939

Speech by Sir Edward Boyle to the 1969 Conservative Party Conference, MS. 660/22942

A Policy Statement for Education, NACE, 1971

Letter from Lord Boyle to Sir Richard Webster, 29 June 1972 MS. 660/22944

The Cox Papers

Letter from Walter James to Anthony Dyson, 29 August 1968

Letter from Cox to Dyson, November 1968

'Back to Education'

Letter from Angus Maude to Cox, 19 December 1968

Letter from Angus Maude to Cox, 2 January 1969

Letter from Angus Maude to Cox, 3 January 1969

Letter from Cox to Maude, 9 January 1969

Letter from R. R. Pedley to Cox, 11 November 1968

Letter from Tibor Szamuely to Cox, 15 December 1968

Letter from Maude to Cox, 22 January 1969

Letter from Maude to Cox, 24 February 1969

Letter from R. Langstone to Maude, 22 April 1969

Letter from Maude to Cox, 8 May 1969

Letter from Cox to Bantock, 21 April 1969

Letter from Bantock to Cox, 25 April 1969

Letter from Boyson to Cox and Dyson, 15 April 1969

Letter from E. Powell to Dyson, 21 March 1969

Letter from S. Hastings to Dyson, 24 April 1969

Letter from R. Bell to Dyson, 7 October 1969

Letter from V. Goodhew to Dyson, 9 October 1969

Letter from Maude to Cox, 16 June 1969

Letter from Maude to Cox, 21 May 1969

Letter from Maude to Cox, 20 August 1969

Letter from Cox to Maude, 22 August 1969

Letter from Bantock to Cox, 30 October 1969

Letter from Bantock to Dyson, 28 April 1970

Letter from M. Thatcher to Cox, 3 August 1970

Letter from Cox to Thatcher, 14 September 1970

Letter from Thatcher to Dyson, 1 December 1969

Letter from Lord Belstead to Anthony Royle, 17 December 1970

Letter from Powell to Dyson, 26 November 1970

Letter from Cox to Bantock, 11 January 1972

Letter from Bantock to Cox, 13 January 1972

Evidence submitted by the NCES to the Bullock Committee of Inquiry, January 1973

Letter from Sir Desmond Lee to Sir Alan Bullock, 20 January 1973

The Need for a New Conservative Policy on Secondary Education, paper presented by Cox to N.W. Area, CNACE, 8 November 1975

Letter from Cox to Boyson, 18 November 1976

Letter from A. Flew to the CQS (NDG)

Letter from N. St John-Stevas to Cox (NDG)

Letter from Boyson to Cllr. K. Eastham, November 1978

Letter from C. Meakin to Boyson, 30 September 1978

Circular letter from T. Radcliffe, Acting Chairman N.W. Area Advisory Committee on Education (Sub-Committee for Greater Manchester) (NDG)

Letter from S. Woodley to Cox, 7 January 1981

The Fisher Papers

Letter from F. von Hayek to Fisher, 1 January 1980

Letter from M. Thatcher to Fisher, 20 February 1980

The Longden Papers

Statement on Secondary Education, paper prepared by the Conservative Party National Advisory Committee on Local Government, June 1965

Topical Commentary: Comprehensive Schools, S. W. Herts Conservative and Unionist Association, February 1966

Letter from Longden to Sir Edward Boyle, 25 May 1966

Circular letter from Longden to members of the Divisional Executive, S. W. Herts, May 1966

An Approach to Secondary School Reorganisation, CRD memorandum, 5 December, 1966

Letter from Longden to Conservative members of LEAs, June 1967

Tory Policy For Secondary Education, letter from Longden to the Editor, The Sunday Times, 28 June 1967

CSC Newsletter, October 1967

Trends in Education, paper presented by Longden at Swinton Conservative College, 20 October 1970

Letter from K. Andrews to Longden, 27 January 1972

Speech by M. Thatcher to the AMA, Manchester, 29 December 1972

The Crisis in Education — A Voucher System to Improve Response to Parental Needs And Enhance Equality of Opportunity For Scholars, paper prepared by H. N. Paulley, 17 November 1972

Copy of letter from Anthony Barber to Lt. Cmdr. H. N. Paulley, 30 January 1973

The Seldon Papers

Letter from Seldon to Professor C. B. Cox, 31 May 1977

Vouchers To Universalise Parental Choice in Education: Response to Secretary of State for Education on Administrative Questions, FEVER, March 1982

The Education Voucher System: A Scheme for Greater Parent Involvement and Higher Standards in our Schools, R. Garwood Scott, M. Seldon and L. Whetstone, in consultation with the Committee of the FEVER (NDG)

Letter from Seldon to Lord Harris of High Cross, 2 July 1981

FEVER — A National Campaign for Parental Choice in Education (NDG)

The Case For Education Vouchers, summary of lecture delivered by Jack Wiseman to the NCES, Portman Hotel, London, 12 January 1975

The Income Graded Voucher System For Schools (NDG)

Other unpublished sources

Jefferys, K. (1984), 'The educational policies of the Conservative party, 1918–44', PhD, University of London

Memoirs

Butler, Lord (1971) *The Art of the Possible*, London, Hamish Hamilton.

Callaghan, J. (1987) *Time and Chance*, London, Collins.

Eccles, Lord (1967) *Life and Politics*, London, Longmans.

Hailsham, Lord (1975) *The Door Wherein I Went*, London, Collins.

Prior, J. (1986) *A Balance of Power*, London, Hamish Hamilton.

St John-Stevas, N. (1984) *The Two Cities*, London, Faber and Faber.

Secondary sources

AHIER, J. and FLUDE, M. (Eds) (1983) *Contemporary Education Policy*, Beckenham, Croom Helm.

ALPORT, C. *et al* (1950) *One Nation: A Tory Approach to Social Problems*, London, Conservative Political Centre.

AMIS, K. (1978) 'Speaking up for excellence' in CORMACK, P. (Ed) *Right Turn: Eight Men Who Changed Their Minds*, London, Leo Cooper.

ANDERSON, D. *et al* (1981) *The Pied Pipers of Education*, London, Social Affairs Unit.

ARMSTRONG, E. (1987) 'The case for morale rearmament', *Times Educational Supplement*, 5 June, p. 4.

BALDWIN, R. (1982) 'Secondary schools — Too important for dogma', *The Cambridge Review*, 26 February.

BANTOCK, G. (1984) *Studies in the History of Educational Theory Vol 2, The Minds and the Masses, 1760–1980*, Hemel Hempstead, Allen & Unwin.

BARNES, J. (1968) 'Reform at the centre', *Swinton Journal*, 14, 1, spring.

BARTON, L. and WALKER, S. (Eds) (1984) *Social Crisis and Education Research*, Beckenham, Croom Helm.

BEHRENS, R. (1980) *The Conservative Party from Heath to Thatcher*, Farnborough, Saxon House.

BELOFF, M. (1985) 'Education — the enemy within', *The Daily Telegraph*, 27 November, p. 18.

BENNETT, N. (1976) *Teaching Styles and Pupil Progress*, London, Open Books.

BERLINER, W. (1978) 'Tories in public policy split over exam league tables', *Times Educational Supplement*, 29 September.

BLAKE, LORD and PATTEN, J. (Eds) (1976) *The Conservative Opportunity*, London, Macmillan.

BLAKE, R. (1986) *The Decline of Power 1915–1964*, London, Paladin.

BOGDANOR, V. (1976) 'Education' in BLAKE, LORD and PATTEN, J. (Eds) *The Conservative Opportunity*, London, Macmillan.

BOGDANOR, V. (1977) 'Reflections on the great debate', *Centre Forward*, 1, October/November, pp. 14–22.

BOGDANOR, V. (1979) *Standards in Schools*, Kay-Shuttleworth Papers on Education No. 1, NCES, September.

BOYSON, R. (Ed) (1970) *Right Turn*, London, Churchill Press

BOYSON, R. (1971) 'Roll back the state', *Swinton Journal*, 17, 4, winter, pp. 23–31.

BOYSON, R. (Ed) (1972a) *Education: Threatened Standards*, London, Churchill Press.

BOYSON, R. (1972b) 'Turn of the tide in education', *The Daily Telegraph*, 21 January.

BOYSON, R. (Ed) (1973a) *The Accountability of Schools*, London, Churchill Press.

BOYSON, R. (1973b) 'Levelling down the schools', *The Daily Telegraph*, 10 July.

BOYSON, R. (1975) *The Crisis in Education*, London, Woburn Press.

BOYSON, R. (1977) 'Towards the Tory future?', *Times Educational Supplement*, 28 January.

BRITTAN, S. (1968) *Left or Right: The Bogus Dilemma*, London, Secker & Warburg.

BUTLER, D. and KAVANAGH, D. (1984) *The British General Election 1983*, London, Macmillan.

BUTT, R. (1969) *The Power of Parliament*, London, Constable.

BUTT, R. (1973) 'Tories who go too unwillingly to school', *The Times*, 11 January.

BUTT, R. (1975) 'Politics and education' in COX, C. B. and BOYSON, R. (Eds) *Black Paper 1975*, London, Dent, pp. 42–5.

BUTT, R. (1986a) *The Unfinished Task: The Conservative Record in Perspective*, London, Centre for Policy Studies, pp. 9–10.

BUTT, R. (1986b) 'Why Sir Keith should go now', *The Times*, 27 March, p. 16.

BUTT, R. (1987) 'Custodians of inequality', *The Times*, 19 February, p. 12.

CARLISLE, M. (1986) 'Build on what we have', *Education*, 25 April, p. 386.

CCCS EDUCATION GROUP (1981) *Unpopular Education: Schooling and Social Democracy in England Since 1944*, London, Hutchinson.

COLERAINE, LORD. (1970) *For Conservatives Only*, London, Tom Stacey.

CORBETT, A. (1969) 'The Tory educators', *New Society*, 22 May pp785–7

CORMACK, P. (Ed) (1978) *Right Turn: Eight Men Who Changed Their Minds*, London, Leo Cooper.

COWLNG, M. (Ed) (1978) *Conservative Essays*, London, Cassell.

COX, C. B. (1984) '*Critical Quarterly* — twenty-five years', *Critical Quarterly*, 26, 1. 2, spring/summer, p. 3.

COX, C. B. and BOYSON, R. (Eds) (1975) *Black Paper 1975*, London, J. M. Dent & Sons.

COX, C. B. and BOYSON, R. (Eds) (1977) *Black Paper 1977*, London, Temple Smith.

COX, C. B. and DYSON, A. (Eds) (1969a) *Fight for Education: A Black Paper*, London, Critical Quarterly Society.

COX, C. B. and DYSON, A. (Eds) (1969b) *Black Paper Two*, London, Critical Quarterly Society.

COX, C. B. and DYSON, A. (Eds) (1970) *Black Paper Three*, London, Critical Quarterly Society.

COX, C., JACKA, K. and MARKS, J. (1975) *Rape of Reason: The Corruption of the Polytechnic of North London*, London, Churchill Press.

CROSLAND, S. (1983) *Tony Crosland*, London, Coronet.

DALE, R. (1983) 'Thatcherism and education' in AHIER, J. and FLUDE, M. (Eds) *Contemporary Education Policy*, Beckenham, Croom Helm.

DAVID, M. (1980) *The State, The Family and Education*, London, Routledge & Kegan Paul.

DAVIES, B. (1986) 'Halting progress: Some comments on recent British educational policy and practice', *Journal of Education Policy*, 1, 4, pp. 349–59.

DEVLIN, T. and WARNOCK, M. (1977) *What Must We Teach?*, London, Temple Smith.

DEWEY, J. (1934) *A Common Faith*, Terry Lecture, Yale University Press.

DONOUGHUE, B. (1987) *Prime Minister: The Conduct of Policy Under Harold Wilson and James Callaghan*, London, Jonathan Cape.

DUNSTAN, J. (1978) *Paths to Excellence and the Soviet School*, Slough, NFER.

DYSON, A. (1969) 'If 'progressives' have their way . . .', *Daily Telegraph*, 29 July.

EDWARDS, T., FULBROOK, M. and WHITTY, G. (1984) 'The state and the independent sector: Policies, ideologies and theories' in BARTON, L. and WALKER, S. (Eds) *Social Crisis and Educational Research*, Beckenham, Croom Helm.

FENWICK, I. (1976) *The Comprehensive School 1944–1970*, London, Methuen.

FINCH, J. (1984) *Education and Social Policy*, London, Longman.

FINN, D. (1987) *Training Without Jobs: New Deals and Broken Promises*, Basingstoke, Macmillan.

FITZ, J., EDWARDS, T. and WHITTY, G. (1986) 'Beneficiaries, benefits and costs: An investigation of the assisted places scheme', *Research Papers in Education*, 1, 3, October.

FLETCHER, R. (1984) *Education in Society*, Harmondsworth, Penguin.

FLEW, A. (1976) *Sociology, Equality and Education: Philosophical Essays in Defence of a Variety of Differences*, London, Macmillan.

FLEW, A. (1987) *Power to the Parents: Reversing Educational Decline*, London, Sherwood Press.

FROOME, S. (1977) 'The Bullock Report' in COX, C. B. and BOYSON, R. (Eds) *Black Paper 1977*, London, Temple Smith, pp. 29–33.

GAMBLE, A. (1974) *The Conservative Nation*, London, Routledge & Kegan Paul.

GAMBLE, A. (1981) *Britain in Decline*, Basingstoke, Macmillan.

GASH, N. (1984) 'Myth of the two Tory parties', *The Daily Telegraph*, 8 October, p. 18.

GILMOUR, I. (1971) *The Body Politic*, London, Hutchinson.

GREEN, A. (1988) 'Lessons in standards', *Marxism Today*, January, pp. 24–30.

GRIGGS, C. (1979) 'The Conservative approach to education' in RUBINSTEIN, D. (Ed) *Education and Equality*, Harmondsworth, Penguin.

GRIGGS, C. (1980) 'The language of education', History Workshop Conference.

HALL, S. and JACQUES, M. (Eds) (1983) *The Politics of Thatcherism*, London, Lawrence & Wishart.

HAMPSON, K. (1986) 'A time to wait and a time to act', *Times Higher Education Supplement*, 25 April, p. 6.

HOLMES, M. (1985) *The First Thatcher Government 1979–1983: Contemporary Conservatism and Economic Change*, Brighton, Wheatsheaf.

HONEY, J. (1981) 'Quietly slumbers the don: The case for contracts' in ANDERSON, D. *et al* (Eds) *The Pied Pipers of Education*, London, Social Affairs Unit, pp. 24–8.

HOPKINS, A. (1978) *The School Debate*, Harmondsworth, Penguin.

HOWARD, A. (1987) *RAB: The Life of R. A. Butler*, London, Jonathan Cape.

HOWARTH, T. (1969) *Culture, Anarchy and the Public Schools*, London, Cassell.

HOWARTH, T. (1985) *Prospect and Reality: Great Britain 1945–1955*, London, Collins.

HOWELL, D. A. and BROWN, R. (1983) *Educational Policy-Making: An Analysis*, London, Heinemann.

HUSEN, T. (1979) *The School in Question: A Comparative Study of the School and its Future in Western Societies*, Oxford, Oxford University Press.

JAMES, P. (1980) *The Reorganisation of Secondary Education*, Windsor, NFER.

JONES, A. (1984) 'Turning the tide in education', *Crossbow*, autumn, pp. 28–34.

JONES, K. (1983) *Beyond Progressive Education*, London, Macmillan.

JOSEPH, Sir K. (1959) 'Way ahead for welfare', *Crossbow*, winter, pp. 28–34.

JOSEPH, Sir K. (1976) *Stranded in the Middle Ground*, London, Centre for Policy Studies.

JOSEPH, Sir K. (1987) 'Escaping the chrysalis of statism', *Contemporary Record*, 1, 1, spring, pp. 26–31.

JOSEPH, Sir K. and SUMPTION, J. (1979) *Equality*, London, John Murray.

JUDGE, H. (1984) *A Generation of Schooling: English Secondary Schools Since 1944*, Oxford, Oxford University Press.

KAVANAGH, D. (1987) *Thatcherism and British Politics: The End of Consensus?*, Oxford, Oxford University Press.

KEEGAN, W. (1984) *Mrs Thatcher's Economic Experiment*, Harmondsworth, Penguin.

KNELLER, G. F. (1984) *Movements of Thought in Modern Education*, New York, John Wiley.

KOGAN, M. (1971) *The Politics of Education*, Harmondsworth, Penguin.

KOGAN, M. (1975) *Educational Policy-making: A study of Interest Groups and Parliament*, London, George Allen & Unwin.

KOGAN, M. (1978) *The Politics of Educational Change*, London, Fontana.

KOGAN, M. (1985) 'Education, policy and values' in MCNAY, I. and OZGA, J. (Eds) *Policy-making in Education: The Breakdown of Consensus*, Oxford, Pergamon, p. 12.

LAYTON-HENRY, Z. (Ed) (1980) *Conservative Party Politics*, London, Macmillan.

LETWIN, O. (1986a) 'Good schools for all at minimum cost', *The Times*, 6 February, p. 12.

LETWIN, O. (1986b) 'Putting education on the right lines', *Sunday Telegraph*, 13, April, p. 18.

LEVITAS, R. (Ed) (1986) *The Ideology of the New Right*, Cambridge, Polity Press.

LEWIS, R. (1975) *Margaret Thatcher*, London, Routledge & Kegan Paul.

LONGDEN, Sir G. (1985) 'The original "One Nation"', *Crossbow*, August.

MACLURE, S. (1969) 'Education: The backlash starts', *The Observer*, 23 March.

MCNAY, I. and OZGA, J. (Eds) (1985) *Policy-making in Education: The Breakdown in Consensus*, Oxford, Pergamon Press.

MARKS, J. (1984) *Peace Studies in our Schools: Propaganda for Defencelessness*, London, Women and Families for Defence, September.

MAUDE, A. (1964) *Good Learning*, London, Michael Joseph.

MAUDE, A. (1968) *Education: Quality and Equality*, CPC No. 391, February.

MAUDE, A. (1969a) *The Common Problem*, London, Constable.

MAUDE, A. (1969b) 'The egalitarian threat' in COX, C. B. and DYSON, A. (Eds) *Fight for Education: A Black Paper*, London, Critical Quarterly Society, p. 8.

MORGAN, D. (1984) 'The right approach to education', *The Salisbury Review*, winter, pp. 6–7.

NORTHAM, R. (1939) *Conservatism The Only Way*, London, The Right Book Club.

NORTON, P. and AUGHEY, A. (1981) *Conservatives and Conservatism*, London, Maurice Temple Smith.

O'KEEFE, D. (Ed.) (1986) *The Wayward Curriculum*, London, Social Affairs Unit.

OLLERENSHAW, DAME K. (1973) 'The crystal ball-planning and population changes', *Education* 6 July, pp. 11–12.

O'SULLIVAN, J. (1968) 'The liberal hour', *Swinton Journal*, 14, 2, summer, pp. 3–7.

PATTEN, C. (1980) 'Policy making in opposition' in LAYTON-HENRY, Z. (Ed) *Conservative Party Politics*, London, Macmillan.

PATTEN, C. (1983) *The Tory Case*, Harlow, Longman.

PHELPS, B. (1983) *Power and the Party: A History of the Carlton Club 1832–1982*, London, Macmillan.

PHILLIPS, N. R. (1978) *The Quest for Excellence: The Neo-Conservative Critique of Educational Mediocrity*, New York, Philosophical Library.

POWELL, J. E. (1953) 'Conservatives and social services', *The Political Quarterly*, April–June.

RAMSDEN, J. (1980) *The Making of Conservative Party Policy: The Conservative Research Department Since 1929*, London, Longman.

RANSON, S. (1985) 'Contradictions in the government of educational change', *Political Studies*, 33, 1, March, pp. 56–72.

RHODES-JAMES, R. (1972) *Ambitions and Realities: British Politics 1964–1970*, London, Weidenfeld and Nicholson.

RIDDELL, P. (1983) *The Thatcher Government*, Oxford, Martin Robertson.

RUBINSTEIN, D. (Ed) *Education and Equality*, Harmondsworth, Penguin.

RUSSEL, T. (1978) *The Tory Party: Its Policies, Divisions and Future*, Harmondsworth, Penguin.

SALTER, B. and TAPPER, T. (1981) *Education, Politics and the State*, London, Grant McIntyre.

SALTER, B. and TAPPER, T. (1985) *Power and Policy in Education: The Case of Independent Schooling*, Lewes, Falmer Press.

SCRUTON, R. (1980a) *The Meaning of Conservatism*, Harmondsworth, Penguin.

SCRUTON, R. (1980b) 'Humane education', *The American Scholar*, September, reprinted in SCRUTON, R. (Ed) (1981) *The Politics of Culture and Other Essays*, Manchester, Carcanet.

SCRUTON, R. (1981) *The Politics of Culture and Other Essays*, Manchester, Carcanet.

SCRUTON, R. (1984) 'Why teach philosophy to children who can't add up?', *Daily Mail*, 3 February, p. 6.

SELDON, A. (1981) *Churchill's Indian Summer: The Conservative Government 1951–1955*, Sevenoaks, Hodder & Stoughton.

SELDON, A. (1983) 'The new economics', *Journal of Social, Political and Economic Studies*, 8, 1, spring, pp. 3–42.

SELDON, A. (1986) *The Riddle of the Voucher*, London, Institute of Economic Affairs.

SEWILL, B. (1959) 'Reshaping welfare', *Crossbow*, summer.

SEXTON, S. (1977) 'Evolution by choice' in COX, C. B. and BOYSON, R. *Black Paper 1977*, London, Temple Smith, pp. 86–9.

SHARP, R. (Ed) (1986) *Capitalist Crisis and Schooling: Comparative Studies in the Politics of Education*, Melbourne, Macmillan.

SIMON, B. (1985) 'The Tory government and education, 1951–60: Background to breakout', *History of Education*, 14, 4, pp. 283–97.

SIMON, B. (1986) 'The 1944 Education Act: A Conservative measure?', *History of Education*, 15, 1, pp. 31–43.

SMART, N. (Ed) (1968) *Crisis in the Classroom*, London, Hamlyn.

SPEARMAN, D. (1976) 'Tell immigrants what to expect', *Daily Telegraph*, June.

ST JOHN-STEVAS, N. (1978) 'Farewell to education — with a peep of protest', *Times Educational Supplement*, 1 December.

STEPHENSON, H. (1980) *Mrs. Thatcher's First Year*, London, Jill Norman.

SZAMUELY, T. (1968) 'Intellectuals and Conservatism', *Swinton Journal*, 14, 1, spring, p. 5.

TAPPER, T. and SALTER, B. (1978) *Education and the Political Order*, London, Macmillan.

TAPPER, T. and SALTER, B. (1986) 'The assisted places scheme: A policy evaluation', *Journal of Education Policy*, 1, 4, pp. 315–30.

THEAKSTON, K. (1987) *Junior Ministers in British Government*, Oxford, Basil Blackwell.

UTLEY, T. E. (1968) 'The future of private education', *Swinton Journal*, 14, 1, spring, pp. 24–30.

VAIZEY, J. (1983) *In Breach of Promise*, London, Weidenfeld & Nicholson.

VAIZEY, J. and CLARKE, C. (1976) *Education: The State of Debate*, London, Duckworth.

VAIZEY, LORD (1984) 'Schoolroom savings: the £7bn equation', *Director*, September, pp. 50–51.

WALDEGRAVE, W. (1978) *The Binding of Leviathan*, London, Hamish Hamilton.

WAPSHOTT, N. and BROCK, G. (1983) *Thatcher*, London, Macdonald/Futura.

WARNOCK, M. (1977) *Schools of Thought*, London, Faber.

WEINER, M. (1985) *English Culture and the Decline of the Industrial Spirit, 1850–1980*, Harmondsworth, Penguin.

WILBY, P. and MIDGLEY, S. (1987) 'As the new right wields its power', *The Independent*, 23 July.

WILLETTS, D. (1987) 'The role of the Prime Minister's policy unit', *Public Administration*, 65.

WOLPE, A-M, and DONALD, J. (Eds) (1983) *Is There Anyone Here from Education?*, London, Pluto.

WORSTHORNE, P. (1971) *The Socialist Myth*, London, Cassell.

WORSTHORNE, P. (1987) *By the Right*, Dublin, Brophy Books.

WRIGHT, N. (1977) *Progress in Education*, London, Croom Helm.

Index